P9-APB-543

Photoshop® Studio Secrets™, 2nd Edition

DEKE McCLELLAND AND KATRIN EISMANN

PHOTOSHOP®
STUDIO SECRETS™, 2ND EDITION

IDG BOOKS WORLDWIDE, INC.

AN INTERNATIONAL DATA GROUP COMPANY

Foster City, CA ▲ Chicago, IL ◆ Indianapolis, IN ▼ New York, NY

Photoshop® Studio Secrets™, 2nd Edition

Published by
IDG Books Worldwide, Inc.
An International Data Group Company
919 E. Hillsdale Blvd., Suite 400
Foster City, CA 94404
www.idgbooks.com (IDG Books Worldwide Web site)

Copyright © 1999 IDG Books Worldwide, Inc. All rights reserved. No part of this book, including interior design, cover design, and icons, may be reproduced or transmitted in any form, by any means (electronic, photocopying, recording, or otherwise) without the prior written permission of the publisher.

Library of Congress Catalog Card Number: 98-075152

ISBN: 0-7645-3271-5

Printed in the United States of America

10 9 8 7 6 5 4 3

2K/RV/RS/2Y/FC

Distributed in the United States by IDG Books Worldwide, Inc.

Distributed by Macmillan Canada for Canada; by Transworld Publishers Limited in the United Kingdom; by IDG Norge Books for Norway; by IDG Sweden Books for Sweden; by Woodslane Pty. Ltd. for Australia; by Woodslane (NZ) Ltd. for New Zealand; by Addison Wesley Longman Singapore Pte Ltd. for Singapore, Malaysia, Thailand, and Indonesia; by Norma Comunicaciones S.A. for Colombia; by Intersoft for South Africa; by International Thomson Publishing for Germany, Austria and Switzerland; by Distribuidora Cuspide for Argentina; by Livraria Cultura for Brazil; by Ediciencia S.A. for Ecuador; by Ediciones ZETA S.C.R. Ltda. for Peru; by WS Computer Publishing Corporation, Inc., for the Philippines; by Contemporanea de Ediciones for Venezuela; by Express Computer Distributors for the Caribbean and West Indies; by Micronesia Media Distributor, Inc. for Micronesia; by Grupo Editorial Norma S.A. for Guatemala; by Chips Computadoras S.A. de C.V. for Mexico; by Editorial Norma de Panama S.A. for Panama; by Wouters Import for Belgium; by American Bookshops for Finland. Authorized Sales Agent: Anthony Rudkin Associates for the Middle East and North Africa.

For general information on IDG Books Worldwide's books in the U.S., please call our Consumer Customer Service department at 800-762-2974. For reseller information, including discounts and premium sales, please call our Reseller Customer Service department at 800-434-3422.

For information on where to purchase IDG Books Worldwide's books outside the U.S., please contact our International Sales department at 317-596-5530 or fax 317-596-5692.

For consumer information on foreign language translations, please contact our Customer Service department at 800-434-3422, fax 317-596-5692, or e-mail rights@idgbooks.com.

For information on licensing foreign or domestic rights, please phone +1-650-655-3109.

For sales inquiries and special prices for bulk quantities, please contact our Sales department at 650-655-3200 or write to the address above.

For information on using IDG Books Worldwide's books in the classroom or for ordering examination copies, please contact our Educational Sales department at 800-434-2086 or fax 317-596-5499.

For press review copies, author interviews, or other publicity information, please contact our Public Relations department at 650-655-3000 or fax 650-655-3299.

For authorization to photocopy items for corporate, personal, or educational use, please contact Copyright Clearance Center, 222 Rosewood Drive, Danvers, MA 01923, or fax 978-750-4470.

LIMIT OF LIABILITY/DISCLAIMER OF WARRANTY: THE PUBLISHER AND AUTHOR HAVE USED THEIR BEST EFFORTS IN PREPARING THIS BOOK. THE PUBLISHER AND AUTHOR MAKE NO REPRESENTATIONS OR WARRANTIES WITH RESPECT TO THE ACCURACY OR COMPLETENESS OF THE CONTENTS OF THIS BOOK AND SPECIFICALLY DISCLAIM ANY IMPLIED WARRANTIES OF MERCHANTABILITY OR FITNESS FOR A PARTICULAR PURPOSE. THERE ARE NO WARRANTIES WHICH EXTEND BEYOND THE DESCRIPTIONS CONTAINED IN THIS PARAGRAPH. NO WARRANTY MAY BE CREATED OR EXTENDED BY SALES REPRESENTATIVES OR WRITTEN SALES MATERIALS. THE ACCURACY AND COMPLETENESS OF THE INFORMATION PROVIDED HEREIN AND THE OPINIONS STATED HEREIN ARE NOT GUARANTEED OR WARRANTED TO PRODUCE ANY PARTICULAR RESULTS, AND THE ADVICE AND STRATEGIES CONTAINED HEREIN MAY NOT BE SUITABLE FOR EVERY INDIVIDUAL. NEITHER THE PUBLISHER NOR AUTHOR SHALL BE LIABLE FOR ANY LOSS OF PROFIT OR ANY OTHER COMMERCIAL DAMAGES, INCLUDING BUT NOT LIMITED TO SPECIAL, INCIDENTAL, CONSEQUENTIAL, OR OTHER DAMAGES.

Trademarks: All brand names and product names used in this book are trade names, service marks, trademarks, or registered trademarks of their respective owners. IDG Books Worldwide is not associated with any product or vendor mentioned in this book.

is a trademark under exclusive license to IDG Books Worldwide, Inc., from International Data Group, Inc.

ABOUT IDG BOOKS WORLDWIDE

Welcome to the world of IDG Books Worldwide.

IDG Books Worldwide, Inc., is a subsidiary of International Data Group, the world's largest publisher of computer-related information and the leading global provider of information services on information technology. IDG was founded more than 30 years ago by Patrick J. McGovern and now employs more than 9,000 people worldwide. IDG publishes more than 290 computer publications in over 75 countries. More than 90 million people read one or more IDG publications each month.

Launched in 1990, IDG Books Worldwide is today the #1 publisher of best-selling computer books in the United States. We are proud to have received eight awards from the Computer Press Association in recognition of editorial excellence and three from Computer Currents' First Annual Readers' Choice Awards. Our best-selling *...For Dummies®* series has more than 50 million copies in print with translations in 31 languages. IDG Books Worldwide, through a joint venture with IDG's Hi-Tech Beijing, became the first U.S. publisher to publish a computer book in the People's Republic of China. In record time, IDG Books Worldwide has become the first choice for millions of readers around the world who want to learn how to better manage their businesses.

Our mission is simple: Every one of our books is designed to bring extra value and skill-building instructions to the reader. Our books are written by experts who understand and care about our readers. The knowledge base of our editorial staff comes from years of experience in publishing, education, and journalism — experience we use to produce books to carry us into the new millennium. In short, we care about books, so we attract the best people. We devote special attention to details such as audience, interior design, use of icons, and illustrations. And because we use an efficient process of authoring, editing, and desktop publishing our books electronically, we can spend more time ensuring superior content and less time on the technicalities of making books.

You can count on our commitment to deliver high-quality books at competitive prices on topics you want to read about. At IDG Books Worldwide, we continue in the IDG tradition of delivering quality for more than 30 years. You'll find no better book on a subject than one from IDG Books Worldwide.

IDG BOOKS WORLDWIDE

John J. Kilcullen

John Kilcullen
Chairman and CEO
IDG Books Worldwide, Inc.

Steven Berkowitz

Steven Berkowitz
President and Publisher
IDG Books Worldwide, Inc.

*Eighth Annual
Computer Press
Awards ≥ 1992*

*Ninth Annual
Computer Press
Awards ≥ 1993*

*Tenth Annual
Computer Press
Awards ≥ 1994*

*Eleventh Annual
Computer Press
Awards ≥ 1995*

IDG is the world's leading IT media, research and exposition company. Founded, in 1964, IDG had 1997 revenues of $2.05 billion and has more than 9,000 employees worldwide. IDG offers the widest range of media options that reach IT buyers in 75 countries representing 95% of worldwide IT spending. IDG's diverse product and services portfolio spans six key areas including print publishing, online publishing, expositions and conferences, market research, education and training, and global marketing services. More than 90 million people read one or more of IDG's 290 magazines and newspapers, including IDG's leading global brands — Computerworld, PC World, Network World, Macworld and the Channel World family of publications. IDG Books Worldwide is one of the fastest-growing computer book publishers in the world, with more than 700 titles in 36 languages. The "...For Dummies®" series alone has more than 50 million copies in print. IDG offers online users the largest network of technology-specific Web sites around the world through IDG.net (http://www.idg.net), which comprises more than 225 targeted Web sites in 55 countries worldwide. International Data Corporation (IDC) is the world's largest provider of information technology data, analysis and consulting, with research centers in over 41 countries and more than 400 research analysts worldwide. IDG World Expo is a leading producer of more than 168 globally branded conferences and expositions in 35 countries including E3 (Electronic Entertainment Expo), Macworld Expo, ComNet, Windows World Expo, ICE (Internet Commerce Expo), Agenda, DEMO, and Spotlight. IDG's training subsidiary, ExecuTrain, is the world's largest computer training company, with more than 230 locations worldwide and 785 training courses. IDG Marketing Services helps industry-leading IT companies build international brand recognition by developing global integrated marketing programs via IDG's print, online and exposition products worldwide. Further information about the company can be found at www.idg.com.   10/8/98

Shame on me for missing your birth,
but I'll be there when you die,
then we'll regroup and make plans after that.

We're soulmates, baby — my beautiful E.P.

— Deke

To all my teachers and mentors: From Mrs. Maybe and
Mrs. Armstrong to Willie Osterman, Judy Levy,
Douglas Ford Rea, and Jeff Weiss. The lessons you
taught me I still learn from today.

— With deepest appreciation, Katrin

FOREWORD

As the editorial lead for the largest gathering of Photoshop users in the country, I have spent many years consuming books, articles, and lectures on how to best use what is arguably the most powerful and deep imaging application in the world.

Like many Photoshop users, I have examined the dozens of technical reference books that have been written by Photoshop experts over the years. These books tend to serve as deeper, more insightful replacements for the documentation that is included with the software. These books talk about the *right* way to use the program, and dissect what menu commands and filters do to your images.

Photoshop Studio Secrets, 2nd Edition is definitely a breath of fresh air. It takes an approach that not only reveals crucial features of the software, but also opens up completely new avenues to using those capabilities.

I had the pleasure of working with artist Glenn Mitsui a few years back when we put together the first Technique Conference, where artists (not techie Photoshop users) came together to show off their art and discuss how they used Photoshop to create it. It opened my eyes to some amazing Photoshop realities.

I saw artists who broke several cardinal rules (they used Contrast and Brighness instead of Levels or Curves). They created stunning compositions without touching the Layers palette. They used the data-destroying Dodge and Burn tool to create very cool 3D effects. In a nutshell, they used Photoshop *wrong*, but after seeing their creations, I learned that there is no *right* way to use Photoshop. These artists were too busy creating award-winning art to bother with convention.

Several of these artists and their innovative approaches have been profiled in this book. The combination of their unconventional techniques with Deke McClelland's and Katrin Eismann's supreme product knowledge and ability to translate these techniques onto paper have created a book that clearly demystifies while it inspires.

I have learned a lot from this book. I hope you enjoy it as much as I did.

Steve Broback
President and CFO
Thunder Lizard Productions

PREFACE

When I was in grade school, I read an account of Pablo Picasso eating a fish and admiring the way its exposed skeleton lay on his plate. Perhaps on a whim, perhaps merely to impress his interviewer, he gathered the skeleton and worked it into a slab of clay. Then, he molded the clay into a new plate from which he might later suck the bones of another fish.

This simple — if not entirely spontaneous — examination of the artistic cycle has stuck with me ever since. What we see inspires us; what we create becomes a thing from which we can derive use, pleasure, and future inspiration. The beauty of the cycle is that the more you make, the better you become. In other words, as you make art, it makes you.

The purpose of this book is to observe what modern Picassos do with their fish. The only difference is that instead of using skeletons and clay, these artists use digital photographs and a computer program called Photoshop.

YOU ALREADY KNOW HOW TO USE PHOTOSHOP

Katrin and I won't take up your time explaining the fundamental principles of using Photoshop. This topic is well covered in my *Macworld Photoshop 5 Bible* and *Photoshop 5 for Windows Bible* (IDG Books Worldwide, 1998), in addition to scads of other perfectly excellent books.

Nor is this a cookbook of graphic formulas with a blow-by-blow account of every brushstroke the artists apply. Again, that's been done — and done quite well — by several authors before us.

YOU WANT TO KNOW HOW TO MAKE ART

I like to think this book is something that hasn't been done before. In the pages that follow, Katrin and I examine proven secrets from top artistic and photographic studios. This is a book of techniques, ideas, philosophies, and inspiration directly from the artists' mouths.

The best way to decide whether this book works for you is to understand our method in creating the book. If you don't care for the method, chances are that the book's content won't suit your needs. But if the method appeals to you, I'm guessing that you'll find plenty to like.

- **I would be the student, not the teacher**: The very first thing I decided was that if I was going to write yet another Photoshop book, I had better learn something from it. There was no point in sitting down and rehashing yesterday's well-heeled tips and tricks. I resolved to seek out fresh insights that I had never heard, or perhaps even considered. As it turns out, I succeeded. Speaking purely personally, every chapter is an eye-opener.

- **Get the best artists**: I decided to concentrate exclusively on the best and the brightest artists in the business. I never sent out a mass e-mail encouraging artists to send me their tips. Undoubtedly, this would have unearthed lots of golden nuggets, but it would have required that I spend too much time sifting through the gravel. Instead, with the help of the able folks at Thunder Lizard Productions, Katrin and I found the artists whose techniques we most trust and whose work we most admire. Happily, nearly everyone agreed to participate, including several artists who have never consented to show their work in a Photoshop book before.

- **Focus on clearly defined topics and explore them in depth**: This book covers 21 topics from 21 artists in 21 chapters. That means you get to spend a leisurely amount of time looking over the artists' shoulders as they concentrate on the tasks that are most near and dear to their hearts.

- **Cover challenging topics that affect working professionals**: Rather than focus exclusively on Photoshop's features — such as masking or color corrections — this book tackles broad artistic topics. These chapters go beyond the narrow confines of the program and examine the larger Photoshop process. Glenn Mitsui explains how to meet the demands of art directors; Bud Peen mixes watercolor and quill pen with digital media; Katrin Eismann explores the world of digital cameras; Eric Chauvin tells how he creates animated matte paintings for feature films. Even the Photoshop-centered topics — such as Eric Reinfeld's examination of text effects or Greg Vander Houwen's meditations on layers — resonate with each artist's unique perspective.

- **Respect the artist**: One of the unfortunate trends in publishing is that most computer graphics books treat their artists as commodities. An image and its artist may rate no more than a single caption or paragraph. Whether it's because the author didn't have the expertise to dig deeper or the artist was too busy to share, this practice short-changes the artist and reader alike. You may learn a little about how the piece was created, but you rarely find out why. I decided to give the artists a chance to show who they are, how they got there, and why they do what they do. By conducting exhaustive, free-form, and sometimes fatiguing interviews, Katrin and I were able to generate a picture of who each person is, largely in the artist's own voice.

Of course, the qualities that permeate my other books are here, too. I try to keep things lively and interesting throughout. (If the text isn't fun to read, there's no way it's going to compete with all this gorgeous artwork!) And while the information comes from some very experienced sources, there's nothing here that a reasonably proficient Photoshop user can't understand.

ABOUT THE WHOLE PLATFORM THING

This is a cross-platform book, which is to say that it's written for both Macintosh and Windows users. If I write "⌘/Ctrl+K," for example, it means to press ⌘+K if you're working on the Mac or Ctrl+K on the PC. A few differences exist between Photoshop for the Mac and Photoshop for Windows, but nothing that affects the content of this particular book.

However, if you take a quick look at the computers that the artists in this book use, you'll notice a strange phenomenon. Virtually every one of them uses a Mac. Ben Benjamin and Michael Ninness also use PCs on the job, and Robert Bowen uses a UNIX-based SGI machine. But the computers with which they spend most of their time are Macs.

Does this mean that Macs are the best computers for artists? Or is it simply an indication that these folks have been working on Macs for so long that they don't know any better? I don't know what the reason is, and more important, I don't care. The machines they use are their business.

In fact, the only reason I bring it up is that some folks may wonder why I didn't work a little harder to find artists who prefer Windows. My frank answer is that doing so would have been pointless and counterproductive. I didn't observe any racial, sexual, religious, geographic, or age-based quotas in selecting these artists. Why in the world would I have given even a passing thought to the computer they use? All that matters is that the information in this book is as equally applicable to Photoshop for Windows as it is to Photoshop for the Mac.

SOME MORE PERSONAL TESTIMONY

In short, of all the Photoshop books on the market, this is the one I would be the most likely to buy. It's the one book I've written that reveals mysteries that were previously outside my range of knowledge on virtually every page. That's because this is less a cohesive book than a compilation of 21 unique seminars presented by 21 eminent artists. My biggest contribution is a sense of enthusiasm and wonder as the information unfolds.

As is so often the case, I started thinking I knew everything, only to learn I knew nothing. Read these pages and delight in the discovery of how little you once knew.

— Deke McClelland

CONTENTS AT A GLANCE

FOREWORD VII

PREFACE IX

PART I: GENERAL TECHNIQUES 1

Chapter 1 Sketch to Execution: The Commercial Art Process 3

Chapter 2 Working Stock Photography into Graphic Art 19

Chapter 3 Creating Budget 3-D Characters 33

Chapter 4 Integrating Natural Media into Digital Art 41

Chapter 5 Merging Past and Present with Sumi Brushstrokes 53

Chapter 6 Enhancing Vector Artwork 71

Chapter 7 The Face-Melting Power of Distortions 85

Chapter 8 Abstract Expressionism to Commercial Design 95

Chapter 9 Special Type Effects 115

Chapter 10 The Tao of Layering 129

PART II: SPECIFIC APPLICATIONS 143

Chapter 11 High-Resolution Imaging for Advertising 145

Chapter 12 Fine Art Printing 161

Chapter 13 Pixels to Platinum 175

Chapter 14 Photographing for Photoshop 199

Chapter 15 Fashion Photography 213

Chapter 16 Creative QuickTime VR 235

Chapter 17 The Quick Guide to Digital Cameras 259

Chapter 18 Photoshop in Motion 273

Chapter 19 Inventing Photo-Realistic Worlds 285

Chapter 20 Creating Images for the World Wide Web 299

Chapter 21 Buttons, Buttons, Buttons 311

APPENDIX ABOUT THE CD-ROM   323

INDEX   327

ABOUT THE AUTHORS   334

COLOPHON   335

END-USER LICENSE AGREEMENT   336

CD-ROM INSTALLATION INSTRUCTIONS   342

CONTENTS

FOREWORD vii

PREFACE ix

PART I : GENERAL TECHNIQUES 1

CHAPTER 1

SKETCH TO EXECUTION: THE COMMERCIAL ART PROCESS 3

FEATURING GLENN MITSUI

Who Is Glenn to Talk? 3

The Client and You 6
    Developing Quality Concepts 7
    The Importance of Communication 7

Art on the March 7
    Medical Objectives and Intestinal Diagrams 8
    Sketch and Concept 9
    Tracing the Sketch in Freehand 11

GLENN SAYS, ONE SKETCH, ONE CONCEPT 11

Rasterizing and Tracing in Photoshop 11
Making the Beveled Body Outline 12
Adding the Background Stuff 12
Binding the Books 13
Creating the Globes 14
Hanging the Internal Organs 15

CHAPTER 2

WORKING STOCK PHOTOGRAPHY INTO
GRAPHIC ART 19

FEATURING GORDON STUDER

Is It Ethical? 21

The Trend Toward Stock Photography 21

Gordonian Geometry 23
    Mixing Static Backdrops 24
    The Central Stock Subject 24

ALIGNING VECTOR ART WITH IMAGERY 24

    Adding the Computer 26
    Composition and Drop Shadows 26
    Tha Anatomically Precise Hand 28
    The Final Adjustments 28

Free-Form Image Chopping 29
    Rough Pixels Inside Smooth Outlines 30
    Cacophony of Kitties 30

Has Photoshop 5 Ruined Gordon? 30

CHAPTER 3

CREATING BUDGET 3-D
CHARACTERS 33

FEATURING MIKE STRASSBURGER

Mike's First Encounter with 3-D 33

The Budget Approach to 3-D 34
    Friskets for the Airbrush 35
    Drawing Paths 36
    Making the Layers 36
    Painting the Highlights and Shadows 38
    Those Glassy Eyes 39

Sometimes, Ignorance Really Is Bliss 39

CHAPTER 4

INTEGRATING NATURAL MEDIA INTO DIGITAL ART   41

FEATURING BUD PEEN

Bud's Natural Media Epiphany   41

Part I: A Conventional Beginning   43

Part II: Shifting into Digital   44
  Combining the Artwork   44
  Coloring the Lines   45
  When You Find a Good Thing . . .   46

Vector Variations   46
  Paths Instead of Watercolor   47
  Embracing Synthetic Media   49

You Use *What*-Peg   50

So Much Media, So Little Time   50
  The World of the Tactile   50
  The World of the Screen   51

CHAPTER 5

MERGING PAST AND PRESENT WITH SUMI BRUSHSTROKES   53

FEATURING HIROSHI GOTO

Inspiration and Process   54

Sketch to Mask   56

Masks to Color   59

Making the Background   61

Compositing   63

Gallery Conversations   65
   The Fish   65
   Cherry Blossoms   66
   The Peony   67

Painting with Watercolors   67

The Final Print   68

In Closing   68

CHAPTER 6

ENHANCING VECTOR ARTWORK   71

FEATURING RON CHAN

Portrait of a Vector Guy   71
   Fear of Photoshop   74
   The Attraction of Pixels   74

Adding Textures to an Illustration   75
   Making the Texture   75
   Bringing in Paths from Illustrator   75

DRAGGING PATHS FROM ILLUSTRATOR   76

   Filling Paths with Textures   76
   Repeat, Repeat, Repeat   77

The Big Oil Texture   78

The Customized Fade Texture   79

Layers in Focus   80

Chan's Imaging Reflections   82

CHAPTER 7

THE FACE-MELTING POWER OF DISTORTIONS   85

FEATURING MARK MOORE

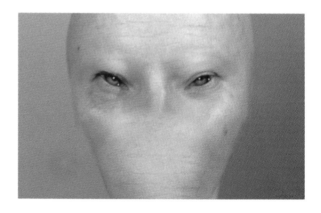

The Visual Effects Art Director at Work   85
   Dissecting the Alien   86

Transforming Sir Guy into Bones   87
   The Immutable Law of Alien Light Bulbs   88
   Masking Features with Forehead   88
   Making the Fierce Little Eyes   89
   Expanding the Cranium   90

CLEANING UP DISTORTION BLURS 91

  Restoring the Nutrient Input Orifice 92
  Alien Intervention 92
  From Photoshop to Creature Shop 93

Kids, Don't Try This at Home 93

CHAPTER 8

ABSTRACT EXPRESSIONISM TO COMMERCIAL DESIGN 95

FEATURING ULRIK CLAESSON

Artistic Randomness 96
  Claesson's Channel Strategy 98
  Simulated Moonscape 99
  More Channel Madness 100
  Adding Color 102
  Managing File Size 103

The Beauty Is in the Details 103

Old and New Merge 106

Commercial Design 110

CHAPTER 9

SPECIAL TYPE EFFECTS 115

FEATURING ERIC REINFELD

The Basic Approach 115
  Clipping Image Against Image 118
  Expanding the Type for the Halo 118

THE BENEFITS OF LAYERED TYPE 119

  Blurring and Dodging 119

Creating Source Variations 120
  Changing the Weight 120
  Making Outlines 121
  Soft Emboss Effects 121

MOVING THROUGH THE LAYERS 121

  The Solid Black Layer 122

Assembling the Actual Composition 122
  The First Emboss Effect 122
  The Red Inner Emboss 123

Inner Emboss Highlights   124
The Big Background Emboss   125

Roughing It   126

Eric's Closing Pearls of Wisdom   127

CHAPTER 10

THE TAO OF LAYERING   129

FEATURING GREG VANDER HOUWEN

Dropping the Dome   132
The Light from on High   133

Using Layer Options   133
Dropping Out and Forcing Through   134
Never Try to Mask Lightning   134

Tonal Adjustments in Layer Masks   135
Gradient Layer Masks   135
Tonal Edge Adjustments   137
Quick Effect Masks   138

Walking the Virtual Mile   138
Building the Layers   138
Striking Base Camp   141
The Finishing Touches   141

GREG KEEPS THE SKETCH HANDY   142

Following the Path That Is Always in Motion   142

Base Camps and Serious Alterations   129

Roughing Out a Composition   130
Chain Sawing a Layer Mask   132

PART II SPECIFIC APPLICATIONS 143

CHAPTER 11

HIGH-RESOLUTION IMAGING FOR ADVERTISING 145

FEATURING ROBERT BOWEN

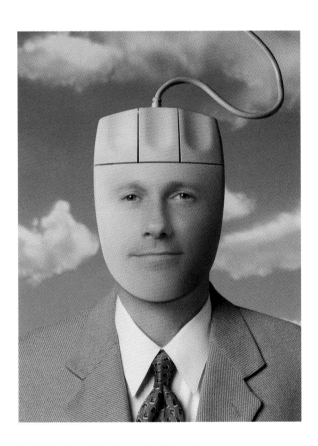

Bob's Exploration into the Unreal 145

Managing Populations of a Few Million Pixels 149
  Working with Super-Huge Files 150
  CMYK Files and RGB Transparencies 150

Case Studies and Nonexistent Worlds 150
  Staging an Illustration 150
  Drinking with Dolphins 152

TEXTURING GRADIENT SKIES 153

Crafing a Spontaneous Snapshot 154

BOB URGES YOU TO GO ALL THE WAY 156

The Physics of Cloning Sheep 157

THE INFINITE DINER 158

And Now for Something Completely Different 158

CHAPTER 12

FINE ART PRINTING 161

FEATURING KARIN SCHMINKE

The Messy World of Mixed Media 163

Painting and Printing, Printing and Painting 163
  Creating the Subimage 164
  Printing the Subimage 164
  Creating the Inset Image 164

A Gold Background for the Inset Image   165
Testing the Overprint with Acetate   166
Overprinting the Inset Image   166

Printing on Black   168
Painting onto a Printed Template   169
Printing onto Acrylic   169

Printing onto Liquid Photo Emulsion   170

Protecting Your Ink-Jet Artwork   171

Shopping for a Fine-Art Printer   171

Why Mix Digital with Traditional   173

CHAPTER 13

PIXELS TO PLATINUM   175

FEATURING DAN BURKHOLDER

Eureka!   178

Calibrate or Do Not Pass Go!   179

The Camera as Notebook   181

Input   182
High-Tech Backlash   183

The Digital Darkroom   184

Matching the Film Grain   187

Creating the Light   188

From Grayscale to Bitmap   191

Working with the Service Bureau   193

The Film Is Done!   193

Additional Finesse   195

Working with a Gallery   197

Discovering Style   197

CHAPTER 14

PHOTOGRAPHING FOR PHOTOSHOP   199

FEATURING JEFF SCHEWE

How Exactly Do You Dress Up a Pig   199

Matching Backgrounds   201

Mixing Multiple Live Elements   203
   Meticulous Paths for Intricate Edges   204
   All Against a Gradient Background   204

Playing with Scale   205

Reflections and Refractions   208
   With and Without Flakes   208
   Inner and Outer Refractions   209
   Reinstating the Reflections   210
   Sprinkling the Snowflakes   210

Merging Passion and Profit   210

CHAPTER 15

FASHION PHOTOGRAPHY   213

FEATURING WERNER PAWLOK

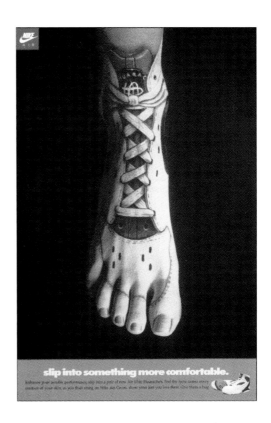

Concept, Photography, Digital Imaging   215
   Nailing the Concept   215
   Choosing the Film   216
   Shooting for Digital   216
   After the Shoot   218

Fashionable Photoshop   218

Beauty Is Pixel Deep   220
   The Plexiglas Tunnel   221

PHOTOSHOP 5.0 NAVIGATION SHORTCUTS   222

Image to Layout   224

Photoshop or Reality?   226

Mask This!   228
   Pawlok's Hair Mask Technique   228

A Beautiful Challenge   232

CHAPTER 16

CREATIVE QUICKTIME VR   233

FEATURING JANIE FITZGERALD

QTVR and the Photographer   235
   Fitzgerald's Commercial Work   236
   Fitzgerald's Personal Work   240
   The VrView Web Site   241

QTVR in a Nutshell   243

Photography for QTVR   244

Photoshop Production for QTVR   245

Proportion and Color   248

Imaginary Spaces   252

Not Just Photographs   254

Virtual Galleries   256

Full Circle   257

CHAPTER 17

THE QUICK GUIDE TO DIGITAL CAMERAS   259

FEATURING KATRIN EISMANN

Is a Digital Camera Right for You?   259
   Time Waits for No One   262
   A Matter of Quality   262
   The Cost of Doing Business   265

Film Still Has Its Merits   265

Selecting the Best Camera   266

Shooting and Editing Your Photos   267

KATRIN'S LOW-END TIPS   268

Adjusting Lighting Irregularities   268
Fixing Rainbows   269
Simple But Special Effects   270

Keeping Your Photos Safe   271

CHAPTER 18

PHOTOSHOP IN MOTION   273

FEATURING WILL HYDE

Video Imaging 101   274
Pixels Per Frame   274
Real-Time Editing   277

Setting Up Text Effects in Photoshop   277
Conveying Transparency to After Effects   278
Hyde Prepares the Haze   279
Animating the Text   281

Rotoscoping with Masks   282

CHAPTER 19

INVENTING PHOTO-REALISTIC WORLDS   285

FEATURING ERIC CHAUVIN

The Basic Matte Process   286
Can't Afford the High-End?   287
Little Images for Big Movies   287

The Empire Shuttle Bay   288
Painting the Void of Space   289
Playing with the Light   290
The Tiny Bay Across the Way   290

The Architecture of Cloud City   290

ELIMINATING FILM GRAIN   291

Adding Buildings in the Sky   292
Turning Down the Lights   292
The Teaming Masses   293

The Dinosaur Movie That Never Got Made   294
Modeling Dinotopia   294
Integrating the Natural World   295
The Cascading Falls   296

Eric's Intermittent Flashes of Fame   297

CHAPTER 20

CREATING IMAGES FOR THE WORLD WIDE WEB   299

FEATURING BEN BENJAMIN

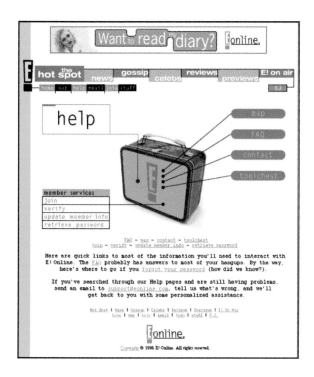

Ben Would Kill for a Kilobyte   299

The Melrose Mystery   301
   A Tawdry Little Cyberplace   301
   Designing Pages in Illustrator   302
   Exporting the GIF Image Map   303
   Anticipating 256-Color Monitors   304

HOW BEN ANTICIPATES 256-COLOR
MONITORS   305

   Exploiting Browser Caching   305

Animated Banner Ads   306
   Hyping Talk Soup   306
   Compiling the Frames in GIFBuilder   307
   File Size, Dimensions, and Duration   309

LOOPING WITH A LOW SOURCE   309

CHAPTER 21

BUTTONS, BUTTONS, BUTTONS   311

FEATURING MICHAEL NINNESS

Study Agriculture   Learn a New Language   You Can Be Mechanical   Learn to Love Symbols

The Basic Beveled Square   312

MYKE SAYS, "WORK BIG"   313

Making Buttons with Clipping Groups   314
   Etching Type into the Beveled Square   317
   Mass Button Production   317

Creating a Stamped Button   318
   The Simple Emboss Approach   318
   The Slightly More Elaborate Lighting Effects
   Method   320

APPENDIX A

ABOUT THE CD-ROM   322

INDEX   327

ABOUT THE AUTHORS   334

COLOPHON   335

END-USER LICENSE AGREEMENT   336

CD-ROM INSTALLATION INSTRUCTIONS   342

NAATA PRESENTS THE

1994

FRANCISCO ASIAN AMERICAN

INTERNATIONAL

FILM FESTIVAL

PART I
GENERAL
TECHNIQUES

Sketch to Execution: The
   Commercial Art Process 3
Working Stock Photography into
   Graphic Art 19
Creating Budget 3-D
   Characters 33
Integrating Natural Media into
   Digital Art 41
Merging Past and Present with
   Sumi Brushstrokes 53
Enhancing Vector Artwork 77
The Face-Melting Power of
   Distortions 91
Abstract Expressionism to
   Commercial Design 101
Special Type Effects 137
The Tao of Layering 151

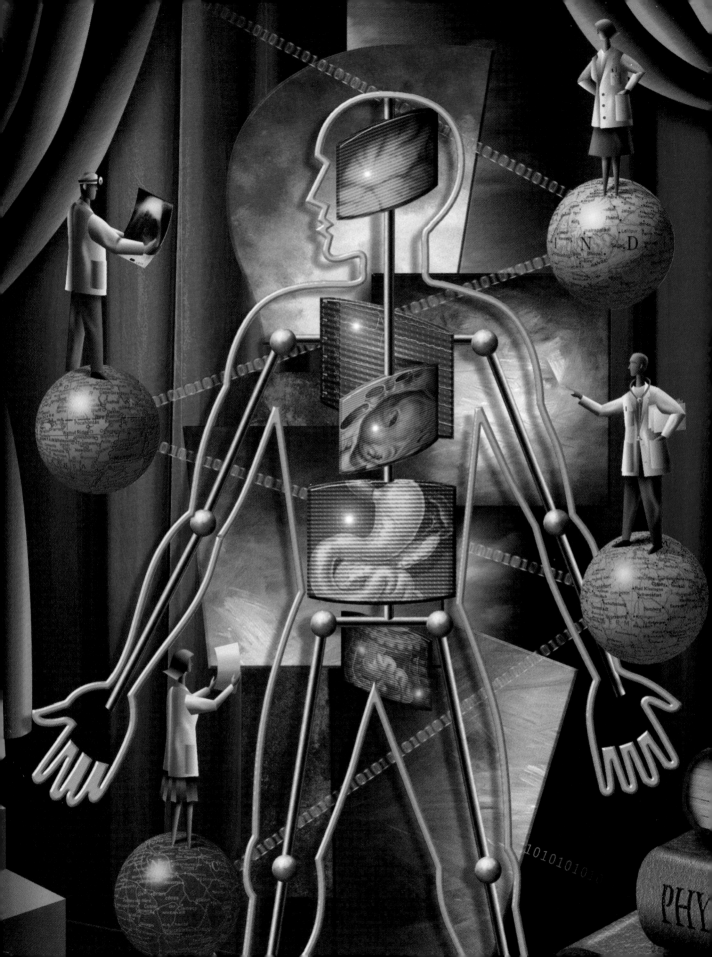

CHAPTER 1
SKETCH TO EXECUTION: THE COMMERCIAL ART PROCESS

Photoshop is, by most accounts, a powerful and well-constructed program, arguably the staple application of the professional graphics industry. But it's the program's price that really forces you to treat it with reverence. Unless you're a highly paid professional type who gets a kick out of image editing in your spare time, Photoshop is too expensive to purchase as a lark. After sinking $500 into the software, and who knows how much into learning it, the best way to recoup your costs is to make money with the program.

We're not proposing to share with you some magic formula for breaking into the computer graphics market. Nor do we have a secret list of art directors who are looking for fresh talent. (If we did, we'd be filming infomercials and setting up 900 numbers instead of writing this book.) Having only a vague recollection of the random turn of events that got us where we are today, we're hardly in a position to coach.

But with the help of veteran computer artist Glenn Mitsui, we can paint a picture of what it's like to create a commercial project from start to finish. If you've never sold a piece of artwork to a high-end client, then this little tour is the next best thing to serving six months as a studio apprentice. And if you already make a tidy living with Photoshop, we think you'll find Mitsui's approach uniquely insightful. This chapter shows Mitsui at work, from initial client contact to final product.

WHO IS GLENN TO TALK?

Before we launch into what Mitsui does, it might help to know a little bit about who he is and what makes

With different styles, you can handle a wide variety of jobs and you're never in a position of having to hammer a round peg in a square hole.

GLENN MITSUI

him an expert on this particular topic. Art directors and colleagues recognize him as a rare chameleon of an artist who can shift styles to accommodate the interests and personalities of his clients. While just about every artist feels compelled to periodically modify his or her style to remain commercially viable, Mitsui seems capable of balancing multiple styles simultaneously.

"If you maintain a single particular style, it's not always possible to force that style into different subject matters. For example, my brightly colored architectural style probably wouldn't work as editorial art for a story about psychology. With different styles, you can handle a wide variety of jobs and you're never in a position of having to hammer a round peg in a square hole. I'm not saying it never works against you — you may find that your identity isn't as strong in one style as in another. And I always have to ask my clients which piece of mine led them to me so I can figure out which style they're looking for. But the mental advantages are well worth it. I don't get bored."

For A'cino, an emerging cosmetics company, Mitsui employed his sleek photo collage style (1.1). "A'cino wanted to create a series of postcards and placards for retail stores. They wanted chic, but they didn't want to look too high tech. So, I tried to create something that was crisp and elegant. And of course, I've always been intrigued by fish swimming beside birds with long legs."

Mitsui used a softer, more traditional style for a poster he did for the Seattle Repertory Theater (1.2).

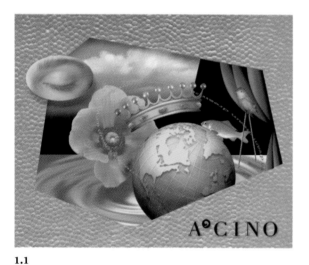

1.1

1.2

ARTIST:
Glenn Mitsui

ORGANIZATION:
Studio M D
1512 Alaskan Way
Seattle, WA 98101
206/682-6221
glenn@studiomd.com

SYSTEM:
Power Mac 7100/66
1GB storage

RAM:
106MB total
70MB assigned to Photoshop

MONITOR:
Radius 17-inch

EXTRAS:
Hewlett-Packard ScanJet IIcx

VERSION USED:
Photoshop 5.0

OTHER APPLICATIONS:
Macromedia FreeHand, FractalDesign Painter, Adobe After Effects

"I'm a big fan of playwright Philip Gotanda, so when they asked me to do a poster for one of his plays, I was very excited. The play's about a 17-year-old girl who grew up on the island of Kauai in the early 1900s. Part of the story is about how she becomes an apprentice for a bitter but very talented pottery artist, and later becomes romantically involved with him. So, I wanted to integrate the elements of natural art, with natural brushstrokes, pottery shards, and the fire from the kiln."

Folks in the computer industry are likely to see a starkly different side of Mitsui. "Resolution Technology asked me to create an ad for a 3-D program of theirs that allows artists to create realistic fly-throughs and landscapes. My approach to it was to build a volumetric person made up of various inter-active elements (1.3). It resembles a 3-D rendering, but I created everything using layers and gradients in Photoshop."

1.3

WORK HISTORY:

<u>1982</u> — Worked as technical illustrator on graveyard shift at Boeing; discovered that women's bathroom had a nap couch.

<u>1987</u> — Created corporate presentation slides on Genigraphics system for Magicmation.

<u>1990</u> — Started Studio M D with Jesse Doquilo and Randy Lim; purchased first Macintosh system.

<u>1992</u> — Started creating full-page feature artwork for *Macworld* magazine.

<u>1995</u> — Became board member and speaker for American Institute of Graphics Arts; served as panel judge for SigGraph fine arts competition.

FAVORITE '70s TV SHOWS:

"Green Hornet" (because Bruce Lee played Kato) and "Long Street" (because Bruce Lee played Kung Fu instructor)

1.4

Mitsui used the theme of paper kites to symbolize the different nationalities represented at San Francisco's Asian American International Film Festival (1.4). "The Festival includes Chinese films, Japanese films, Korean, Thai, Indonesian, and all kinds of other contributions. I wanted to show that although we're all different in a lot of ways, we're blown by the same wind. Here I tried to emphasize the printed quality of the paper by exaggerating the creases and wrinkles and keeping the halftone dots in the eyes."

One of Mitsui's most recent stylistic developments is what he calls his "big hurkin' icons with Spirograph" approach. "The image of the two hands (1.5) was one of the illustrations I proposed to demonstrate compatibility issues for a new chip from Fujitsu. I feel like this style really emphasizes the power of the line. It lets me elicit humor, anger, and other raw emotions using quick icons. It's like a logo — it either succeeds or fails on first glance."

THE CLIENT AND YOU

Initial contact with a client usually starts with a phone call or e-mail from an art director. "By the time you hear from an art director, the client has probably already seen your work." Does the art director already

1.5

have a sketch or visual idea in mind? "Sometimes, but mostly not. If I'm doing magazine art, I probably get a copy of the article. If it's an ad, I might get the ad copy or they might send me the product. But the client usually relies on me to come up with a visual concept that relates to what they do."

DEVELOPING QUALITY CONCEPTS

The art director is the client's one and only representative. To satisfy the client, you have to include the art director fully in the decision-making process. "Most problems occur when you don't involve the client enough. The last thing you want to do is surprise your client, like so many digital artists do. That usually happens when you take a concept and run with it on the computer before anybody but you has seen it.

"You can't just tie together a bunch of special effects and expect your artwork to sell. A good illustration is 90 percent concept and 10 percent execution. The concept has got to be strong. If you go to the computer right away, without completely developing the idea, you get 90 percent technique and 10 percent concept. That's simply not going to fly with high-end clients.

"It's really easy to take an idea too far, too fast, when you're working in a program like Photoshop. That's why I develop the concept with traditional pencil sketches. If I'm on a deadline, I sit down and force the sketches to work. If I have a week to come up with a concept, I sketch when I'm feeling creative. But as a rule, I avoid the computer altogether until the art director has signed off on the concept."

THE IMPORTANCE OF COMMUNICATION

Much as we might like to hope that talent always wins, commercial art is a business like any other. The most successful artists are generally the ones who take the most care in securing and maturing personal relationships. Your ability to get work hinges on effective communication. "If you exclude art directors from the creative process, it can be a big strike against you, particularly if you've never worked with them before. You can almost guarantee that they're going to find things wrong. Whereas, if you get their input at the very beginning and you maintain good relationships, then you avoid surprises and get more

jobs in the future. Talk about the project up front. If you don't understand something at the beginning, feel free to ask dumb questions until you know who your client is and what he wants. Don't be nervous, don't feel like you have to apologize. Just patiently feel him out. Now you're working with the art director to get something that he can be comfortable with bringing to his client, and will fight for."

But accommodating your client doesn't mean you have to behave like a wimp. Mitsui advocates that you agree to a reasonable fee up front and stick to it. "The client signs a job estimate before I put pencil to paper for the first sketch. It's a standard contract that I and the others at Studio M D put together a few years back. The estimate is pretty much the exact fee, unless some special circumstances come along. I usually allow for a couple of rounds of revisions before I start charging hourly for anything beyond that. If you do good stuff, and you're predictable and reliable, then you'll always be in demand."

ART ON THE MARCH

Mitsui's work for Advanced Medical Ventures probably illustrates the trials and rewards of creating computer art as well as any piece he's created. "It was an interesting job, all right." The assignment was to create a cover for a medical conference brochure. "The conference was about disorders of the upper stomach. The panelists at this conference were all leading experts in the field of digestive disorders. A bunch of other doctors who treat this illness were invited to come and participate in the audience. Everybody had a keyboard. They posed all questions and received consensus answers from the panelists. There was even going to be a satellite link to show operations beforehand. I can honestly say, it was unlike anything I had done before."

Objective #1: Define dyspepsia, appreciate its epidemiology and clinical significance, and understand the importance of dysomitility in its pathogenesis.

Objective #2: Understand the natural history of gastro-esphageal reflux disease (GERD), the importance of erosive compared to non-erosive esophagitis, and the complications of GERD.

1.6

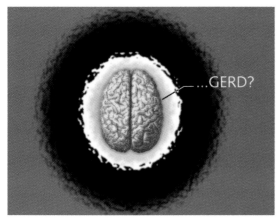

...GERD?

1.7

MEDICAL OBJECTIVES AND INTESTINAL DIAGRAMS

"I didn't know anything about stomach disorders — you know, my stomach seems to be working okay — but I agreed to do the job because it sounded like it would be different. Then, the art director faxed me these two objectives that he wanted me to cover in the artwork (1.6). I don't usually get a list of objectives from a client — not like this, anyway. I looked them over, but for all I could tell, they were written in Greek."

Did the objectives imply that Mitsui should show GERD in action? Was he supposed to highlight the importance of understanding GERD? Or was his mission to produce the artwork while suffering the complications of GERD? Mitsui responds, "I see you have a sense of some of the questions that were going through my head (1.7). Part of the excitement and challenge of being an artist is that you learn so much. Even when you don't want to learn, you get to. It's quite thrilling."

So, how does Mitsui gain a clear understanding of a job when he embarks into such incredibly alien territory? Does he go to the library and search through a few medical encyclopedias? "No way. That might help me understand GERD, but it doesn't get me any closer to knowing the client. The only thing to do is talk and talk and talk to the art director. I ask every dumb question I can think of until I come across something I can work with. It's better to look like a dope up front than create an illustration that doesn't suit the client's needs."

To make things more interesting, the art director asked Mitsui to integrate some existing diagrams into his artwork. "He said, 'I'm going to totally leave the creative aspects up to you. But I have a couple of images that I want you to include in your illustration.' And then these intestinal tracts come through (1.8). I thought, whoa, these are pretty. I mean, what is that yellow thing back there? Did this guy swallow a whole cob of corn or something? What in the world am I going to do with this stuff?"

But the client is always right. Who knows, a couple of intestinal diagrams might provide the creative spark that Mitsui is looking for. "Whenever I have something weird like this, I always leave it until the last. That way, I can sit around and worry about it the whole time I'm working on the illustration. It provides motivation."

SKETCH AND CONCEPT

"My personal objective in this project is to come up with a piece of artwork that looks cool and doesn't gross people out. In my first sketch (1.9), I had a little trouble focusing. I think it's Abe Lincoln in a lab coat surrounded by some fire. Even though I didn't use any of this, it was an important part of the process. When you're under a deadline, you don't have any choice. You have to work it out until you hit something that really works for you. For me, sketching is the best way to develop a concept.

"Then, I started brainstorming a little. I looked around the room, paged through books. At some point, I saw some clothes on a hanger, and it reminded me of this petroglyph (1.10). I read the petroglyph as a wire structure with these deelee-boppers hanging down from it, kind of like pots and pans. That's when the basic concept clicked. The body would be the frame, and the organs would hang inside it, like a primitive Visible Man."

With this concept in mind, Mitsui began to sketch in earnest. He quickly settled on a frontal view of the body with the head turned in profile. Then, he arranged a series of globes around the body (1.11). "The conference includes speakers and doctors from all over the world. So the globes demonstrate the international feel of the event.

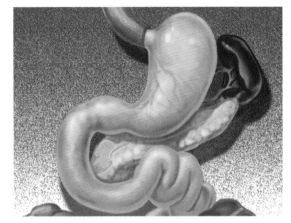

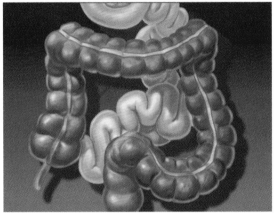

1.8

Reprinted with permission from Advanced Medical Ventures. Artwork by Linda Nye.

1.9

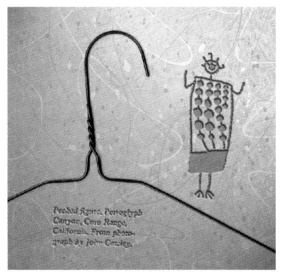

1.10

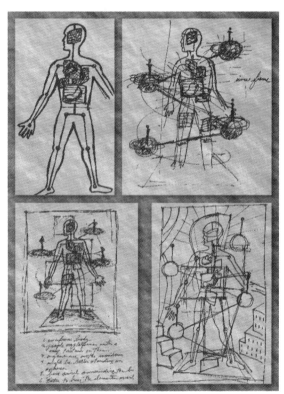

1.11

"As I sketch, I write myself little notes in the margins. These include little comments and ideas I want to remember, things I need clarification on, and questions that I have to ask the client. You have to make a real effort to stay on top of the client's needs. By keeping notes, I make sure I don't forget something that could gum up the works."

Mitsui's final sketch adds structure to the illustration (1.12). "The wireframe could look a little flimsy if I just stuck it against a neutral background. By adding some simple, block-like objects — the steps, the curtains, the books — I could convey depth without distracting attention from the primary element. It makes the sketch feel like a more substantial piece of artwork."

At this point, Glenn faxed his sketch to the art director for approval. "He signed off on it right away." Did the quick approval surprise Mitsui? "No, it was a solid concept. After working this long, I think I have a pretty good sense of whether I've nailed it or not. If I don't think I have it, I don't send it."

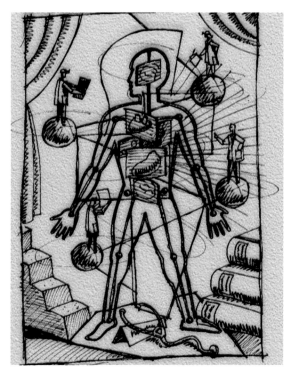

1.12

TRACING THE SKETCH IN FREEHAND

After getting the sketch approved, Mitsui scanned it into Photoshop and scaled it to get the proper width and height dimensions. Then, he saved the sketch as a TIFF image and imported it into FreeHand. Inside FreeHand, Mitsui used the pen tool to trace the main outlines. As we'll see, these paths later served as template elements and selection outlines in Photoshop.

Mitsui likes FreeHand for its simplicity. "It's the 7-Eleven of graphics programs. If you need a Twinkie, you go to 7-Eleven, get in and get out. No one gets hurt. FreeHand is the same way. You get in, trace your paths, get out. No thinking necessary. I don't expect much from it, and it gives me very little in return."

We should mention that Mitsui is still using FreeHand 3.1, a program that was last seen in stores about four years ago. "Sure, it's old, but it's easy to use and it does everything I need it to. I can fly around and trace all the paths I need in 15 minutes or so. I don't think I even have the colors loaded anymore; I just use it in black and white."

RASTERIZING AND TRACING IN PHOTOSHOP

"I saved the illustration in the Illustrator 3 format, because that's the best FreeHand 3.1 can do. Then, in Photoshop, I rasterized it at 300 pixels per inch. Since all the paths were black, I opened it as a grayscale image so it came up as fast as possible."

Mitsui had no intention of integrating the FreeHand drawing directly into his final artwork; it was merely an architectural template, cleaner and more precise than the original pencil sketch. And in Photoshop, the best place to put a template is in a separate channel. "I went to the Channels palette. Because it was a grayscale image, there was only one channel there. I duplicated it to a second channel and inverted it so it appeared white against black (1.13)."

GLENN SAYS, ONE SKETCH, ONE CONCEPT

"Once I get it right, I send just the one sketch. A lot of artists get indecisive and send off two or three sketches just to be safe. That's a bad idea because it confuses the client and asks him to think about issues that are really your responsibility. You have to say, 'Here's my vision. Do you like it, yes or no?' If no, then we talk. If yes, I move on. It's a very clean process this way."

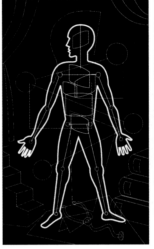
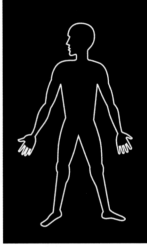

1.13   1.14

Mitsui converted the file to the RGB mode and filled the RGB image with black to clear out the rasterized drawing. (The inverted template remained safe in the alpha channel.) He then returned to the alpha channel, now the fourth channel, and traced most of the template outlines with Photoshop's pen tool. "One of the things about using FreeHand 3.1 is that you can't bring the paths over directly. But that's okay. Tracing them again gives me the opportunity to further refine the drawing."

MAKING THE BEVELED BODY OUTLINE

So Mitsui redraws every single path? "Not all of them. The outline of the body is something I used as is. I went back to the FreeHand file and copied the body path and pasted it into a file all by itself. Then, I brought that over as a fifth channel in my Photoshop image (1.14). This outline was thick enough to use as a mask all by itself."

The body outline was the first image element that Mitsui added to his illustration. He started by ⌘/Ctrl-clicking the fifth channel in the Channels palette to convert it into a selection outline. Then, he filled the selection with yellow (1.15). To add a beveled edge to the body outline (1.16), Mitsui relied

on the third-party Inner Bevel filter, which is part of the Eye Candy plug-in collection from Alien Skin Software. But he could have just as easily applied an Inner Bevel layer effect in Photoshop 5.0.

ADDING THE BACKGROUND STUFF

Mitsui blocked in his background objects on separate layers using gradient fills and stock images. He started by creating red drapes in the upper left corner of the illustration (1.17). Each fold of the drapery is the result of converting one of his paths to a selection and then filling it with a red-to-black gradation. To make the soft blue drapes at the rear of his virtual auditorium (1.18), he imported a stock photo from the PhotoDisc image library. The floor of the stage (1.19) is a wood pattern that Mitsui shot himself. Like the red drapes, Mitsui created the green steps by converting paths to selection outlines and filling the selections with gradations.

No one can accuse Mitsui of being stingy with his gradient shadows. "My motto is simple. No shadow bad; plenty shadow good." But the astute viewer will notice that Mitsui plays fast and loose with his imaginary light source. "When my students tell me, 'Mr. Mitsui, your light source is inconsistent,' I just say, 'So?' Then they say, 'Your perspective is all screwy,' and I say, 'Yup.' I had my fill of paying attention to that kind of thing when I worked as a draftsman at

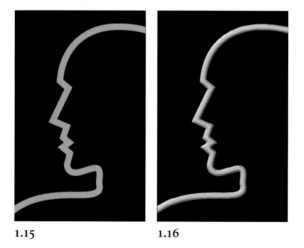

1.15   1.16

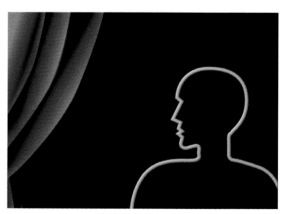

1.17

Boeing. This is my world, darn it. Everybody else is just a nut trying to get a squirrel."

Was it possible Mitsui was inspired by French post-impressionist Paul Cézanne, who purposely violated perspective in order to focus on abstracted details in his artwork? "Oh, yeah, I'm big on violating stuff. But seriously, people don't come to me to create technically accurate illustrations. They're looking to me to create a mood and a feel and a dynamic."

BINDING THE BOOKS

To highlight the scholarly nature of the conference, Mitsui's sketch called for books in the lower right corner of the artwork. He created the basic book shapes by reshaping and cloning elements from real books (1.20). But the bindings were generic hardcover fabric with no markings to identify them as medical volumes (1.21). The challenge was to take

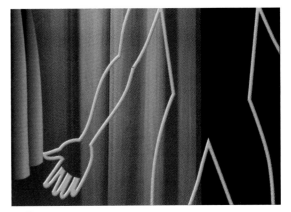

1.18

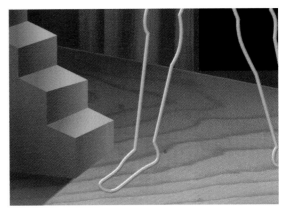

1.19

1.20

1.21

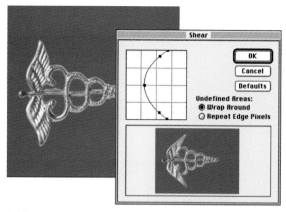

1.22

1.23

1.24

1.25

words such as Anatomy and Physiology and wrap them onto the curved spines of the books.

"Filter ➢ Distort ➢ Shear is great for faking 3-D effects. Here, I used the Shear filter to distort the text and medical emblem horizontally (1.22) so they appeared to bend around the sides of the books. Then, I just rotated the elements to match the angle of the spines (1.23). I used to do this kind of stuff in Ray Dream Designer, but now I totally avoid 3-D programs. I never did enjoy working in Ray Dream or any of them."

CREATING THE GLOBES

For each of his four globes, Mitsui started with a small, square scrap from a scanned map (1.24). Then he applied the Glass Lens Bright filter from Kai's Power Tools 2 to wrap a circular area of the map around a 3-D sphere (1.25). "I bet I could've come up with something similar using the Spherize filter that's included with Photoshop, and layering on a couple of radial gradations. But some of those simple KPT filters are really useful."

Mitsui wanted to colorize each globe with a different hue, so he converted the globe to a grayscale image. Then, he indexed the color palette using Image ➢ Mode ➢ Indexed Color. This permitted him to modify the palette using Image ➢ Mode ➢ Color Table. "When you choose the Color Table command, Photoshop lets you edit all 256 colors in the indexed palette (1.26). I just dragged across all the colors in the palette. Then, Photoshop asked me to specify the darkest color in the table and the lightest color. I set them both to shades of blue. Then, Photoshop automatically blended between them (1.27)."

Why not use the Hue/Saturation command? "I don't feel like I have enough control over the process with that command. The ramping between light and dark colors is uneven. As a result, the colors tend to get too hot, and an image like this might start to band. With the Color Table command, I can precisely control the tonal range of colors in one fell swoop." After colorizing each globe, Mitsui selected it with the elliptical marquee tool and dragged it over into his composition (1.28).

HANGING THE INTERNAL ORGANS

"So here I am, almost done with the job. One of the last things I have to do is insert the organs into the artwork. I've put it off as long as I can (1.29).

"By now, I've already decided that I'm going to frame the organs inside slanted viewing screens which will hang from the frame that I've set up inside the body. But I'm still a little nervous about integrating the client's images. These doctors are used to seeing internal organs. But it's up to me to make the artwork palatable to a general audience. I don't want some older couple to walk by the conference room and run away screaming when they see the artwork."

To get a feel for how the organs were going to work, Mitsui started with one of the more enlightened representatives, the brain (1.30). "The brain is another PhotoDisc image. This is one of those cases where I really have to rely on a stock image. I can't walk outside and say, 'Excuse me, could I, uh, saw your head open? It'll only be for a minute. I have some twine here to tie things back up when we're through.' That's just not going to cut it."

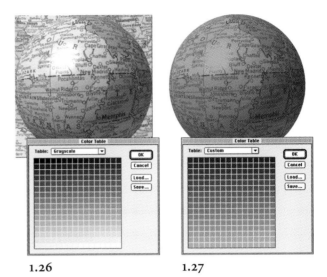

1.26   1.27

1.28

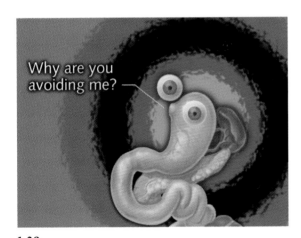

1.29

Reprinted with permission from Advanced Medical Ventures. Artwork by Linda Nye.

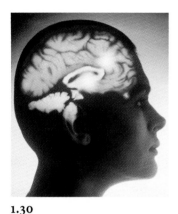

1.30

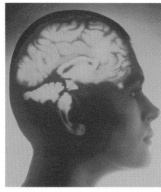

1.31

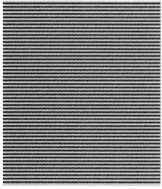

1.32

1.33

Mitsui converted the brain to grayscale and colored it green using the Color Table trick described earlier (1.31). "I wanted to simulate the look of those old-style green-and-black monitors." To create the effect of interlaced screen lines, Mitsui opened the green brain inside Fractal Design Painter, which offers better texturing capabilities than Photoshop. He selected a horizontal line pattern included in Painter's Art Materials palette (1.32). Then, he applied it to the brain as a paper texture (1.33). (This effect is not impossible to perform in Photoshop, it's just harder. You'd have to load the pattern into a separate alpha channel and apply it as a texture map using the Lighting Effects filter.)

After saving the brain out of Painter, Mitsui opened it up again in Photoshop and copied it to the Clipboard. Then, he returned to his medical composition and selected the path that traced around the outline of the monitor inside the head. He converted the path to a selection and chose Edit ➤ Paste Into to paste the green brain inside. Then, he slanted the brain to match the angle of the monitor using Edit ➤ Transform ➤ Skew (1.34).

"To give the monitors some depth, I beveled the edges with the Alien Skin filter. That didn't always produce the effect I was looking for, so I hand-brushed in a couple of highlights and shadows along the edges of the paths. Then, I hit each monitor with the Lens Flare filter to create a little reflection on the screen (1.35)."

1.34

1.35

Mitsui performed the same steps on the other organs with one exception. "I colored the main stomach image orange to set it off from the others (1.36)." Did the client have any problem with Mitsui de-emphasizing the organs by framing them inside monitors? "No, they loved it. I think they understood that it was a modern treatment of the subject that tied in well to the conference angle. You have these little doctor figures analyzing the big body and commenting on the screens. It's like he's their virtual patient."

We imagine the conference organizers were proud indeed to display this piece on the cover of their handouts. It establishes a bold and authoritative mood for the event from the outset, before a word is spoken on stage. The illustration tastefully introduces the topic at hand, explains the relationship between the experts and international attendees, highlights the role of technology at the event, and delivers the scene inside a lush and palpable diorama. Every need satisfied according to plan. This is one conference where the artist will get invited back.

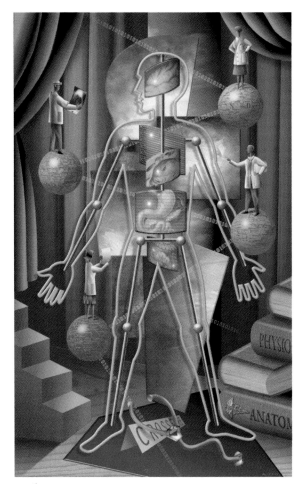

1.36

CHAPTER 2
WORKING STOCK PHOTOGRAPHY INTO GRAPHIC ART

There's a certain tiresome machismo associated with owning big, expensive computer gadgetry. When guys brag about their big disk arrays and their monster memory upgrades, we have to excuse ourselves and visit the little boy's and girl's room. Like everybody else out there, we fully admit that we personally have far too much capital sunk into our machinery, but it's because we can't manage to get by on less, not because we derive any pleasure from owning excessive equipment. Deke, in particular, is one of those crusty old codgers who still remembers fondly how he wrote, designed, and laid out his first book on a Mac 512Ke with two 400K floppy drives and no hard disk. Sure, he lived in a state of perpetual digital torment, but he was too young and stupid to know any better. The fact is, computers are like a sick addiction; we can't seem to live without them, but it's unbecoming to take pride in our depraved predicaments.

Refreshingly, professional illustrator Gordon Studer represents the other extreme. He proves that you can make a living with Photoshop without making the slightest attempt to keep up with the Joneses. Until recently, Studer got by with a Quadra — roughly equivalent to a 486 PC — equipped with 16MB of RAM and a 200MB hard drive. When we first wrote this several months after the release of Photoshop 4, Studer was making due with Version 2.5, which, as veteran devotees may recall, lacks layers. He even used a Zip cartridge as a scratch disk. Studer admitted this might not be the wisest solution in the world. "An Adobe representative came up to me once and said, 'You can't tell people that. They're going to

The idea is to strip the forms down to their bare minimum and play with unrelated abstractions inside the forms. If the photograph wasn't there to identify the image, it would break down into a bunch of concentric squares.

GORDON STUDER

destroy their computers!' But I've been doing it for about two years and I haven't had any problems."

What was Studer doing with his wee system? Creating illustrations that blend his primitive, whimsical style with volumes of royalty-free stock photography and occasional 35mm snapshots. Therefore, Studer's economical system matched his economical approach. "The funny thing is, I get nearly all my images from maybe a dozen PhotoDisc and Adobe CDs. I get my faces from 'Retro Americana' and 'Beyond Retro' (2.1) and my hands from a collection called 'Just Hands.' The 'Retro' collections are wildly popular, but the way I use the photos, no one even recognizes where they come from. I combine a man's head with a woman's eye and another guy's mouth. Then I carve them into simple geometric shapes (2.2). I use the same photos over and over again, but no one tells me, 'Man, I'm getting tired of that image.' All they see is the artwork."

2.1

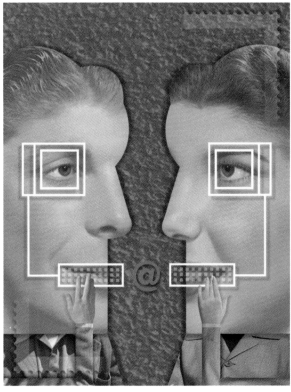

2.2

ARTIST:
Gordon Studer

STUDIO:
1576 62nd Street
Emeryville, California 94608
510/655-4256
gstuder363@aol.com

SYSTEM:
When this chapter was first written:
Quadra 840AV
200MB storage
Now:
Power Mac G3/266
6GB storage

RAM:
When this chapter was first written:
16MB total
8MB assigned to Photoshop
Now:
96MB total
60MB assigned to photoshop

MONITOR:
Apple 17-inch

EXTRAS:
Microtek 300-dpi scanner, PhotoDisc and
Adobe Image Library royalty-free images

VERSION USED:
When this chapter was first written:
Photoshop 2.5.1
Now:
Photoshop 5.0

You can test Studer's hypothesis by trying to spot a separate illustration printed later in this chapter that repeats one of the stock photographs shown here. As you'll discover, the simple act of modifying the shape of the face lends the revised subject its own distinct appearance.

IS IT ETHICAL?

Some might take exception to an artist who makes a living off repurposing a small collection of photographs. Setting aside the fact that the illustrations in this chapter are stylistically unique — being both compositionally and creatively independent of the photographs that populate them — Studer makes ethical use of what is generally accepted to be an ethical system of distribution. A reputable multiuse image dealer such as PhotoDisc or Digital Stock pays its photographers royalties based on how many copies of a CD it sells. Digital Stock estimates that its photographers earn on average $50,000 in the first year for a collection of 100 images — a figure that exceeds the average per-person royalties paid out by traditional stock agencies.

As artists who likewise rely on royalties for a chunk of our income, we would argue that Studer's repeated use of an image is no less scrupulous than you making repeated use of a technique that you learn in this book. It is exceedingly important to observe codes of professional behavior, but it is equally important to evaluate new practices with an open mind. Otherwise, digital manipulation makes pirates and scalawags of us all.

THE TREND TOWARD STOCK PHOTOGRAPHY

Studer's reliance on stock photography is a fairly recent phenomenon. "I made a whole style change about three years ago. Prior to that, I was doing really graphic stuff with sharp lines and abstract forms (2.3). But I grew tired of the fact that everything was so flat. So I started to experiment with textured patterns and designs. To avoid the computer look, I scanned in photographic textures and dropped them inside my basic shapes. It was like I had wrapped my artwork in a series of fabric coatings, giving the shapes a richness they didn't have before (2.4).

OTHER APPLICATIONS:
Adobe Illustrator, Adobe After Effects

WORK HISTORY:
1978 — After deciding football wasn't going to pan out, took up fine arts at Penn State.

1983 — Studied at Corchrain School of Arts; got job as paste-up artist and spot illustrator for Red Tree Associates.

1988 — Left *Oakland Tribune* for *San Francisco Examiner*; was introduced to Illustrator and computer design.

1990 — Created first piece for *MacWeek* "MacInTouch" column, which continued every week for seven years.

1994 — Shifted artistic style from high-contrast graphics to stock photo collage.

1998 — Took up After Effects, illustrated children's book about cats.

FAVORITE WORKING WARDROBE:
Bathrobe ("I got a new one and I just love it.")

2.3

2.4

2.5   2.6

"About this same time, I was playing around with deconstructing my artwork, reducing it to stark 'circle-head' characters (2.5). It was successful with my editorial clients, but the corporate and ad people were turned off. It was just too weird for them. Then I hit on something that really surprised me. If that same weird shape was filled with a photograph (2.6), no one seemed to have a problem with it. The client was able to make the jump. It was like the photograph identified the face as a person instead of a space alien. Then I was free to do whatever I wanted with the outline.

"To keep things interesting, I believe in making a stylistic shift every three or four years. Right now, I'm working on another shift. I'm trying to push the geometry of the shapes even further. For example, I have this one image that's cut out into completely abstract forms that don't even vaguely resemble a head outline (2.7). The idea is to strip the forms down to their bare minimum and play with unrelated abstractions inside the forms. If the photograph wasn't there to identify the image, it would break down into a bunch of concentric squares." From Studer's work of simple abstraction, the photo extends a fragile thread that touches the real world.

GORDONIAN GEOMETRY

"I have two ways I work. One is really geometric — all right angles and circles. Another is more free-form with random cutouts. The illustration I made for Coca-Cola (2.8) is an example of the geometric look. Normally, when you think geometry, you think precision and order. But here, it's a complete abstraction. Nothing in real life is this exact, so the geometry takes you farther away from the real world."

2.7

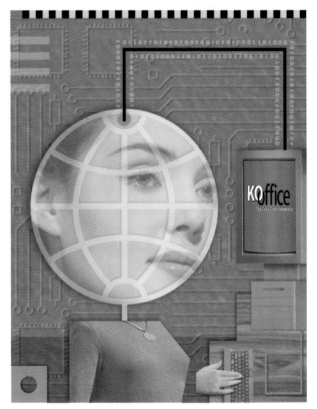

2.8

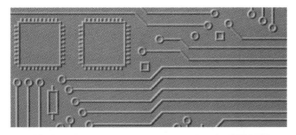

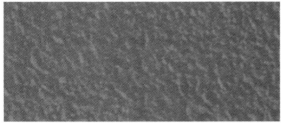

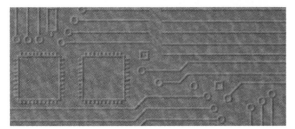

2.9 (top), **2.10** (middle), **2.11** (bottom)

2.12

2.13

MIXING STATIC BACKDROPS

"Because I'm working without layers, I have to start at the back of the image and work my way forward. So I always lay in the background first." For the Coca-Cola illustration, Studer rendered a circuit board pattern he created in Illustrator and applied the Emboss filter inside Photoshop (2.9). Then he opened a cork texture (2.10), copied the circuit board, and pasted it on top. To merge the two images, he applied the Luminosity blend mode and set the Opacity to 50 percent (2.11).

Studer frequently wallpapers his artwork with static, textured backgrounds. "The cork and chip patterns are good examples. I use these backgrounds, or slight variations on them, in a lot of my work. Like I might colorize the cork brown in one image (2.12) and blue in another (2.13). The idea is to set up similar worlds, so each illustration feels like a room inside the same home."

THE CENTRAL STOCK SUBJECT

"After the background, I lay in the big forms. Usually that's the face, because I like to work everything off the main head in the image (2.14). I always start with a grayscale image. Even if it's in color, I make it

---

ALIGNING VECTOR ART WITH IMAGERY

Aligning an object-oriented pattern such as Studer's circuit board with a face (2.13) or other image can be a tricky matter. Except for scaling, rotating, and the like, you can't edit the pattern in Photoshop, so it's important to nail the alignment in Illustrator or FreeHand. "Before I create the pattern, I save a 72-ppi version of the Photoshop image as an EPS file. Then in Illustrator, I choose Place Art, which gives me a template for how the photographic part is laying out. I can draw the circle exactly around the eyeball or the chip around the mouth. I even have a little circle around the nostril. Then I delete the template, save the illustration, and import it into Photoshop."

grayscale. Then I convert the image to RGB and colorize it, as opposed to trying to make it look realistic
(2.15). The colorizing reminds me of the way I used
to work — with pure flat-color fills. Sometimes I add
stylized highlights like rosy cheeks, but only to reaf-
firm the retro look. The images don't seem like photographs to me; they're more like scraps of color. I
like to think of a face as just a big piece of yellow."

Studer's colorizing isn't the vanilla Hue/Saturation
type. It's really more of a duotone effect, with hues
ranging from yellow to red. "I use the Variations
command to saturate the image with yellows and
reds. In this case, I selected the Midtones radio button and nudged the slider bar toward Coarse. Then I
clicked twice on the Yellow thumbnail and twice on
Red (2.16). It's way easier than creating a real duotone, and it gets me the hyper-saturated colors I'm
looking for. Awhile back, Glenn Mitsui showed me a
trick where he gets a similar effect by indexing the
image and modifying the color table (see Chapter 1).
But I don't know — that seems like more work."

2.14 (TOP), **2.15** (BOTTOM)

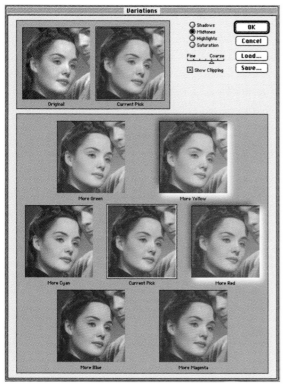

2.16

2.17   2.18

To define the shape of the head, Studer superimposed a globe illustration he created in Illustrator. He filled the artwork with white (⌘/Ctrl+Shift+Delete in Photoshop 5) and dropped it on the woman's face (2.17). Then he lowered the Opacity to 50 percent to merge globe and face into one element (2.18).

ADDING THE COMPUTER

"I have a small collection of computer pictures that I use over and over (2.19). All of them come from photos I shot myself. For a really brief period of time, I had a $20,000 Kodak digital camera on loan. I just went hog wild with it — I tried to photograph as many things as I could. Then I cut and pasted pieces of the monitors and computers to get a more stylized look. There's a geometric monitor, an orthogonal one, and another that's really irregular. I also colorized the images, airbrushed in shadows, and did whatever it took to convert the computers from photographs to graphics."

COMPOSITION AND DROP SHADOWS

After selecting the least dimensional of his monitors, Studer copied the head and monitor and pasted each one at a time against his background (2.20). "You can see even in the early composition how I'm using simple geometry. The head's a circle, the monitor comes in at 90 degrees. The head is vertically centered on the background, and the green screen of the monitor is exactly centered with respect to the head.

"As each element goes in, I give it a drop shadow. Everyone has a method for making shadows, and whatever yours is, I'm sure it's as good as mine. I'm just going for the basics — feathered edges, black fill. When I add a shadow, it's not intended to convey perspective. I want it to look like I cut out a bunch of photographs and laid them on top of the background (2.21)."

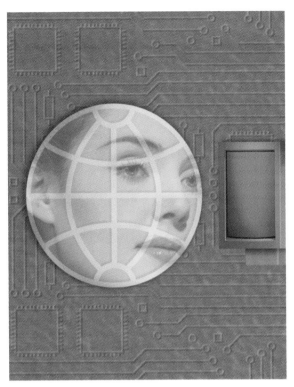

2.20

2.19

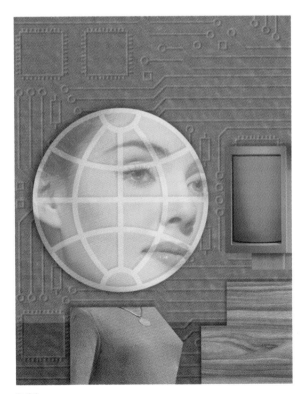

2.21

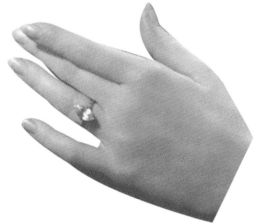

2.22 (TOP), 2.23 (MIDDLE), 2.24 (BOTTOM)

THE ANATOMICALLY PRECISE HAND

Second only to faces in Studer's stock photo library are hands. For the Coca-Cola illustration, Studer wanted to add a single hand operating the keyboard. After finding a stock hand that fit his needs (2.22), he colorized it with the Variations command. "I can basically replay the last colorization I applied by pressing the Option/Alt key when I choose the Variations command. If the lighting isn't quite the same, I might have to tweak the settings a little, but usually it only takes a couple of seconds to get it dead on."

Instead of cutting the hand into an abstract shape, Studer carefully selects each and every finger (2.23). "You can't abstract hands the way you can faces. Fingers make hands what they are. Besides, I like the way the detailed treatment of the hands plays off the simple geometry of the head." Studer retouched away the ring by cloning from the third finger. Then he flipped and rotated the hand so it rested on top of the keyboard, detached from the body without even a hint of arm. "Again, the hand sits at a right angle (2.24). Despite the detailing, I have to make it conform to the geometry of the overall illustration."

THE FINAL ADJUSTMENTS

"To make that alternating yellow/black accent across the top of the art (2.25), I just create a black square, a yellow square, and clone them over and over again. Of course, I never hit it right on, so I leave a big gap at the end and fill it with red." What is the purpose of this accent? "I've used that pattern since day one, and I have no idea why. No sense questioning it — it just is."

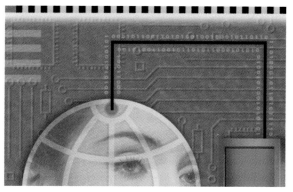

2.25

At this point, the image was ready to send off to the client. But as any working artist knows, the job doesn't necessarily end when you turn in the artwork. "The first image (2.8) is the one I submitted. But the art director had me make a bunch of last-minute changes. He had me change the body — it was too pointy — and he had me flip-flop the entire image. He also wanted me to add a little Coke bottle cap at the top of the forehead (2.26)."

Whenever a client dictates modifications to an illustration, there's a chance for damage. The smallest changes can upset a hearty aesthetic balance and send it teetering headlong into a pile of digital goop. "My biggest concern was the flip. I've had so many images where you flip them and they don't look right at all; everything seems off. But because this one was so geometric, it survived pretty well." We guess if your face can tolerate the occasional mirror image as you comb your hair in the morning, a face in a circle can hold up to reflection as well.

FREE-FORM IMAGE CHOPPING

Not all of Studer's images adhere to strict geometric guidelines. Many of his illustrations deliberately shun order in favor of chaos, with carefully clipped cutouts jockeying for attention inside crowded compositions. In an image he did for *CIO* magazine, the assignment was to show a cat working at a computer while his previous lives look on (2.27). "I had to take this one cat and create a bunch of different variations on him. It gave me the opportunity to focus on one element at a time, completely out of context with the others." Studer carved his subjects into human forms, some resembling cartoon skulls, others suggestive of Jimmy Durante in profile.

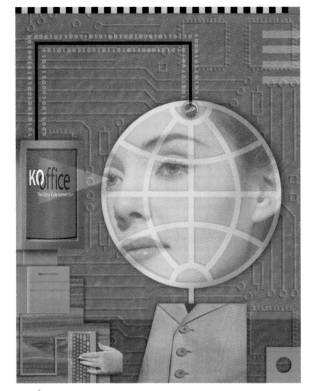

2.26

2.27

"The cats are mine. I just shot them with my camera, went down to a one-hour delivery place, and scanned them (2.28). In Photoshop, I cut and paste the cats into basic arrangements of faces and fur. Then I used the pen tool to shave the cats into the cartoon shapes (2.29)."

ROUGH PIXELS INSIDE SMOOTH OUTLINES

"The resolution of my original photographs was more or less awful. I had to sample them up and sharpen them to get them the way they look in the finished artwork." Is increasing the resolution a wise idea? "If I was working with a flat photograph, probably not. But I've got all kinds of elements coming in

2.28

2.29

at different resolutions. Maybe I'm more cavalier than I ought to be, but I just scale things as I need them. I know I can always deal with any softness or graininess later.

"Besides, I don't think people read a piece of artwork one element at a time; they see the whole piece together, even when it's an obvious composition. The fact that the pen tool edges are nice and sharp makes the entire image look in focus. I've never had a client complain about the resolution or softness of my art."

CACOPHONY OF KITTIES

As before, Studer built his composition off a single image. This time, it was the computer-capable cat in the lower right corner (2.30). But with no layers at his disposal, Studer was cautious not to go too far too quickly. "I put the bodies in first, because the placement was so tricky. After I got the bodies arranged the way I wanted them, I put in the arms and tails (2.31).

"It was a challenge to get all those cats arranged properly. As I positioned each cat body, I just had to hope that I was making the right decisions. Squeezing that last cat in there was the toughest. I specified in my rough that I was going to do nine cats — for each of the nine lives — but it didn't quite fit. I had to call the art director and say, 'Is it okay if he still has a life left? He's still alive; there he is working. I'd hate to think he could get, like, electrocuted and then drop off for good.' I don't think anyone quite bought my argument, but they gave me a break. So eight cats it is."

HAS PHOTOSHOP 5 RUINED GORDON?

Since this chapter was first published, Studer's world has transformed dramatically. He now uses a G3 Power Mac equipped with a 6GB hard drive and 96MB of RAM. He's taken up digital video editing with After Effects. And, yes, he's using Photoshop 5.

The blame must be laid at the feet of Russell Brown, one of Adobe's creative directors and a member of the Photoshop development team. "Russell invited me to an Adobe training event in Santa Fe and talked me into buying a new computer and getting Photoshop 5. I still own my old machine, and I still use Photoshop 2.5 occasionally. But I spend most of my time now in Version 5."

2.30   **2.31**

material? "Oh, no. If anything, I'm getting more retro than ever. Right now, I'm using After Effects to create movies featuring these '40s and '50s characters (2.33). I still use the abstracted forms, but now they're moving. It carries the abstraction one step farther. It adds another layer of realism and depth, where all I really have are these simple shapes."

Is that a good thing? "You know, I think it is. It's made a huge difference in the way I work. I used to have to be so organized. I had to dissect the image from back to front and figure out exactly how it was going to lay out. Now, I just start dumping in images — 40 or 50 layers — and then clean it up from there. I used to work with 8MB images, now they grow to 150MB. You'd think that would slow me down, but it doesn't. I'm working faster than ever."

Layers have also permitted Studer to experiment with new techniques. "Instead of cutting just one face into a shape, now I can merge multiple faces into one (2.32). I might take the eyes from one image and the nose from another. I also have more flexibility when experimenting with color and positioning. I feel like I'm much more versatile. I can throw stuff together that before would have been a nightmare."

What about multiple undos? Do they come in handy? "The undos really help. I talk to artists who have been upgrading Photoshop all along, and they act like they've come up with ways to avoid any need for multiple undos by using layers. But since I came across layers and multiple undos at the same time, I use them both. Constantly."

Such a huge leap forward must be downright life-changing. "You wouldn't believe it. I have so much less stress, I feel like I sleep better. When my clients want changes, it's no problem. I don't have to save a million versions of my artwork to Zip files. I can keep it all together in one file."

After so much modernization, does Studer have any plans to abandon the retro images in favor of newer

2.32

2.33

CHAPTER 3
CREATING BUDGET 3-D CHARACTERS

From your computer's perspective, 3-D artwork is the pinnacle of artistic achievement. Armed with the proper software, you can set up an intricate 3-D landscape, toss in a hundred or so wireframe objects, apply surface textures and patterns, shine a few lights on your subjects, and render the whole thing to a high-resolution image file. The result is so intensely realistic — you swear you can hear your computer clap its hands and scream "It's alive!" as it writes the final kilobyte.

But while 3-D is a big thrill for your processor, its effect on your brain is distinctly less agreeable. You have to master an entire glossary of new terminology, learn to work in a 3-D environment on a 2-D screen, and put up with incessant computational delays that make Photoshop look like a raging speed demon.

When push comes to shove, learning a new 3-D drawing program may be more hassle than its worth. The solution is to fake it in Photoshop.

MIKE'S FIRST ENCOUNTER WITH 3-D

At least, faking it in Photoshop was the verdict of artist Mike Strassburger, cofounder of Modern Dog, a Seattle-based graphic design firm. His job was to jazz up a collection of the studio's cartoon characters that had appeared on a line of K2 skis sold in Japan. By all accounts, Modern Dog's creations were already a hit overseas, helping to distinguish K2's tips from those of its competitors. K2 even went so far as to commission a comic book that explained where the characters came from and how they ended up on the skis (3.1). But as other manufacturers populated

I'm all for automating the process, particularly when it's as easy as applying a filter.

MIKE STRASSBURGER

3.1

33

3.2

Tokyo's sporting-goods showrooms with copycat cartoons, Strassburger looked for ways to remind skiers that his critters were the ones that started the trend.

"The K2 characters have been going on for about three years," recalls Strassburger. "They started out really flat (3.2). Every year, we developed them a little more to compete with the rip-off skis. At first, we just put drop shadows behind them, but they still looked pretty flat. So we decided to go fully 3-D."

Adept at using Photoshop, Illustrator, and QuarkXPress, Strassburger's first inclination was to boldly venture into yet another category of software by investing in a 3-D drawing program. After asking a few friends which program they used, he forked over $900 for StrataStudio Pro.

But things didn't go according to plan. "I had never worked in 3-D, so I didn't understand any of it. I tried drawing a character's head, but I didn't know how to subtract one shape from another, or, well, *anything*. All I could do was make a sphere and push little parts in and out — that was totally out of control. So I just said, 'Ah, forget it.'"

THE BUDGET APPROACH TO 3-D

Strassburger reckoned he could achieve the effects he wanted in Photoshop without going to the trouble of learning a new program. By segregating the illustration into layers and painting in shadows and highlights with the airbrush tool, he developed a technique virtually identical to applying a traditional airbrush inside a frisket. All it took was a bit of forethought and organization.

For starters, members of Strassburger's team sketched trial versions of the characters in Illustrator (3.3). "Sometimes I design the character, sometimes someone else designs it. But I always end up doing the 3-D finishing work."

ARTIST:
Mike Strassburger

COMPANY:
Modern Dog
7903 Greenwood Ave. North
Seattle, WA 98103
206/789-POOP
mike@moderndog.com

SYSTEM:
Power Mac 7200/66
500MB hard drive

RAM:
54MB total
30MB assigned to Photoshop

MONITOR:
SuperMatch 21
with $2,000 metal box that shields electromagnetic waves and gets rid of screen jitters

VERSION USED:
Photoshop 3.0.5

After culling the best characters for the ski logos, he rasterized the artwork inside Photoshop (using File ➤ Open), sizing each character 5 to 6 inches tall at 300 pixels per inch. "The final characters are only about 3 inches tall, but it's always a good idea to work large and downsample later."

FRISKETS FOR THE AIRBRUSH

At this point, you might assume that Strassburger would dive right in and start airbrushing his brains out. However, as with its traditional counterpart, Photoshop's airbrush by itself doesn't provide sufficient control. The airbrush needs a frisket. "Every single element has to be on its own layer so it can mask the airbrush. Eyes, eyelids, eyebrows — they're all separate.

"I use the original character just as a template layer in Photoshop. Then I create my new layers on top of that." Because these are high-contrast characters with lots of smoothly curving edges, Strassburger creates the new layers by tracing the character with the pen tool."

3·3

OTHER APPLICATIONS:
Adobe Illustrator, QuarkXPress, Adobe After Effects, StrataStudio Pro

WORK HISTORY:

<u>1981</u> — Entered graphic design field right out of high school.

<u>1987</u> — Founded Modern Dog with college pal, Robynne Raye.

<u>1992</u> — First computer job revising annual report in PageMaker on borrowed Macintosh SE.

FAVORITE MOUTHWASH:
Drug Emporium house brand version of Listerine, mint flavor ($2 compared with $7).

DRAWING PATHS

But why redraw the paths when they already exist in the original Illustrator file? Can't you simply port the paths over from Illustrator?

"I actually do bring in all the paths from Illustrator just in case. But most of them are no good. When we draw the characters in Illustrator, we do it in the cartoon style where the outlines are fat in some areas and thin in others. As a result, neither the inside nor the outside line is correct."

As we've demonstrated using the head from the scorpion (3.4), the 3-D character doesn't share the flat character's heavy outlines.

(For the sake of comparison, the bottom head shows the original Illustrator paths superimposed on the final 3-D character.) Strassburger was also free to make creative modifications as he redrew the paths. You can see his adjustments to the scorpion in the angle of the cheek, the placement of the right eye, and the size of the pupils.

MAKING THE LAYERS

Strassburger drew the paths and saved each one independently of the other. This made for what amounts to the tidiest collection of paths we've ever seen in a Photoshop document (3.5). He then created a separate layer for each path, converted the path to a selection outline (by pressing Enter on the keypad), and filled the selection with the colors specified in the template.

In most cases, there's a one-to-one correlation between the paths and the layers. But as you can see in Figure 3.5, there are a couple of layers — Eyes and Eye Rear — that seem to have sprung up out of nowhere. The eyes are made up of angled ovals that Strassburger drew with the elliptical marquee tool and rotated in the quick mask mode (3.6). Clearly, there's no sense in using a complicated tool when a simple one will do.

3.4

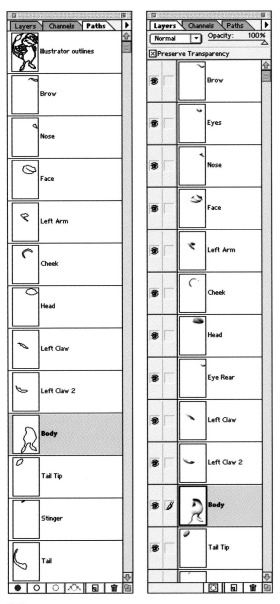

3.5

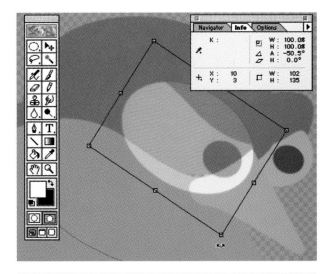

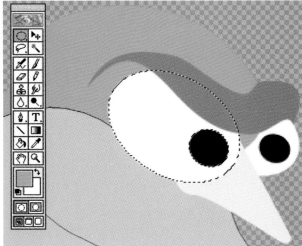

3.6

3.7

TIP

When painting shadows in any color but black, select Multiply from the brush mode pop-up menu in the Airbrush Options dialog box. Similarly, when painting highlights in any color other than white, select the Screen mode. When using black or white, the Normal blend mode will suffice.

PAINTING THE HIGHLIGHTS AND SHADOWS

From here on out, Strassburger applied the tools of traditional shading. He used the dodge tool to paint in highlights and the burn tool to paint in shadows. Since he was shading flat colored areas to begin with, he spent a good deal of time messing with the controls in the Toning Tool Options palette. "When shading the yellow area in the bee's face, I had to set both dodge and burn to the Highlights setting (3.7). Otherwise, the tools wouldn't produce any shading at all."

But Strassburger's favorite shading tool is the airbrush. "I ended up doing more airbrushing than dodge and burn. Using the dodge tool and choosing Highlights or Shadows gave me different looks depending on which color I was painting. It made it look like there was weird lighting going on (as 3.7 illustrates). I realized if I used the airbrush with the foreground color set to black, the effect looked more consistent."

Before applying the airbrush tool, Strassburger was always careful to turn on the Preserve Transparency check box in the Layers palette. Keep in mind that you have to activate the check box for each and every layer in the stack. (Because this gets a little tedious, you can quickly toggle the check box from the keyboard by pressing the / key.) With Preserve Transparency active, each layer acts as a mask for the airbrush — you can't paint where there aren't already pixels.

After shading the individual layers, Strassburger painted the *cast shadows,* in which one layer appears to shade the layers behind it. "You can airbrush all the parts and have them looking exactly right by themselves. But then when you place, say, the head on the body, you need to make sure the head casts a shadow on the body to make the effect believable."

In the flame character, for example, Strassburger painted a large shadow on the red face layer to create the appearance of a shadow cast by the eye (3.8).

"When painting the characters, I always imagined the light was coming from the top left. But as long as you're consistent, it doesn't matter."

THOSE GLASSY EYES

Again, there are simpler ways to create shadows inside a sphere. "Sometimes I painted the eyeballs and bellies with the airbrush tool. But most of the time, I used the Glass Lens filter from Kai's Power Tools (3.9)." If you don't own Kai's Power Tools (KPT), you can achieve similar effects using Photoshop's own Lighting Effects filter. You may even be able to achieve the effect you're looking for with a simple radial gradation. "I'm all for automating the process, particularly when it's as easy as applying a filter."

SOMETIMES, IGNORANCE REALLY IS BLISS

"The whole reason we came up with this technique was we didn't know how to use the proper tools," confides Strassburger. "But even if we had, I'm not sure if we would have attempted something as intricate as the bee or the flame character. I mean, I don't know how hard of a time other people have with computers, but for most artists, I imagine this is an easier way to achieve 3-D effects. And for us at least, it ended up delivering a better effect than if we had gone with a real 3-D program (3.10)."

Does this mean Strassburger has decided to call it quits on 3-D software for good? "No, I eventually figured out how to extrude type in StrataStudio Pro. And recently, I learned how to do much more with it. I probably understand 70 percent of the program. In fact, I just finished rendering the Comedy Central logo in real 3-D, so I'm pretty comfortable with it now."

It just goes to show you, sometimes it's a good idea to buy an application and let it molder on your shelf for a while. It can be quite invigorating to curse yourself for not having the time or energy to learn a new piece of software. Stress sometimes leads to ingenuity, and frustration can fire the creativity of the clever mind. So go for it — buy that 3-D drawing program you've had marked in the catalog for the last five months. You'll be back in Photoshop inventing workaround techniques in no time.

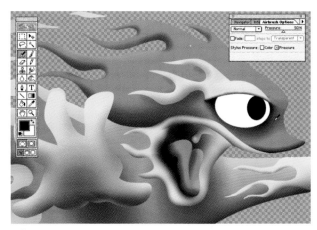

3.8

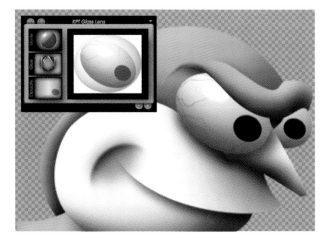

3.9

3.10

CHAPTER 4
INTEGRATING NATURAL MEDIA INTO DIGITAL ART

This book devotes a lot of space to ways that a computer, together with Photoshop, can broaden your creative range and make you more productive. But we'd be lying if we characterized any computer — Mac, PC, or otherwise — as the ultimate achievement in artistic machinery.

Probably the most irritating aspect of a typical computer is that it doesn't begin to give you the same tactile feedback as a 25¢ pencil against a nickel sheet of paper. You move your mouse or stylus on a horizontal surface and observe the results a foot or more away on a vertical screen. Meanwhile, the screen provides you with a relatively tiny window into your artwork. As a result, it can be extremely difficult to sketch in, say, Photoshop and accurately gauge issues such as form and composition.

Simply put, you can expend less effort and create better artwork if you draw or paint directly to paper and then scan your artwork into Photoshop for further processing.

BUD'S NATURAL MEDIA EPIPHANY

Veteran freelance illustrator Bud Peen learned this lesson the hard way. "I struggled for weeks trying to create simple watercolors in Fractal Design Painter. I came to hate that program. I really hate it with a passion. It's just so awkward and annoying to work with. Finally, it occurred to me, why am I doing this? Why don't I just paint with real watercolors, then scan in the artwork and modify it in Photoshop? It was like an anvil dropped on my head.

> **The key is to recognize the inherent purpose and limitations of your tools.**
>
> BUD PEEN

"It seems so obvious now. But I think the reason I never really considered it before is that there's a stigma associated with working outside the computer. It started when magazines like *Macworld* required that their artists work on a Macintosh. It built a dividing wall between traditional and nontraditional materials. Nowadays, it's almost like there's this religion where everything has to be created digitally."

If such a religion does exist, Peen has plainly left the fold. In fact, looking at Peen's playful, perspective-irreverent artwork (4.1), you'd swear he'd never touched a computer in his life. The watercolor effects were obviously created using real brushes dipped into real water-soluble pigments and dabbed onto real pieces of paper. (Shocking, really — we can hardly believe our editor lets us relate such appalling news.) But in truth, these are layered Photoshop files scanned in multiple passes and finished with the airbrush tool. As you'll discover in this chapter, Peen could not have achieved these effects without the aid of a computer.

4.1

ARTIST:
Bud Peen

COMPANY:
Bud Peen Illustration
2720 Madeline Street
Oakland, CA 94602
510/482-8302
http://www.budpeen.com
bud@budpeen.com

SYSTEM:
PowerWave 604/150 (Power Computing)
1GB storage

RAM:
80MB total
12MB to 30MB assigned to Photoshop

MONITOR:
Old Radius 19-inch (planning on getting
professional Sony model)

EXTRAS:
Epson 1200e scanner with transparency
adapter

VERSION USED:
Photoshop 5.0

"The key is to recognize the inherent purpose and limitations of your tools." Photoshop, for example, easily outperforms the $30,000 stat camera, but doesn't hold a candle to the $3 pen nib. By contrast, conventional illustration tools permit you to quickly create elements, but compositing and production are nothing short of tortuous. By merging natural media with digital tools, Peen has learned to command both ends of the process. The result is a style that favors efficiency and control without wearing its method on its sleeve.

PART I: A CONVENTIONAL BEGINNING

Peen's illustrations typically comprise a series of calligraphic outlines laid against a brightly colored watercolor background. After getting the client's approval for his rough pencil sketch — which he draws meticulously on ledger paper — he traces the sketch onto five-ply bristol using graphite paper (it's like carbon paper except with graphite on it). "It's a very primitive method, but I don't know of any better way." He then paints the watercolors over the graphite lines on the bristol board (4.2).

Isn't it a little unusual to apply the watercolors before the line work? "Yeah, it's completely opposite the way most people do it. But I found that most artists are a little sloppy with the watercolors if they apply them second. The background becomes an afterthought. By painting the watercolor first, it makes me spend more time and get the colors just right. For me, the watercolor is the most important part of the illustration."

After the watercolors dry, Peen draws to registration dots on the bristol board. He then places a sheet of translucent Duralene on top of the bristol and copies the registration dots to ensure proper alignment. Finally, Peen traces along the graphite lines using a Gillot Extra Fine quill pen. "Once the line work dries, I'll go in with a single-edged razor and scrape away mistakes and sharpen up some of the lines.

"At this point the line work is all black (4.3). Now, in the old days, I would submit the bristol and Duralene as a composite mechanical and specify a flat process color for the line work. But the lines just sat there like lumps on top of this very expressive watercolor background. I was never really happy with that."

OTHER APPLICATIONS:
Adobe Illustrator, Adobe Streamline, Macromedia Director, QuarkXPress, Strata StudioPro (still learning)

WORK HISTORY:
1977 — After graduating from college, set up silk screening department in Santa Rosa print shop.
1979 — Worked for New York advertising agency.
1983 — Spent a year in Paris studying fine art and sculpture.

1989 — Commissioned by *PC World* to create five illustrations in CorelDraw; work came out flat and lifeless.
1995 — Gave up trying to create natural effects on computer and purchased scanner to integrate traditional media into digital workflow.

FAVORITE MOVIE GENRE:
Submarine flicks ("I often shout 'Dive! Dive!' when the phone is ringing off the hook and work is piling up.")

4.2   4.3

4.4

PART II: SHIFTING INTO DIGITAL

This sounds like a job for Photoshop. "There's something liberating about having a scanner hooked up to a computer. Once I crossed that threshold and decided that I could create things outside the computer and bring them in, everything started falling into place. I discovered I could do things that I never could before."

To prepare the watercolor and Duralene for scanning, Peen carefully aligns the registration dots and slices a common straight edge along the tops of both sheets. "This way, I can place the top of each page flush with the edge of the scanner to ensure vertical alignment inside Photoshop." He scans the watercolor in 24-bit color at 300 pixels per inch. Then he scans the line art in black and white at the same resolution.

COMBINING THE ARTWORK

Peen opens both images in Photoshop. Using the Canvas Size command, Peen crops the taller of the two images to match the shorter one, making sure to crop away from the bottom. Then he drags the line art and Shift-drops it into the watercolor image, resulting in a new layer. Pressing the Shift key during the drop confirms that the two images are aligned vertically.

As things stand, the black-and-white line layer hides the watercolor background. To get rid of the white pixels, Peen goes to the Channels palette and ⌘/Ctrl-clicks the RGB composite channel. This selects the white pixels and leaves the black lines deselected. Pressing the Delete key makes the white go away. Then Peen deselects the image (⌘/Ctrl+D) and ⌘/Ctrl+Shift drags the lines into horizontal alignment with the watercolor background (4.4).

4.5

4.6

COLORING THE LINES

Now for the fun part. Peen turns on the Preserve Transparency check box in the Layers palette so he can paint exclusively inside the quill lines. Then he uses the airbrush to add colors at will (4.5). "I'll use the eyedropper to lift colors from the watercolor layer. Then I'll adjust the color to darken it up in the Colors palette. The colors in the lines are always related to the colors in the background (4.6).

"If I wanted colored lines before Photoshop, I had to resort to dipping a brush into as many as 20 colored inks. It was incredibly complicated. Now it's not only easier and less messy, but I have much more control." One look at Peen's colored lines by themselves (4.7) illustrates just how much better Photoshop handles coloring functions than traditional media. "And I can go back and change colors with complete flexibility."

4.7

Does Peen experiment much with the Layer palette's blend modes before flattening the line art into the watercolor? "If the line work is really defining, I'll leave the blend mode set to Normal to make the lines opaque. But if I'm doing more subtle work, I'll apply the Multiply mode to burn the lines into the watercolor."

WHEN YOU FIND A GOOD THING . . .

Just for the sheer heck of it, we've included two additional examples of Peen's artwork showing the progression from scanned watercolors (4.8) to black line art overlay (4.9) and final airbrush-colored lines (4.10). "What I love about this technique is that I can place the lines on the watercolor work and see right away how the lines react to the watercolors. There's a degree of immediacy that you simply can't get with conventional mechanicals."

VECTOR VARIATIONS

Although flexible, Peen's watercolor approach isn't right for every job. Sometimes Peen wants a more synthetic look; other times the Photoshop approach simply isn't practical. "I originally wanted to create the Antiquarian Book Fair poster (4.11) using watercolor and quill pen. But it was such a large piece — over 30 inches tall — that I simply couldn't make it work inside Photoshop. I tried to airbrush one of the lines and it took like five minutes. So I was forced to turn to Illustrator instead."

4.8   4.9   4.10

In this case, Peen scanned his quill-pen illustrations — one for the title, another for the reading minstrel — and converted it to vector objects using automatic tracing program Adobe Streamline. Peen then positioned the quill paths on a layer inside Illustrator and created the color paths on a separate layer in the background.

PATHS INSTEAD OF WATERCOLOR

Why discuss a piece of Illustrator artwork inside a Photoshop book? Because this poster was a step in discovering additional ways to color lines inside Photoshop. "I began to experiment using Illustrator paths as a background element instead of watercolor."

For instance, in the case of the Emale graphic (4.12), Peen started as usual by inking in the line art, scanning it, and converting the lines to paths with Streamline. Then he used Illustrator's brush tool to paint in color on a separate layer behind the line art. "Generally, I don't like Illustrator's brush tool. But it came in handy here."

4.11

4.12 (TOP), 4.13 (MIDDLE), 4.14 (BOTTOM)

After saving the background paths and line art as independent files, Peen opened the background paths in Photoshop and airbrushed in a few dollops of color to add a hint of depth to the flat fills (4.13). He then opened the line art and dragged it over as a separate layer. And finally, he turned on the Preserve Transparency check box and painted color inside the lines (4.14).

In case you're wondering what font Peen used for Emale, the answer is none. "The type was a piece of quill pen artwork. I introduced it as a separate layer inside Photoshop."

4.15

EMBRACING SYNTHETIC MEDIA

"I think the *Predicting Doom* piece I did for *InfoWorld* (4.15) is a really nice one because it allowed me to really push the synthetic aspect of the artwork. I used Illustrator blends to feather the sky and ground. You can even see the banding — it doesn't even remotely resemble watercolors, which is the way I wanted it."

As usual, Peen brought in the line art through Streamline. But when processing more complicated artwork like this, Streamline has something of a problem. "The program traces paths from the outside in. It actually stacks on top of each other areas of black and white. This means the white areas are opaque, which prevents the colored fills from showing through.

"To fix this in Illustrator, I go ahead and slip a dark box behind the traced paths so I can see which areas are opaque (4.16). Then I start selecting paths from the outside in and convert them into compound paths until all the interiors become transparent (4.17). It sounds like a lot of work, but it usually ends up being only about eight or nine paths that have to be converted."

4.16

4.17

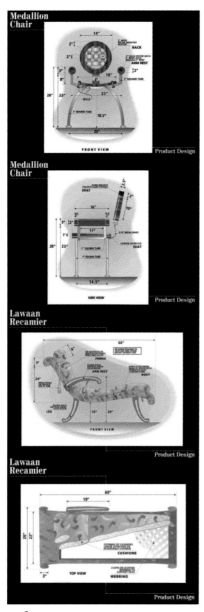

4.18

YOU USE *WHAT*-PEG

Peen's colors are so vivid, you might think he spends a lot of time worrying about CMYK conversions and color matching. "I stick with RGB for the sake of e-mail. My colors are bright, but I'm not that concerned about specific color palettes. I just want small file sizes."

And with commercial printers urging their clients to submit printer-ready EPS files, what format does Peen use? "JPEG, actually. I've been using JPEG files for years without any problems. And they take far less time to e-mail to my clients." Chalk up another one for the independent-minded artist.

SO MUCH MEDIA, SO LITTLE TIME

"Illustrating is all about solving problems within a framework of equations that you use on a regular basis. That's why I like the computer; it gives you so many different chances to exercise your options. With traditional art, the closer you get to the end, the fewer options you have. But with a computer, you never reach a dead end. You can always strip out elements or undo steps. You have this incredible freedom to experiment, from the beginning all the way to the end."

THE WORLD OF THE TACTILE

Lately, Peen's artistic interests have been leading him into still other traditional and nontraditional media. "I'm a sculptor by training. So in addition to my illustrations, I've been dabbling in furniture design (4.18). It started a couple of years ago when I sent off a few drawings of lamps and clocks to a Dallas-based furniture artist named Lam Lee. I didn't expect much, but he just went nuts. He told me, 'Your work fills my heart with great joy.' It was wonderful! I've never had a client tell me that before. So he asked me to design a whole line of furniture. I use Photoshop to prepare the mechanical sketches for the factories, which lets me integrate different colors and materials very quickly. The frames are made of wood, then they cover it with these little tiles of beautiful stone. It looks great, but it's incredibly heavy."

THE WORLD OF THE SCREEN

If you're more interested in something that you can bring into your house without the help of three hardy workmen, then you can find Peen's illustrations in the *National Geographic* online Fantastic Forest project (4.19). Designed by multimedia artist Brad Johnson, this award-winning site is definitely worth a visit — especially if you have kids. In addition to Peen's forest elements — each created as an independent water-color — Fantastic Forest offers excellent examples of Shockwave sounds and objects. Of particular interest, you can build your own forest using a few of Peen's watercolors (4.20). To see it for yourself, go to *http://www.nationalgeographic.com/modules/forest.*

4.19 (TOP), **4.20** (BOTTOM)

CHAPTER 5
MERGING PAST AND PRESENT WITH SUMI BRUSHSTROKES

The tools artists, photographers, and designers use influence how they work and what they produce. This is equally true for digital, as well as conventional, tools. All too often, software features, the latest plug-ins, or trendy special effects carry a digitally produced image as much as (or more than) the skill or sensitivity of the artist. We need only remember the morph, fractal, or KPT phases that have passed over us in the past few years to see how quickly a fad comes and goes. It's certainly rare to find an artist working with Photoshop who draws deep inspiration from studying the masters, artisans, and diverse century-old art forms. Enter Hiroshi Goto.

Hiroshi Goto — illustrator, artist, and president of the successful design firm HI! Seisaku-Shitsu — lives and works in Tokyo, Japan. Goto blends the old and new in a fascinating and seductive manner. His passion for the modern world of computer graphics and design is balanced by a profound appreciation for the history of his native culture. Spending much of his time in the tea establishments of the historical city of Kanazawa, playing the *shamisen* stringed instrument, and singing the Naga-uta, the world of the geisha is strongly reflected in Goto's art.

Goto did not follow a direct path into the fields of art and graphic design. "After graduating from junior high school, I went on to become a hair designer, studying hair design at night and working as a stylist during the day. I began to doubt my choice and, thanks to an introduction arranged by my mother, I was able to find a job at a design office. I went on to study graphic design through practical work experi-

Working with Photoshop allows me to accomplish what was previously achieved through tedious hand-craftsmanship, copy machine work, film processing techniques, and a touch of luck.

HIROSHI GOTO

ence, visiting as many design offices as I could to gain knowledge about the industry. Ten years ago I established my own design office, HI! Seisaku-Shitsu, and two years after that I first came in contact with the Macintosh computer. At that time it was still unusual in Japan to do graphic design work on a computer, since it's compatibility with the Japanese language was quite insufficient (to put it politely). Every day of work was a constant trial-and-error process, requiring infinite patience."

Goto's images combine traditional drawing and painting techniques with Photoshop, which he uses to color drawn image elements and merge them with scanned backgrounds. "Working with Photoshop allows me to accomplish what was previously achieved through tedious hand-craftsmanship, copy machine work, film processing techniques, and a touch of luck. Most importantly, when I work with Photoshop I can see the results immediately. Looking back, I began to see the emergence of Photoshop as a revolution in art and design and became hooked on using it to produce original pieces of art. It has taken me three or four years to develop my own personal style, and I am still fascinated by working with the latest technology to create traditional yet modern images."

INSPIRATION AND PROCESS

Twentieth century Japan is a country of contrasts, where tradition and cutting-edge technology mingle at will. Goto's work reflects this and speaks of a place where the digital and the traditional balance one another. The *Morning Glory* image is a perfect example. "This image was created specifically for the *Photoshop Studio Secrets* book, and I might say that it is my favorite of all the pieces I have created so far (5.1). I like to go out drinking in the old part of town, sometimes until the early morning hours. One morning as I came home at around 5a.m., the morning glories (hence the name) were in full bloom. Since they droop and wilt as soon as the summer heat finds them, I had never seen them in this richness before. After looking at the blue flowers in full bloom covered in morning dew, I was inspired by the feeling of freshness that they gave me to create a new painting."

5.1

ARTIST:
Hiroshi Goto

ORGANIZATION:
HI! Seisaku-Shitsu
404 Kagurazaka Heights
Tsukiji-Cho 15
Shinjuku-ku, Tokyo
Japan
(011) 81-3-5227-6720
http://www.haili.com/gallery/
Goto@c-engine.co.jp

SYSTEM:
Power Mac 7200/166 with G3 Card
Mac OS 8.1
2GB storage

RAM:
272MB total
150MB assigned to Photoshop

MONITOR:
Sony 17-inch Multiscan

EXTRAS:
Nikon Coolscan 600 dpi flatbed scanner

VERSION USED:
Photoshop 5.0J

PRIMARY APPLICATIONS:
Adobe Illustrator 7.0J, QuarkXPress 3.3J

WORK HISTORY:
1988 — Established HI! Seisaku-Shitsu, a graphic design office.

Goto starts every painting with a pencil sketch of the image (5.2). The sketch then serves as a template, which he places on a light table. He then paints over the sketch on watercolor paper with ink and paint (5.3). "At this point I am already thinking about the Photoshop aspect of the work and am considering which parts of the image need to be on their own Photoshop layer. I make a separate painting for each layer to be. For example, when I painted the *Morning Glory* image, I broke the flower up into blossoms, buds, and leaves, and painted each one of these pieces separately (5.4 and 5.5). Later, each piece became an individual Photoshop layer. It's more practical for me to paint each layer individually with ink and paint than it is to try to separate the elements later in Photoshop. This is an original technique and not a traditional one, reached simply through experimentation." Goto's method of brushwork is also self-taught and he is still refining techniques as he experiments with different types of paper and brushes, and amounts of ink, paint, and water.

5.2

5.3

1990 — Purchased first Macintosh IIcx.

1992 — Received the Adobe Design Contest Adobe Award and started to get serious about creating art on a computer.

1993 — Group exhibitions. First work featured in Japanese magazines and books.

1994 — Selected to create the yearly New Year's card for Japan's National Ministry of Posts.

1996 — Created numerous illustrations for magazine and book covers, and other media forms.

1998 — Keeping very busy creating cover illustrations for magazines and novels, advertisement posters, record jackets, calendars, and a variety of other projects.

FAVORITE MUSICAL INSTRUMENT:

The *shamisen* (which is a three-stringed instrument). "This traditional Japanese art form is not commonly studied today and I find it infinitely interesting. There are no other 'youngsters' in my group so I am a bit spoiled and coddled by my elders."

5.4

5.5

SKETCH TO MASK

Once the sketch and paintings are done, the image is two-thirds of the way to completion. Goto scans each painting at 300 dpi in grayscale mode with his flatbed scanner and brings each file into Photoshop. "The next step is a bit tedious but very important." Goto proceeds to mask out each image element with a high-contrast luminance mask. He starts by duplicating the entire grayscale image file as a new channel (5.6). He then uses Curves to increase the contrast, forcing the background paper to white and darkening the flower itself (5.7). Due to the tonality in the image, light areas often remain in the dark flower, so Goto cleans the mask up with the Dust & Scratches filter (5.8). By inverting the mask he can easily see where the Dust & Scratches filter left artifacts (5.9), which he can erase with the block eraser (5.10).

5.6

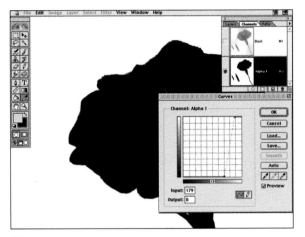

5.7

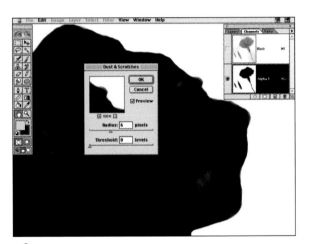

5.8

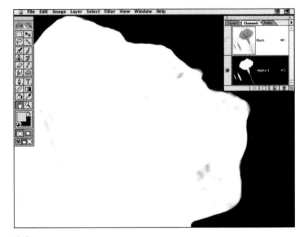

5.9

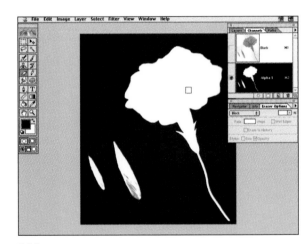

5.10

5.11

NOTE

If you zoom the image out (⌘/Ctrl+minus key) when using the block eraser, the eraser remains the same size of 16 by 16 pixels. By zooming out, you are using a larger eraser in relationship to the image — this is a quick and easy way to clean-up flat areas.

Once the initial mask is complete, it's easy to extrapolate additional masks for each image element (5.11 – 5.14). "However, I must be careful not to leave any jagged edges. Sometimes I have to carefully apply the blur filter or use the blur tool to selectively eliminate them."

5.12

5.13

5.14

MASKS TO COLOR

Before adding color to the image Goto experiments with the Solarize filter to highlight the shadowy areas of the grayscale image. This adds a unique effect reminiscent of traditional woodcut prints (5.15). He then inverts the image. Sometimes this leaves the piece with insufficient tone, so he darkens it using Brightness/Contrast.

The next step is to add color to the image. First he converts the grayscale image to RGB mode. "Often in the final stages I must convert the file to CMYK mode, but I initially work in RGB because CMYK does not provide the color palette that I need. Since I take my files out to different output devices, some of which require RGB data while others work with CMYK data, I keep the files in RGB as long as possible and check them with CMYK preview in Photoshop (⌘/Ctrl+Y) to see how the CMYK transform will effect my color palette. If the change is too extreme, I use Select Color to select the out-of-gamut colors and then use Hue/Saturation to desaturate those colors."

By loading the individual alpha channels and working with image adjustment layers, Goto can add color piece by piece and is able to return to each adjustment layer to fine-tune the color and tonality. He starts with Color Balance to get the initial color (5.16) and then uses Hue/Saturation (5.17) to fine-tune the

5.15

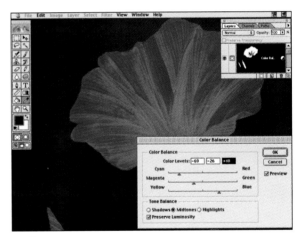

5.16

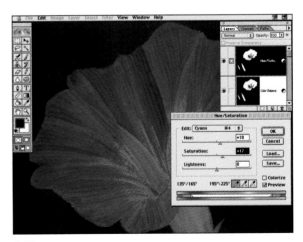

5.17

5.18

intensity of each piece, as you can see in the final flower (5.18).

"Although I create the image in pieces, I visualize the complete piece as a whole. I find that a real living object is far more unique and intricate than anything that springs from my imagination. Referring back to my original concept of the *Morning Glory* image (still residing in my head), I turn to the computer. I try to think of my own mind as another filter for the image." Notice how Goto has separated the leaves from the blossom (5.19). Although many people would overlook the common green leaves and tendrils, he has composed and colored them beautifully so they become supporting vines for the rich blue blossoms (5.20).

5.19

5.20

MAKING THE BACKGROUND

Once all the image elements have been masked, toned, and colored accordingly, Goto creates a unique background for the image. He has different ways of doing this. "Sometimes I try to find a section of the image in which nothing is drawn and which may contain scan irregularities or show the texture of the paper. I enlarge these areas, heighten their contrast, add texture with the Noise and/or Motion Blur filters,

and finally add color with the previously mentioned technique."

For the *Morning Glory* piece, Goto created a pattern from the painting of the branches and leaves of the plant (5.21). Working intuitively, he used the Transform function to distort the shape of the image, applied the Motion Blur filter (5.22), and heightened the contrast of the image (5.23 and 5.24).

Eventually, the image is broken down enough to become an abstract pattern (5.25). "By loading the

5.21

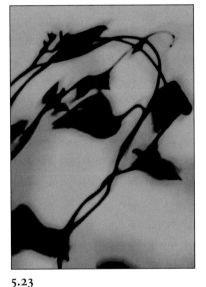

5.23

5.22

5.24

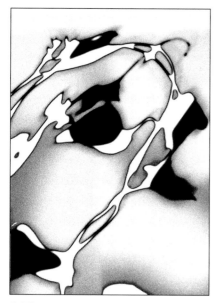

5.25

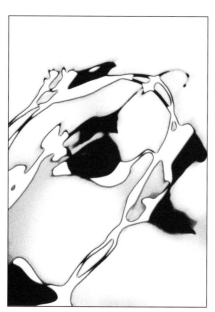

5.26

luminosity of this abstract pattern (⌘/Ctrl+Option/ Alt+tilde) and creating a new alpha channel, I can use the pattern as an alpha channel for the background layer. After loading the selection, I continue to experiment with inverting colors, using the Solarize filter as I go (5.26). Most importantly, I have no fixed technique for backgrounds and often simply go with the creative flow to make them. If you can believe it, sometimes I even end up using scans of my own fingerprints for backgrounds!"

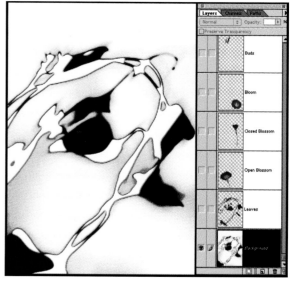

5.27

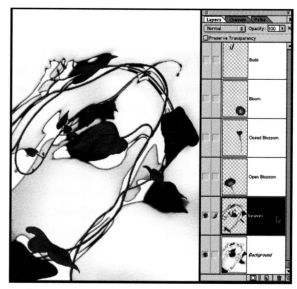

5.28

COMPOSITING

"Once the background is ready, I select each piece of the painting and bring it to the background file as a new layer. I align the pieces with prepared guidelines to bring everything into position, and the piece is finished. Since I have sketched, painted, and scanned the pieces to scale, the compositing aspect of my images is rather straightforward (5.27–5.32)."

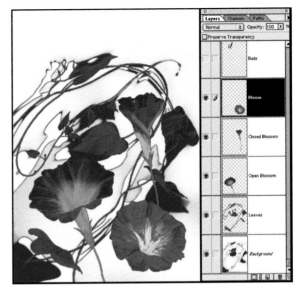

5.31

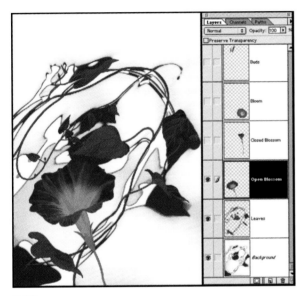

5.29

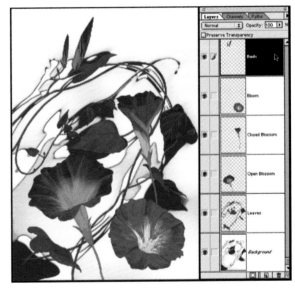

5.32

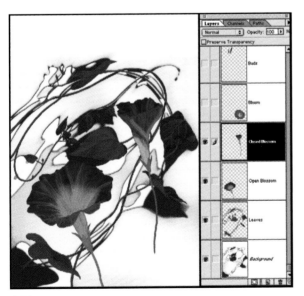

5.30

5.33

To finish an image, Goto signs each piece with the traditional Tenkoku seal. Traditionally, it has been applied to Nihon-ga paintings and written materials in Japan as a simplified pen-name for an author or artist. It features the name "Hiroshi" written in a typestyle called Tensho. Goto actually carved this stone seal and uses a scanned version of the seal's impression to sign his artwork (5.33). Interestingly enough, the layer with the seal on it is the only time that Goto uses a blend mode other than Normal. He uses Multiply to darken the seal to make it look as if it was actually printed onto the paper.

Here you see the final composited painting (5.34) with a detail view that reveals the fine color and textured tonality contrast between the background and subject (5.35).

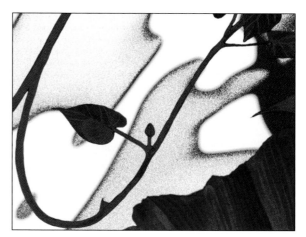

5.35

5.34

GALLERY CONVERSATIONS

One of the images that we were most taken by is the hauntingly beautiful image of a light lily on a very dark background (5.36). This piece was used for the cover of a Japanese novel entitled *Yogare*. *Yogare* is a sorrowful word from the Heian period that describes a situation in which a man promises to meet his lover at nighttime, but grows tired of the woman and decides not to meet her. Goto wanted this image to express the painful nighttime longing of a woman for her man, and this led to a piece featuring the contrast of a white lily floating in the depths of a dark background.

"It is not often that I find work in which a black background is required. It depends on the work in question, but generally Japanese clients seem to dislike dark backgrounds. I myself have a preference for them."

THE FISH

The ornamental fish is another icon of traditional Japanese culture. "You can find this fish in people's aquariums all over Japan. It is black, has eyes that bulge out of its head, and is described by the Japanese name *demekin* (5.37). The tail of the demekin is truly beautiful, and to accent it I used a softly curving image of water in the background. To create the background, I drew a series of curved lines in FreeHand, imported them to Photoshop, and then used the Shear and Blur

5.36

5.37

filters to mimic the graceful motion of flowing water. I pasted this shape into an alpha channel, loaded the channel to the image, inverted it, and added color with the Color Balance and Hue/Saturation technique described earlier."

CHERRY BLOSSOMS

The cherry blossoms that bloom in spring are an integral aspect of traditional Japanese culture, annually awakening the country with festivals, concerts, and celebrations. As Goto explains, "The theme for this television station poster was 'Spring in Japan' (5.38). I tried to attain light and airy colors to match the feeling of spring. The blue background represents the color of the Japanese spring sky. By using a pale pink color blending into the sky background, I tried to express the gentle, bright, and cheerful feeling of

5.38

spring. Finally, I used the noise filter to imitate the pollen in a natural cherry blossom (5.39). Expanding the texture of paper from the scanned painting and adding color and shadows created the background. Each flower petal required its own Photoshop layer and level of transparency."

5.39

THE PEONY

For the *Peony* painting (5.40), Goto essentially used the same technique described earlier, although it may seem more complex because this oriental flower has a very complex shape and the petals are in multiple folds. "The work in Photoshop was not especially difficult but the original painting took most of a day. The background image is meant to remind one of a gold *byobu* folding screen."

PAINTING WITH WATERCOLORS

In interviewing Hiroshi, we were quite surprised to find out that he doesn't paint with Photoshop and, therefore, doesn't use a pressure-sensitive tablet for his work. "I am still considering studying traditional watercolor technique. When it comes to the use of color and composition, I refer to the traditional Nihon-ga paintings for inspiration and ideas. I make quite a few trips to museums and galleries to view the Nihon-ga and am constantly studying a variety of books on the subject. The feature that strikes me most about traditional Nihon-ga is the bold sense of design style and that even though objects are not drawn in perspective, the viewer still gets a strong sense of depth from the paintings as a whole. One of my favorite painters is Kiichi Suzuki of the famous Rinpa Group, active in the latter half of the Edo Period (1615–1868). The Rinpa style arose in the Momoyama period (1573–1615) and was characterized by an emphasis on two-dimensional design, striking color patterns, and the previously mentioned bold sense of design style."

Goto uses the Tarashikomi (spilling ink) method characteristic of the Rinpa style to draw the branches and stems of plants. Before the first brushstrokes have dried, he allows more concentrated ink to run

5.40

through parts of the painting. So rather than mimicking paint with a computer, Goto paints with the real thing, allowing the serendipity of the flow of ink to add to the image.

THE FINAL PRINT

We were curious as to how Goto submits work to his clients and his solution illustrates the conundrum that many digital artists experience. "I submit work in various forms, but when it is required to submit an image as data, I do so with a file converted to CMYK on an optical disk. Somehow it seems that every time I do this, responsibility for the color reproduction always comes back to me and this often becomes a hassle. So whenever possible, I submit a piece already

output in the original RGB mode using a Fuji Pictography 4000 continuous tone, high-resolution printer. For my personal exhibition work, I print each piece on Japanese *washi* paper using the IRIS 3047 printer. With this method I can create large poster size prints — but interestingly enough extremely high-resolution images are not necessary to create very good results. Since the washi soaks up a portion of ink, I get a slight blurring of the dots, and even a 150 dpi file offers remarkable quality."

IN CLOSING

In closing, we'd like to extend a sincere thank you to Jade Carter for his accurate translations and extreme patience.

CHAPTER 6
ENHANCING VECTOR ARTWORK

I f there's one program that every computer artist uses, it has to be Photoshop. Some folks are primarily vector artists; others are famous for their 3-D work, and still others do videos and animation. But they all spend some amount of time in Photoshop — sketching roughs, rasterizing artwork, editing renderings, and performing hundreds of other chores. It's the closest thing there is to an industry-standard graphics application.

So call us sick, but we thought it'd be a lot of fun to find a prominent computer artist who *didn't* use Photoshop. Had never touched it. Simply didn't have any call to play with it. There must be — oh, gosh — two or three such examples in the country, but the best one we know is Ron Chan. Chan is a San Francisco-based freelance artist who is best known for his Illustrator work. Our job — invite Chan to join the Photoshop-using majority and turn him into a pixel kind of guy. Resistance is futile; Chan will be assimilated.

PORTRAIT OF A VECTOR GUY

Just to give you a sense of who Ron Chan is, we've taken the liberty of including a few examples of his artwork over the years. These pages feature an early cover from *Macworld* magazine (6.1), the ubiquitous announcer guy who long adorned Macromedia Director boxes (6.2), and the eye-catching mandrill roll-out for Illustrator 5 (6.3). If you're more interested in type tricks, check out the cover of the *TV Guide* big fall preview issue (6.4) or the more interesting version that was deemed too chaotic for the publication's audience (6.5). Sadly, the artwork didn't

As I see it, Illustrator is the creation tool and Photoshop is the editing tool. My goal is to take the strengths of both and marry them into a single überprogram.

RON CHAN

6.1

quite measure up to Chan's expectations. "I thought the *TV Guide* cover would be a great job because my mom would see it," the artist confides. "But she forgot to buy it that week."

6.3

6.2

Whether Mother Chan is aware of it or not, everything her son creates is pure PostScript vector art. Sharp outlines, stylized forms, vivid colors — this stuff wouldn't know a pixel from a pancake.

ARTIST:
Ron Chan

STUDIO:
24 Nelson Avenue
Mill Valley, CA 94941
415/389-6549
http://www.ronchan.com
ron@ronchan.com

SYSTEM:
PowerWave 604/150 (Power Computing)
6GB storage

RAM:
160MB total
80MB assigned to Photoshop

MONITOR:
ViewSonic PT810

VERSION USED:
Photoshop 5.0

OTHER APPLICATIONS:
Adobe Illustrator, Fractal Design Painter,
Macromedia Director

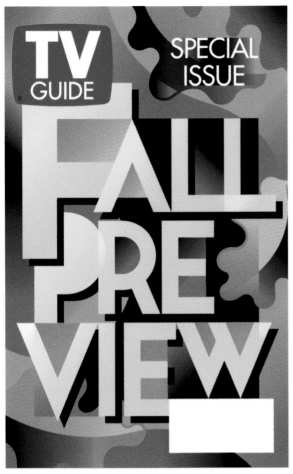

6.4

6.5

WORK HISTORY:

<u>1979</u> — Instead of going to art school, started working at Hallmark Cards ("so I never really did learn how to draw").

<u>1984</u> — Hired as part-time staff artist at the *San Francisco Chronicle*.

<u>1986</u> — Tested illustration program from Adobe code-named Picasso (later named Illustrator).

<u>1989</u> — Created cover for first all-digitally produced issue of *Macworld* magazine.

<u>1995</u> — Cover for "Fall Preview" issue of *TV Guide*.

<u>1997</u> — Participated in this book, forever changing the way he works!

FAVORITE CHILDHOOD TOY:

Major Matt Mason ("When you bend the arms too much, the wires pop out and poke you.")

FEAR OF PHOTOSHOP

Chan is obviously both talented and technically proficient. He was one of the first artists to ever touch Illustrator, a year before Adobe released it publicly. So why this avoidance of Photoshop? It can't be ease of use, because it's more difficult to manipulate a Bézier curve in Illustrator than change the color of a pixel in Photoshop. And it can't be that he doesn't own a copy of the program, because he's had it on his hard disk for years. Just what is the story?

"For one thing, I'm used to manageable file sizes. A really complicated magazine cover might take up 700K to 800K in Illustrator. To have an equivalent resolution in Photoshop, it'd have to be at least 20MB. To me, that seems like an enormous file. I can't quickly e-mail it to a client." And for Chan, JPEG compression isn't an option because it would gum up his high-contrast edges. "Then there's the problem of archiving. Right now, I can put two or three years of work on a Zip cartridge. If I used Photoshop, that would hold maybe two or three jobs.

Photoshop also makes you worry about resolution all the time, where Illustrator doesn't. But, I suppose it ultimately boils down to the fact that I'm making a steady living using Illustrator and I haven't really been forced to use Photoshop."

Chan considers and then adds, "Well, not until you started bugging me."

THE ATTRACTION OF PIXELS

But surely Photoshop offers some advantages over Illustrator. "Blends in Illustrator are a real chore. You have to set up a beginning and ending shape, and you have to enter the right number of steps to avoid banding. In Photoshop, adding a blend is as easy as filling a feathered selection or painting with a soft brush. Glows and shadows are especially easy to throw together. And you can get a more natural, less sterile effect.

"Another thing I'd like to do with Photoshop is add textures. I've been looking at some WPA silk-screens from the 1940s that combine gritty textures with high-contrast poster art. I suppose I could try to get this effect with Illustrator's Ink Pen filter, but it would be so much trouble that I doubt it'd be worth it. Photoshop seems like a much better program for this purpose."

We suggested to Chan another way Photoshop could be used to enhance his artwork. By relegating elements to different layers and discreetly applying the Gaussian Blur filter, he could create a depth-of-field effect. This would impose a sense of visual hierarchy, literally focusing attention on the foreground elements and downplaying the background, as in the revised take on Chan's Sarazen World Open Championship poster (6.6). Chan ventured that he wasn't terribly keen on the idea. "Gee, I don't think I own any 3-D glasses." But he generously gave us permission to take a whack at it ourselves, as we do later in this chapter.

6.6

ADDING TEXTURES TO AN ILLUSTRATION

The first project Chan decided to texturize in Photoshop was a poster he created for a concert featuring young soloists with disabilities (6.7). The piece is clean and precise, composed mostly of simple shapes with flat fills. Chan stripped out the handful of blends that used to serve as highlights and color transitions. In place of these, he resolved to substitute textural fades inside Photoshop.

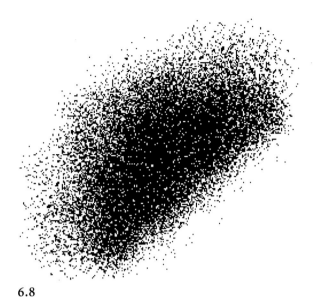

6.8

6.7

MAKING THE TEXTURE

To safeguard the visual harmony of his artwork, Chan decided to start with a single texture pattern and repeat it over and over throughout the image. He created his texture (6.8) by making a transparent image and painting in the empty layer with the airbrush tool set to Dissolve in the Airbrush Options palette. All of the pixels were either black or transparent. Because it's a small trick to later fill the black pixels with color while leaving the transparent pixels intact, this small file is ideally suited to Chan's needs.

BRINGING IN PATHS FROM ILLUSTRATOR

The next step was to rasterize the Illustrator artwork in Photoshop and then transfer Illustrator's paths to use as masks for the textures. "When opening the artwork in Photoshop, I modified the resolution; but I never changed the inch measurements of the image. This way, I could drag individual paths over from Illustrator and have them align exactly.

"I used Illustrator's Trim filter to simplify the illustration so none of the paths overlapped. Mostly, that worked out fine. When it didn't quite work, I used Unite or another Pathfinder filter to get the shapes I wanted. Then I copied the paths I needed, pasted them into Photoshop, and positioned them with the direct selection tool (the white arrow in the same slot as the pen). Actually, I was surprised how well it worked. I didn't have much problem at all lining up the paths exactly the way I wanted them."

6.9

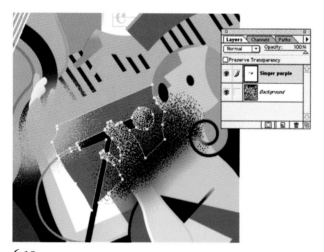

6.10

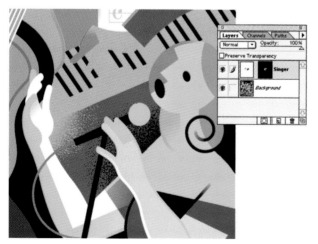

6.11

DRAGGING PATHS FROM ILLUSTRATOR

Whether you're using a Mac or Windows 95, Illustrator 8 and Photoshop 5 can share paths without resorting to the Clipboard. Drag a path from Illustrator and drop it into Photoshop, just as you would to rasterize the path. But before you drop, press and hold the ⌘/Ctrl key. This tells Photoshop to import the path outline directly into the Paths palette.

FILLING PATHS WITH TEXTURES

The best way to see how Chan used the paths to mask his textures is to focus in on a detail in the image. The purple area around the singer's hand and microphone includes a total of four paths. After Chan imported and aligned these paths (6.9), he named them in the Paths palette to ensure that Photoshop didn't automatically delete them when he imported more paths later.

Chan imported his texture (6.8) onto a new layer. He positioned the texture in the area below the microphone and left it painted black. Next, he cloned the texture, rotated it 180 degrees, and positioned the clone to the right of the singer's raised hand. He sampled the lavender color from the piano with the eyedropper. Then with the cloned texture still selected, he filled it with lavender by pressing Shift-Option/Alt+Delete. Chan also used the airbrush (set to Normal) to fill in the texture with a little additional color (6.10).

As you can see, Chan made no attempt to keep his textures inside the lines. This is the purpose of the paths. He converted the paths to selection outlines by pressing Enter. Then he converted the selection to a layer mask by clicking the layer mask icon at the bottom of the Layers palette. The result was a perfect stencil to contain the textures (6.11).

REPEAT, REPEAT, REPEAT

Chan repeated this process over and over again to add texture to the other elements in the image (6.12). The completed image contained 14 layers with as many named paths. "Sometimes I had to edit the layer masks a little to get the textures aligned properly. And once or twice, I played around with the blend mode. When the texture overlapped the black piano keys, for example, I set the layer to Darken so the texture covered only the lavender area."

The final effect is splendid (6.13), but importing all those paths must have gotten a little tedious after a while. "Oh, I don't know; it wasn't too bad. If I did it again, I'd probably use fewer layers. I might also dab on the texture directly using the airbrush set to Dissolve. I guess it took me longer than setting up blends in Illustrator, but I like the effect better, too. And I bet I'll get a lot more efficient with time."

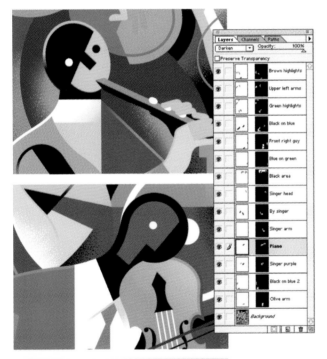

6.12

6.13

6.14

6.15

6.16 (TOP), **6.17** (BOTTOM)

THE BIG OIL TEXTURE

At our urging, Chan experimented with adding textures to a couple of other images at low resolutions. In the case of a client's annual report illustration (6.14), Chan decided to apply a more complex texture over a few large areas of color. He started by creating a grayscale oil paint texture inside Fractal Design Painter (6.15). "I really like the natural media tools in Painter, but I don't like its layering controls. It's just too confusing to mask images." So he rasterized the illustration inside Photoshop, imported the paths he needed for layer masks from Illustrator, and opened the Painter texture.

This time, Chan was able to get by with far fewer layers — six to be exact. "I'd just roughly position and rotate the texture against one of the elements in my illustration. If the texture didn't quite cover an element, I either stretch it or repeat it (6.16)." The texture wasn't designed to repeat, so Chan sometimes had to cover up the seam. "In the red clouds, I had to align the seam above the box — where the clouds are thinnest — to make the seam as unobtrusive as possible (6.17)."

As before, Chan used paths to make layer masks. But how did he color the texture? "Filling the texture with a flat color would have ruined it. I could have colorized the texture with Hue/Saturation, but then I couldn't exactly match the colors I had set up in Illustrator. I tried rendering each texture layer as a duotone, but that was way too much work.

"Finally, I discovered a *reeeally* easy solution. I left the texture layer grayscale and applied the Screen mode with the Opacity set to about 30 percent. This worked great because it made the texture follow the blends from the original illustration. Once I figured that out, it took me like a half hour to finish the whole thing (6.18)."

6.18

THE CUSTOMIZED FADE TEXTURE

According to Chan, his final experiment was the most successful. "I wouldn't have any hesitation about sending this to a client." Chan started by rasterizing the office supply illustration (6.19). Then he created a rough brush texture in Painter (6.20). The problem was, the texture was painted onto a white background, making it nearly impossible to colorize and overlay onto different backgrounds. The challenge: Turn this flat brush into a flexible layer with an accurate transparency mask.

6.19

Selecting the brush with the magic wand or Color Range command wouldn't have caught all the delicate edges in the texture. The correct solution was a bit more obscure, so naturally it fell to us, keepers of obscure facts, to do the honors. We switched to the Channels palette and ⌘/Ctrl-clicked on the top channel item to convert the tonal range to a selection. This selected the white pixels, so we chose Select ➢ Inverse to select the black ones. Then we copied the selection to a new layer (⌘/Ctrl+J). And now for the weirdest step: we pressed Shift+Option/Alt+Delete to fill the texture with solid black. Then we deleted the Background layer, leaving the layered black texture (6.21). It was an exact match to Chan's original.

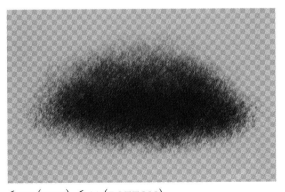

6.20 (TOP), **6.21** (BOTTOM)

Chan then used the texture to create highlights and color transitions, just as he had back in the Young Soloists poster. But this time, instead of using a black-and-white MacPaint-style pattern, Chan's texture supplied a full range of gray values. He was able to colorize it by pressing Shift+Option/Alt+Delete, just as before, because the layer's transparency mask was the only factor controlling the softness of the edges. The result is an elegant rendering that any professional would be proud to see on his or her ink blotter (6.22).

6.22

LAYERS IN FOCUS

The next few paragraphs explain how to add depth to a two-dimensional piece of vector art. But I should warn you up front that this technique is mine, the "me" in this case being Deke. Don't blame Chan; it's not his fault. Although the subject of the technique is Chan's Young Soloists poster, I am the cheeky monkey responsible for its execution.

No doubt, some of you may think it's presumptuous for me to modify another artist's work, even if said artist gave me permission. After all, Chan deliberately violates the rules of depth and perspective in favor of geometric form and a stylized convergence of elements. Isn't it possible that the technique I'm about to suggest may have a trivializing effect on Chan's artwork? I guess it is, particularly with a half-wit like me at the helm. But my philosophy is this: If Leonardo Da Vinci sees fit to give Quasimodo a stab at the *Mona Lisa*, who are we to judge?

The idea is simple: Isolate elements on different planes according to the distance from the viewer, assign each plane to a separate layer, and blur the layers that lie in front or in back of the viewer's plane of focus. You can use different blur filters to get different effects, but for this demonstration, I'll stick with Gaussian Blur.

I assume you recall the unmodified Young Soloists illustration (6.7). Inside Illustrator, I established four planes, each on a separate layer. I placed the clarinet and violin players on the front layer, the singer on the next one back, the guitarist and pianist on the third layer, and the background at the rear (6.23).

Using Illustrator 8, I exported the layered illustration as a layered Photoshop 5 file. This ensured that Photoshop automatically respected each of the four layers created in Illustrator, from background up to clarinet and violin players.

To focus the viewer's attention on the singer, I needed to apply varying amounts of blur to all the other layers. (No sense in sharpening the singer; she's already as sharp as rasterized vector art gets.) Using the Gaussian Blur filter, I applied Radius values of 4.0 to the front layer, 2.0 to the guitarist and pianist, and 10.0 to the background. I also used the Levels command to reduce the contrast of the two rear layers and darken the front layer (6.24).

The effect was too subtle for a Philistine like me. I added some gradations in between layers to serve as simple lighting effects. I started by adding a layer to the front of the stack and drawing a black-to-transparent gradation from the base of the image to the base of the clarinet. I inserted a similar white-to-transparent gradient layer in front of the singer. I also added a circular drop shadow behind her head.

6.23

6.24

6.25

The finished composition imposes a kind of View Master sensibility on Chan's artwork (6.25). What does the artist think? "Mm hmm. And the advantage of this is what?" Not quite the ringing endorsement I was hoping for, but he's not threatening a lawsuit either. All things considered, I'd call that a success.

CHAN'S IMAGING REFLECTIONS

A year after this chapter was first written, Chan now regularly creates his flat vector art in Illustrator (6.26) and adds textures and depth in Photoshop (6.27). As of late, Chan has become more adventurous with his textures, introducing organic elements such as photographic surfaces and airbrushed clouds (6.28).

6.26

6.27

"At first, I had this fear of large files. But I went ahead and upgraded my computer to 160MB of RAM and a 6GB hard drive. Now I can work with large, layered images in Photoshop pretty quickly. Some things are slower than they are in Illustrator, but it's usually worth the wait . . . and the wait and the wait. Gives me time to read the newspaper."

Any complaints? "Photoshop's a great program and everything, but there are a few things that irritate me about both Versions 4 and 5. In particular, I wish I could paste multiple elements into a single layer instead of constantly creating new layers. Then I could set up a single layer mask and paste several images into it. It really should be a toggle — paste as a new layer or paste as a floater. Let me decide."

Would Chan ever create artwork directly in Photoshop? "I don't see what I would gain by doing that. Illustrator's drawing tools give me the precision I expect from the computer. If I want to sketch or paint, I'll turn to traditional tools before Photoshop. As I see it, Illustrator is the creation tool and Photoshop is the editing tool. My goal is to take the strengths of both and marry them into a single überprogram."

6.28

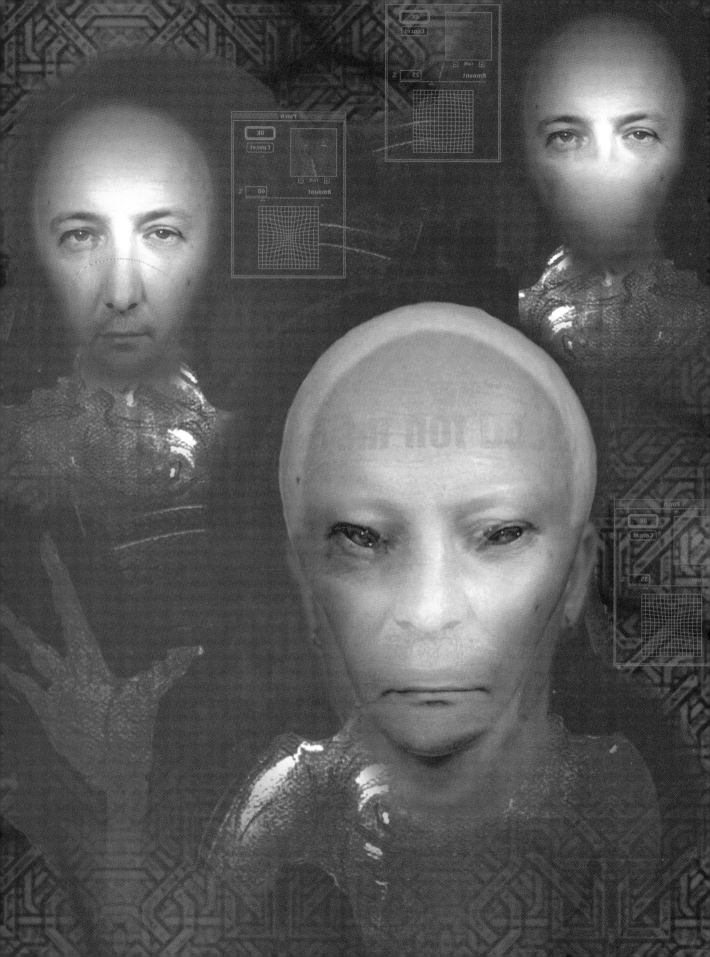

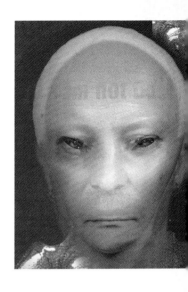

CHAPTER 7
THE FACE-MELTING POWER OF DISTORTIONS

The commands in the Filter ⇨ Distort submenu leave most artists covering their gaping mouths with one hand and scratching their heads with the other. Oh sure, Spherize (7.1), Pinch (7.2), and fellow pixel mutilators are a lot of fun, but what do you do with them? The chance of a client asking you to contort the holy heck out of some poor guy's face seems awfully remote.

To find out how someone might apply these strange commands in a professional capacity, we went to the original stomping ground for the Distort filters, George Lucas' Industrial Light & Magic (ILM). All but a couple of the commands were written by John Knoll, an effects supervisor at ILM. Knoll wrote the filters not only to amuse himself, but also to generate the occasional special effect.

Fellow ILM artist (and subject of this chapter) Mark Moore claims distortions were the feature that first drew him to Photoshop. He recalls his reaction to an early prerelease demonstration of the program just a few months after he joined ILM: "We all knew John was working on an image editor, so we had a rough idea of what to expect. But when he opened up a picture of his wife and applied a few distortions, that's when my jaw fell on the floor. I thought, 'This is going to change how all artwork is done.' And sure enough, it has."

THE VISUAL EFFECTS ART DIRECTOR AT WORK

In order to understand how and why Moore uses distortions, it's helpful to see how his job fits into the special effects puzzle. "When we first start a project,

This is going to change how all artwork is done.

MARK MOORE

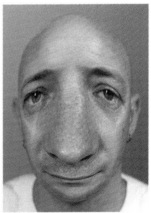
7.1

7.2

the effects supervisor breaks down the script and decides which shots are going to be visual effects. Then I step in and oversee the creation of the story-boards, which are comic book-like panels that illus-trate the effects sequences. After that, I'll pick out key panels and flesh them out into full-fledged concept art. I create detailed pencil sketches to block out the composition and show what the basic scene should look like. Then I'll take the sketches I like and work them into photo-realistic renderings in Photoshop. That way, the director can look at them and get a pretty exact idea of what he can expect."

In 1993, Moore worked as art director on an alien-abduction movie called *Fire in the Sky*. Very briefly, *Fire in the Sky* is the belabored story of Travis Walton, a freelance tree chopper who gets kidnapped by a pack of fiendish extraterrestrials. He spends half the movie missing in action and the other half freaked out by his strange ordeal. The ordeal is revealed near the end of the film in a creepy scene that takes place inside the alien spaceship. Devoid of any dialog — which in this movie is a very, very good thing — it features lead character Travis waking up inside a slimy pod, fighting his way out of a huge cocoon of equally slimy pods, discovering some sleeping aliens, and unwisely electing to pause and scrutinize them. Suddenly, a couple of tiny but feisty aliens seize young Travis, fling him onto an operating table, and prepare him for the most appalling medical examina-tion this side of *Marathon Man*. Et tu, space friend?

According to Moore, this one scene was the begin-ning and end of ILM's involvement in the movie. "We built the entire alien set — including the cocoon and the interior of the spaceship — on our main stage. There was just one actor, D. B. Sweeny, and the rest was puppeteers."

DISSECTING THE ALIEN

Moore was put in charge of designing the main alien, a critter nicknamed Doc. "The director thought that Doc should look like a burn victim. He was basically humanoid, but something was very wrong with him. I also had to make him seem tough but vulnerable. The aliens wore these skintight space suits that looked like the classic large-headed, big-eyed E.T.'s to protect them from our environment (7.3). The idea was that the space suits were organic and actually grew onto their bodies. But inside the ship, it was like being in a big womb, so they could walk around naked. This was also the rationale for why Doc is operating on Travis. The aliens believe we have supe-rior bodies, and they might be able to use them for their own purposes." Ah ha, that explains Ross Perot.

"So I started by putting together some pencil sketches of the operating room and Doc (7.4). The problem was, I couldn't come up with anything that was specific enough. The director wanted to see pol-ished renderings, not sketches. Photoshop was per-fect for this, because I could scan some faces,

---

ARTIST:
Mark Moore

ORGANIZATION:
Industrial Light & Magic
San Rafael, California
mtwo@kerner.com

SYSTEM:
Power Mac 7500/100
2GB storage

RAM:
80MB total
50MB assigned to Photoshop

MONITOR:
Radius 20-inch

VERSION USED:
Photoshop 3.0.5

OTHER APPLICATIONS:
Macromedia FreeHand, Adobe Texture-Maker

WORK HISTORY:
1976 — Turned 20, saw *Star Wars*, understood for the first time what he wanted to do for a living.

rearrange them, and come up with a look that spelled it out very accurately. There was no room for misinterpretation."

Normally at this point, we would include content from the actual movie, just as we do for *The Empire Strikes Back* and *Dynotopia* in Chapter 19. But Paramount — the studio that owns *Fire in the Sky* — wanted to charge us more than we could afford to reprint the images. (We guess that's one way to recoup costs.) So Moore agreed to show us the steps he used to arrive at Doc as applied to a different original image. The result will be a wholly unique character whom we will christen Bones, in deference to a different Paramount-owned character.

For Moore's technique to work, he has to start with a person with a shaved head. Hence, Moore has selected as raw material a fellow ILM employee whose scalp is appropriately bereft of hair (7.5). Known as Sir Guy of Hudson in the credits to *Fire in the Sky*, this mysterious individual served as lead alien puppeteer. It is therefore ironic that in this chapter, he serves as puppet.

TRANSFORMING SIR GUY INTO BONES

"Before I started work on the sketches, I got some books on alien abductions. A couple of them said that the bad aliens are called Grays. They're the ones you look out for. So we decided to make the aliens a sort of gray-brown. Meanwhile, I was working on a

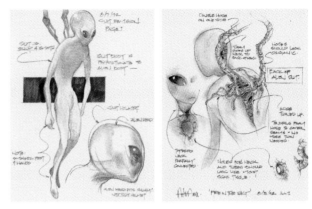

7.3

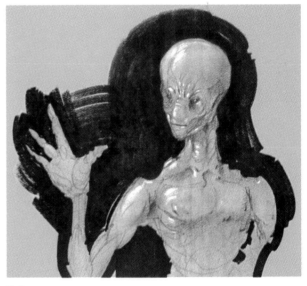

7.4

1982 — Received degrees in Graphic and Industrial Design from the University of Washington in Seattle.

1989 — Landed job as concept artist for LucasArts Attractions, worked on theme park rides including "Star Tours."

1990 — First movie credit, Mechanical Model Design for flying train in *Back to the Future III*.

1993 — Met stop-motion innovator Ray Harryhausen at *Jurassic Park* opening in Los Angeles.

1997 — Visual effects art director for *Star Wars: Special Edition*.

FAVORITE GUILTY PLEASURE:
Godzilla movies ("The only person I've ever talked to who likes Godzilla more than me is Tim Burton.")

7.5

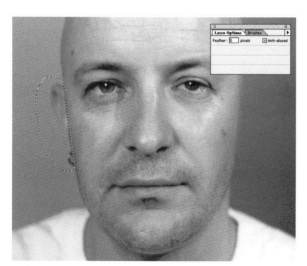

7.6

Mac IIfx at the time (equivalent to a 386 PC), and it was taking forever. So I decided, hey, if they're gray, why not work in grayscale?" For the purposes of this lovely full-color coffee table book, we've colorized the screen shots to get a duotone effect. Having finally gotten our publisher to spring for color, we're dang well going to use it.

THE IMMUTABLE LAW OF ALIEN LIGHT BULBS

When you're crafting an alien, the ears are the first thing you have to change. According to the grand tradition of Movie Logic, alien beings either have big ears or no ears at all. Bones falls into the latter camp. "The helmet design was based on the classic Whitley Strieber *Communion* alien, with a tapering face, giant eyes, and a gentle mouth (7.3). The heads needed to be able to fit inside these light bulb-shaped helmets. So I was trying to streamline the head as much as possible."

Moore used the lasso tool with the Feather value set to 5 to select each ear (7.6). Then he used that selection to grab an empty portion of the background and drag it on top of the ear. To taper Guy's head like a light bulb, Moore selected the bottom half of the face and applied Filter ➢ Distort ➢ Pinch set to an Amount value of 60 percent (7.7).

MASKING FEATURES WITH FOREHEAD

Another feature that aliens frequently lack is the nose. So Moore set about eliminating the nose by cloning the forehead on top of it. He started by setting the Feather value in the Lasso Options palette to 11. Then he selected the area around the nose and mouth (7.8). He moved the selection outline straight up to the forehead, then he ⌘/Ctrl+Option/Alt-dragged to clone the forehead onto the lower half of the face (7.9). Finally, he used the Levels command to darken the chunk of forehead and lessen the contrast (7.10). Then he touched up the edges with the dodge and burn tools.

"Thanks to the fact that Guy is bald, I had a nice big patch of skin I could use to cover up the bottom of the face. If you look carefully, you can see that I have a bit of eyebrow down at the bottom of the chin, but I could easily clone that away if I wanted to. The point is, by cloning bits and pieces of the face, I can match the tone and texture of his skin. You get a halfway realistic effect with little work."

MAKING THE FIERCE LITTLE EYES

"The classic alien has gigantic eyes that make it look cute. We wanted tiny beady fierce eyes so that you'd think, 'Yikes, this guy is scary.' We wanted him to look smart like a human, but cold like a predator.

"I started by going in and painting the whites of his eyes (7.11). For the most part, I just painted in the whites with black using the airbrush. I also highlighted the irises just a bit with the dodge tool and rubber stamped a couple of reflections. I figured the black eyes went a long way toward erasing his humanity.

"The model I used for the movie didn't have eyebrows. I don't know if he had shaved them off or they were super light, but I didn't have to worry about them. Unfortunately, I couldn't ask Guy to shave his eyebrows, so I had to eliminate them by cloning some more of the forehead." As before, Moore selected the area he wanted to replace with the lasso tool, moved the selection outline over a piece of the forehead, and ⌘/Ctrl+Option/Alt-dragged the selection to clone the forehead back onto the eyebrow (7.12). Then he used the dodge and burn tools to touch up the edges.

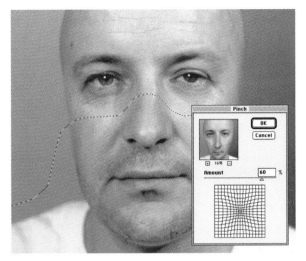

7.7

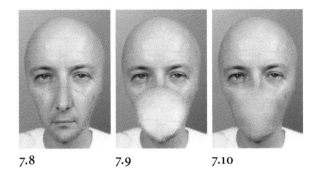

7.8   7.9   7.10

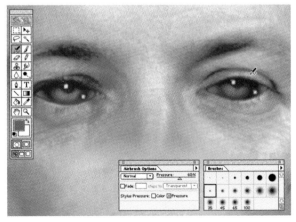

7.11

"Next, I tilted the eyes to give them a kind of cat quality." In each case, Moore selected the eye and pressed ⌘/Ctrl+Option/Alt+T. This simultaneously clones the selection and enters the Free Transform mode. Then he rotated the eye about 20 degrees (7.13). "I purposely rotated the eyes to slightly different angles. Many artists have a habit of maintaining absolute symmetry in Photoshop, and it just doesn't look natural. A little bit of asymmetry really sends the effect home.

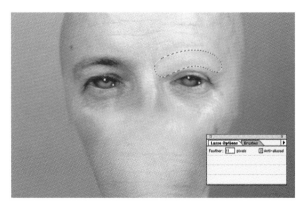

7.12

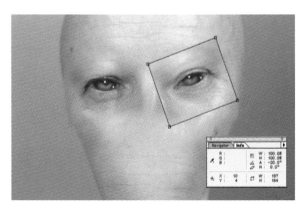

7.13

"To reduce the size of the eyes, I pinched them each 35 percent (7.14). This had the effect of not only shrinking the eyes, but also stretching the bags and wrinkles around the eyes. It helped to age the creature and make it more believable." The finished eyes appear savage and malevolent (7.15), just what you want in a doctor from outer space.

EXPANDING THE CRANIUM

"Guy has such a strong bridge to his nose that I had to touch it up with some more forehead. Again, I just selected the area, moved the selection over the forehead, and cloned the forehead into position (7.16). Then I did the usual Levels adjustment and touch up."

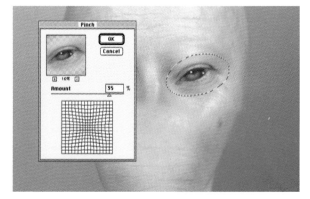

7.14

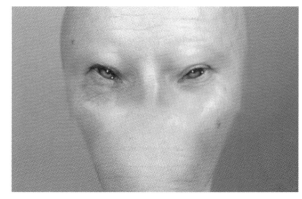

7.15

Moore next selected the top portion of the image and applied Filter ➤ Distort ➤ Spherize (7.17). He set the Amount value to 25 percent to swell the skull ever so slightly (7.18). "After all the work on the eyes, he was starting to look pretty beastly. The brain expansion helped him to look more intelligent."

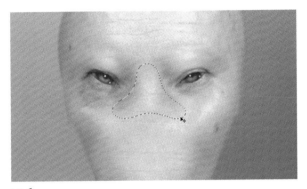

7.16

CLEANING UP DISTORTION BLURS

When you distort feathered selections, you tend to get blurred edges and stretch marks. In the spherized version of Bones (7.18), the stretching is evident under the bridge of the nose, around the eyes, and below the cheekbones. "These motion blur trails are a real telltale sign of digital manipulation. To get rid of them, I'll usually go in and lay down some noise with the Add Noise command set to Monochromatic. That helps to simulate the film grain. Then I'll apply a very low Gaussian Blur radius, maybe 0.3. After that, I'll do spot work with the rubber stamp tool.

"Of course, cleanup takes time, and around here time is a scarce commodity. So we typically toss it together as quickly as we can. Then when the show's released and it's successful, we go back and do it over again like we did with *Star Wars*."

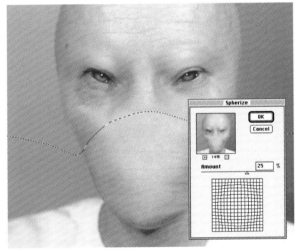

7.17

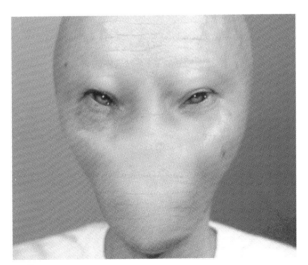

7.18

RESTORING THE NUTRIENT INPUT ORIFICE

"I still wanted my alien to have a mouth, so I went back to the original image and selected the mouth using a feathered lasso. Then I copied the mouth and pasted it into the Bones image. Then I scaled the mouth to make the lips super thin (7.19). It was really fun to have this free-floating mouth because I could nudge it around to get different expressions. I could make him look like a real dummy by positioning the mouth high. If I put the mouth too low, he just looked ridiculous. I even put it on his forehead just for laughs."

ALIEN INTERVENTION

Moore eventually arrived at three variations on the Doc theme, including Bones (7.20) and two additional operating room characters, Intern (7.21) and Nurse (7.22). "You notice I kept Guy's mole in all three images. It's a little detail you don't expect to see in visitors from another planet. But I imagine they have skin blemishes and other defects just like we do."

Moore should know. Legend has it that he was inspired by beings beyond our solar system. "Before the movie came out, there was an article in a local psychic publication. The writer claimed she was notified by aliens that they were controlling the production of the movie. They were paying special attention to the person who was designing the aliens. And I thought, cool, that should speed up the approval process."

We guess it just goes to show you: Even hyperintelligent aliens have their limitations. They may have built the great pyramids and they're clearly the people to call if you need a nice crop circle, but their movie directing skills are a bit hit and miss. *A* for special effects; *D* for drama.

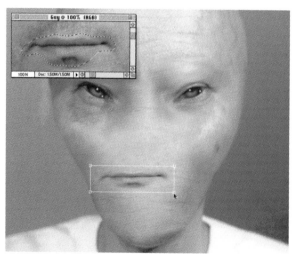

7.19

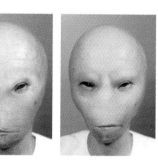

7.20   7.21   7.22

FROM PHOTOSHOP TO CREATURE SHOP

"After the director approved my design for Doc, I sent the Photoshop sketch off to our creature shop and they used it to sculpt the clay model for the puppet. I worked with the creature shop to figure out the depth and decide how the puppet should move. In the end, less turned out to be more. We ended up inserting cables to move his eyes and eyelids. Then we added pulsating areas around his temples. That was all there was to the face. Then the arms and body were puppeted. Somehow he was scarier if he was largely immobile."

KIDS, DON'T TRY THIS AT HOME

Moore is one of the few artists who gets to play with his stuff after he makes it. As visual effects director, he was on hand when the operation scene was filmed, so he had a chance to experience some of the props up close and personal.

In the movie, a big sheet of plastic sucks the actor down onto the operating table. It covers his whole body, including his face. The plastic sinks into the actor's open mouth and it looks to all the world like he's suffocating. "That's actually true. I took a turn as a stand-in and you can't breath at all. There's this huge compressor that sucks the sheet onto you. It was loud as heck. The director's wife, the actress Marilu Henner, was standing there and all I could hear over the motor was her screams. It scared her so bad she ran and hid behind a cabinet. I finally had to break the suction by lifting my leg. After I got my breath back, I asked, 'How was it?' And they said, 'Yeah, it looked great. Real scary.'

"Our big limitation in scripting the operating scene was that none of the people who claim they've been abducted have any marks. So we figured, what kind of operating can you do without leaving scars? We decided to concentrate on the orifices — the eye, the ear, the mouth. We even fooled around with going a little lower. In the final cut, the aliens put a pipe down Travis' mouth. But we were going to have another pipe come in from the other end. At some point, we'd see the pipes right under the skin as the one from above met up with the one from below. But the director was like, 'Er, no. That's just too disgusting.' He might have been right.

"Right after the pipes, the aliens pour some fluid into Travis' eye. Originally, the fluid was going to be really dark, but it didn't read very well on camera. So we decided to try something light. Unfortunately, we were all set up and ready to go. So one of the guys from the model shop ran off and came back with some white stuff. The director asked him, 'What is it?', but the model shop guy just said, 'Believe me, it's safe. I tested it on my own eye.' So we poured it into the actor's eye, and it looked great. You know what it was? Mocha mix." Wow, it's both a stimulant and an eye whitener.

CHAPTER 8
ABSTRACT EXPRESSIONISM TO COMMERCIAL DESIGN

Being an artist requires the powers of observation, interpretation, and expression combined with the propensity to experiment with and learn from your work. Whether we work with words, chisels, pencils, brushes, cameras, or computers, we all share a passion that drives us to create and explore, often late into the night. The problem with many of those late night forays is that we need to get up and go to work the next morning in order to be able to pay for our art supplies and the museum visits that inspire us — oh, and pay the rent, and some food would be useful, too. Some artists solve this problem by divesting themselves from their art during the workday, while others find jobs that allow them to incorporate their artistic skills into their work. Ulrik Claesson is an example of the latter, balancing his passion for art while working as a designer and art director at Clockwork, a leading Swedish Web design company. Clockwork's clients include the international corporations Eurocard, Hoechst, McDonald's, and some of Sweden's most important companies such as Digital Equipment AB, EMA Telstar, and Alcro Färg.

In this chapter, we will have the opportunity to take a look at what motivates and inspires Ulrik in his personal work and how his artistic sensibilities carry over into his commercial work. Claesson explains, "I am interested in the randomness of nature and how that contrasts with man-made constructions. When I work in Photoshop, I use layers and channels to mimic nature's randomness, allowing the masks and selections to work together in unpredictable ways. For me, the creative process is intuitive and inspiring, and I often do not know where I will end up. This is in hard contrast to my professional design work

> *When I work in Photoshop, I use layers and channels to mimic nature's randomness, allowing the masks and selections to work together in unpredictable ways.*
>
> ULRIK CLAESSON

95

where I need to meet specific objectives, deadlines, and expectations. I incorporate my artwork into my design work where applicable, but obviously that doesn't work all the time."

ARTISTIC RANDOMNESS

In the piece *Bodoni* (8.1), Claesson uses layers (8.2) and channels (8.3) in a way we've never seen before, to build up the image and create a seemingly random, yet beautifully designed piece. He started by scanning in used and abused Letraset Pres Type with his flatbed scanner. Before digital page layout and design applications were commonplace, Pres Type was used to lay out comps and package designs. It consisted of a thin wax paper with mirror images of letters that you would rub onto paper. This would reverse the mirror type to create text and layouts. Anyone who has ever used Pres Type will remember the frustration of getting all the letters in a word just right and then cursing under your breath as the last letter slips off axis. Once a sheet of Pres Type is used a few times the wax paper begins to tear, letters get damaged, and the most often used letters run out. Claesson puts this deteriorated type to good use. "I love the blemished surfaces that are created randomly through the passage of time. People try to mimic this deterioration with Photoshop filters, but I don't think that ever looks as good as the actual effect that time has on the material world."

8.1

ARTIST:
Ulrik Claesson

ORGANIZATION:
Clockwork Consulting AB
Tullvaktsvägen 11
SE-115 78 Stockholm
http://www.algonet.se/~meltwood
(personal)
meltwood@algonet.se (personal)
http://www.clockwork.se (professional)
u l r i k . c l a e s s o n @ c l o c k w o r k . s e
(professional)

SYSTEM:
PowerPC G3/225
4GB storage
Mac OS 8.1

RAM:
120MB total
90MB assigned to Photoshop

MONITOR:
17-inch AppleVision with Mactell Vision
3D Graphic Acceleration card

EXTRAS:
Agfa DuoScan Flatbed Scanner

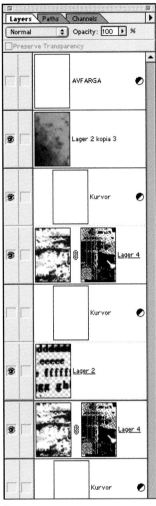

8.2

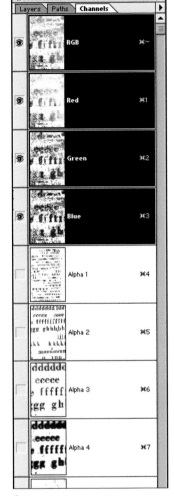

8.3

VERSION USED:

Photoshop 5.0

OTHER APPLICATIONS:

Macromedia FreeHand 5.5 – 8.0

WORK HISTORY:

1986 — Interested in photography throughout high school.

1988 – 91 — Studied design, art, and photography to prepare for college. Discovered using the computer as an art tool.

1990 — Received a degree in design and illustration from RMI-Berghs School in Stockhom, Sweden.

1991 – 92 — Attended DomenArt-School in Gotheburg, Sweden.

1991 – 92 — Student in the academy course "The Computer as Artistic Tool."

1994 — Founded network-based design business: Apelgren & Claesson Design.

1998 — Employed by Clockwork.

FAVORITE FLIGHT SIMULATOR:

A-10 Cuba. "One of the best combat flight simulators ever! It looks simple if you look at the graphics, but you can experiment and fool around with the plane in the A-10 world for a long time without getting bored."

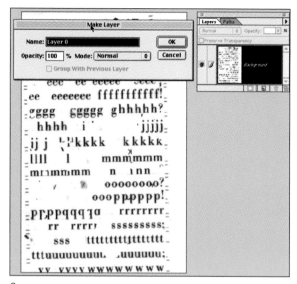

8.4

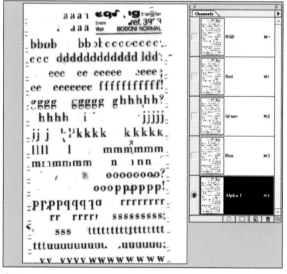

8.5

After Claesson has scanned in the Bodoni sheet of Pres Type, he opens the file in Photoshop and immediately double-clicks it so that the background layer becomes a layer that can support a layer mask (8.4). "By changing the background layer to a normal layer I can also put layers beneath it. This frees me from only working up; I can do a lot more by being able to work freely up and down."

CLAESSON'S CHANNEL STRATEGY

As we mentioned earlier, Claesson works with channels in a way we've never seen. In the *Bodoni* piece, he duplicated one of the color channels as a new channel (8.5) (it didn't matter which one since the image is essentially grayscale). He then zoomed in on the channel to extrapolate new images by selecting an area from this channel (8.6) and copying it into a new

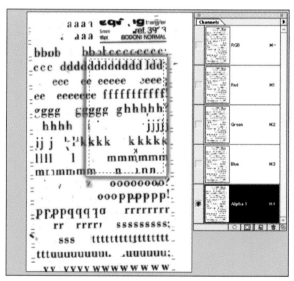

8.6

channel. He used Transform to size the section up to fill the entire channel (8.7). After doing this a few times, the image information started to fall apart. Rather than letting the pixelation take over, Claesson used Curves (8.8) to actually deconstruct the channel information even further (8.9). All the channels he created will later serve as the foundation of the image when he works with layers, layer masks, and adjustment layers to add color and texture to the file.

SIMULATED MOONSCAPE

To add texture to the image and break down the type, Claesson adds photographic elements, additional scanned images, and channels from previous projects. When you first see the channels of the layered Photoshop document, it looks like a picture of the

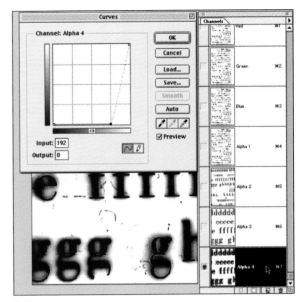

8.8

8.7

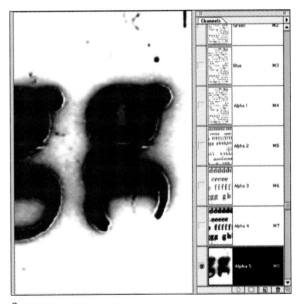

8.9

8.10

8.11

moon's surface (8.10). However, Claesson explains, "I use photography to simulate nature. Rather than walking around with a camera looking for an image, I create it in the studio. In the case of the moonscape, I photographed an extreme close-up of broken plaster with a macro lens to create this abstract yet familiar picture. Echoing nature with my own photographic and digital constructions frees me from relying on the real world around me for source images."

MORE CHANNEL MADNESS

Take a look at one of Claesson's earlier pieces (8.11) and the layer mask (8.12) he used to interact with the typography in the *Bodoni* piece. It takes a true Photoshop fanatic to enjoy the aesthetics of a mask! Claesson mixes and matches channels between disparate images to add complexity to the individual compositions while also developing a relationship between the images that share channels and textures. By inverting the mask from the older image, Claesson created a new channel, which he brought into the *Bodoni* piece (8.13).

"I often look at many of the images that can be found in the channels as art-worthy works in their own right. The same goes for the different 'images' that I see when I turn on and off the eye on the Layers palette." Once the channels are in place, the creative process takes over. With a lot of experimentation, and coffee, Claesson loads channels as selections into empty layers. In this example, he loaded channel #6 into a new layer (Select ➤ Load Selection), inversed the selection (Select ➤ Inverse), and filled the selection with black (Edit ➤ Fill) (8.14).

After dropping the active selection (Select ➤ Deselect), he added an image adjustment layer and grouped it with the layer below (Layer ➤ Group With Previous). By running a radical Curve (8.15), he inversed the tones. Now you may wonder why he didn't just fill the text with white. The decision to work with black or white is actually arbitrary because the image adjustment layer doesn't add to the file size

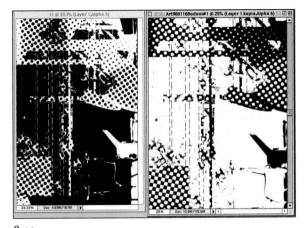

8.12

8.13

and its effect can be changed, reversed, or deleted at any point in the image creation process.

By continuing to experiment with the loading and filling of channels, Claesson builds up pieces of images that layer on top of one another in unpredictable ways, as seen in this layer which combines the plaster moonscape texture with type and the grid-like structure from channel #9 (8.16). When we

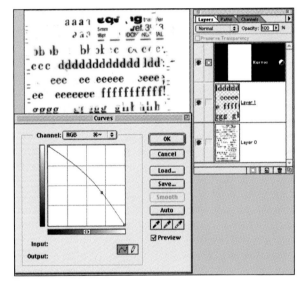

8.15

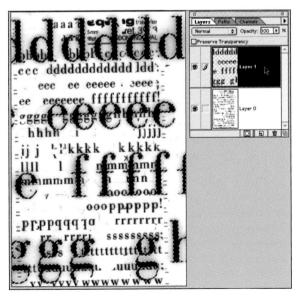

8.14

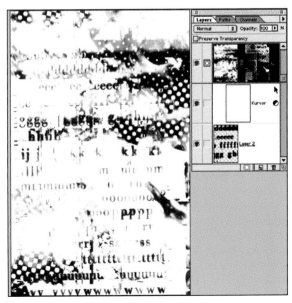

8.16

8.17

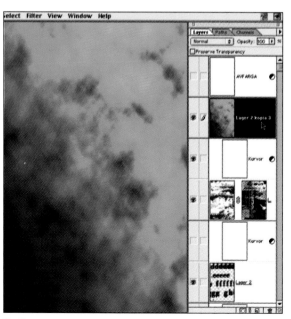

8.18

asked Claesson to deconstruct this piece during our interview, he calmly stated, "That is difficult. Creating these images is not a series of well-planned intellectual steps. I work somewhere deeper, and at the same time I am much more interested in what the image means and looks like to you." Here is the layer isolated by itself (8.17).

ADDING COLOR

Finally, to add color to the image, Claesson duplicated layer #2 (Layer ➤ Duplicate) and ran the Difference Clouds filter with the foreground color set to a bright green to create a fiery effect (8.18). He then changed the blend mode to Screen to colorize the layers beneath (8.19). Once again, there was no

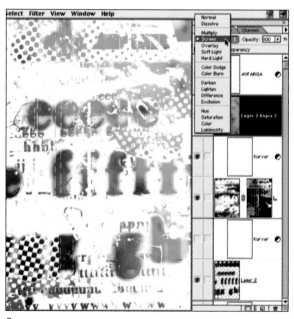

8.19

way to predict what would happen, but the experimentation paid off in the end, as seen in the final piece (8.20).

MANAGING FILE SIZE

All of this work with channels and layers has consequences. A seemingly manageable 10.8MB file has grown to a whopping 115.6MB. "I need to keep the final flattened file size reasonable — not too small because I plan to output these files on a translucent material to be displayed with narrow, light boxes so that all the details and layering that I worked so hard to get comes out."

Sometimes the alpha channels are as beautiful as the images themselves. In this case, a 6.07MB image is obtained (8.21) by removing the channels and flattening the layers of an original 53.6MB image file with 14 layers and 13 channels. These figures (8.22 – 8.24) show some of the complex alpha channels Claesson used to create his final artwork.

THE BEAUTY IS IN THE DETAILS

Claesson sees beauty in individual channels and layers (8.25). When he reaches a stage in the image that feels complete, he creates a mask on a topmost layer to crop out distracting elements (8.26). This enables him to see new images (8.27). These masks act like the cropping blades of a darkroom easel, allowing him to investigate image context, details, and abstractions (8.28). "As you can see in my images, I don't work with recognizable photographs of people, places, or animals. Instead I have limited myself to working with form, color, shapes, and typography. I have consciously limited the types of materials that I work with in order to get total freedom inside of those limits (8.29)."

8.21

8.20

8.22

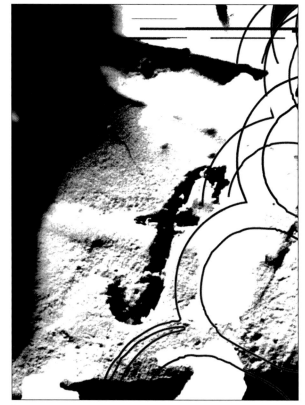

8.23

8.24

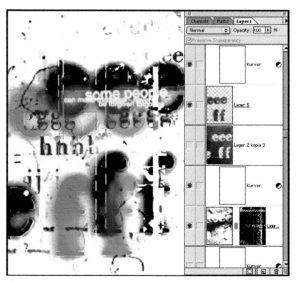

8.25

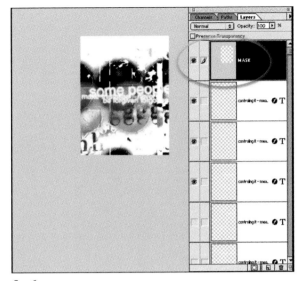

8.26

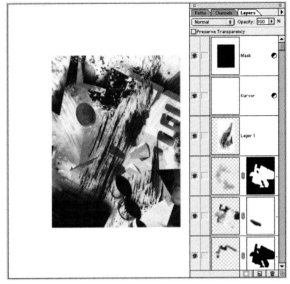

8.27

8.28

8.29

OLD AND NEW MERGE

Claesson was commissioned by *IdN* (International Designers Network) magazine to create a four-color cover (8.30). "The publisher gave me free reign to create the piece showing how new technology and old technology are merging. I've always been interested in how technology, design, and typography are interrelated, and this assignment was the perfect venue to explore these concepts."

This image is also a perfect example of how Claesson's personal work influences his professional work. He started out by collecting shapes and forms from existing documents, channels (8.31), and layers (8.32). This developed into a brainstorm with fascinating edges, textures, and shapes. Finally, to represent the old and new merging in the field of design,

he added channels and layers from a typography study.

The secret behind creating the abstract shapes and edges is in the way Claesson works with the magic wand. "To me the magic wand is more than a tool to simply select a shape or isolate an image element. I'm constantly experimenting with its tolerance settings and studying how it searches. In a way, it mimics the random nature of fractals. As I change the tolerance and keep adding to the selection by holding down the Shift key, I can create abstract shapes and edges that look natural within their randomness." In this example, Claesson worked with the magic wand on the background layer from a typography image. By Shift-clicking he kept adding to the selection (8.33). As the selection grew in both size and interest, he made a new layer by pressing ⌘/Ctrl + J. If you don't see

8.30

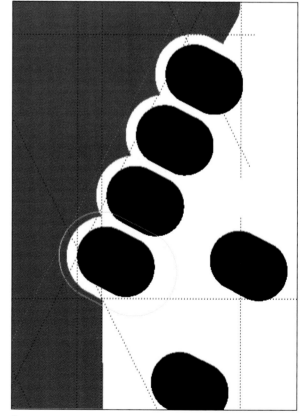

8.31

where Claesson is going with this, look at the rotated file (8.34) and compare it to Claesson's brainstorm file (8.35) and a close-up of the file (8.36).

With this abstract selection, Claesson created a new file and began to combine and merge it with a hiero-glyphic-like text scrap (8.37) to create the final brain-storm. He used the geometric form in a layer mask (8.38) and channel mask (8.39) to allow very subtle tones to come through the image, breaking up the black and gray surfaces with blue tonality (8.40).

8.32

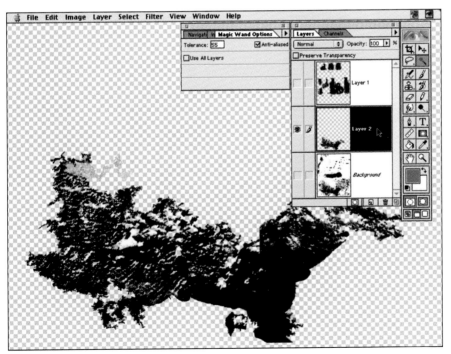

8.33

8.34

8.35

8.36

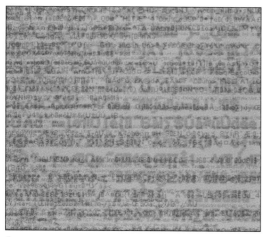

8.37

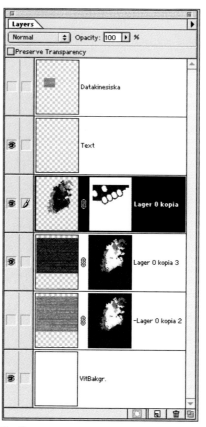

8.38

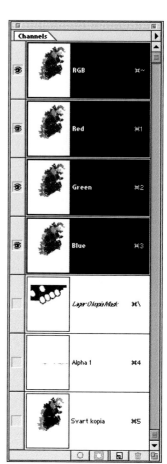

8.39

For the final image, Claesson combined the textured brainstorm file with his familiar palette of typographic elements, layers, and channels. He tied the image together by grounding the composition on a neutral solid color background. Note that the drop shadow Claesson used to separate the central element from the background is not your standard duplicate, fill, and blur drop shadow. Rather he painted the shading by hand. "I'm not interested in the standard filters or effects that ship with Photoshop. Instead I use the standard tools that correspond with the real world. The way I use the magic wand is a good example of that. By painting the shadow, I am interacting with the piece rather than using predetermined values or techniques to create an effect that will most likely look artificial (8.41)."

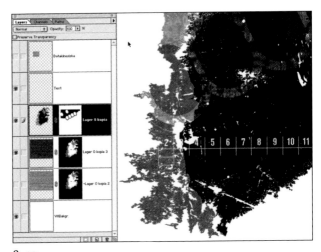

8.40

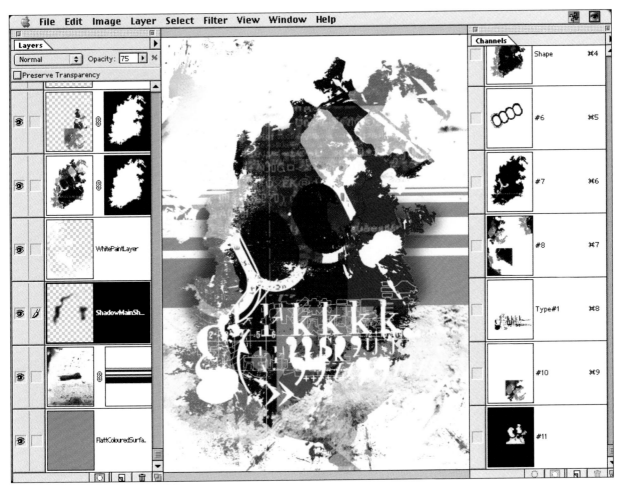

8.41

COMMERCIAL DESIGN

Claesson was commissioned by A.Wingårdh Design to design a corporate identity for a Swedish office supply company that would work well for a variety of tasks, from coarsely screened brown paper bags to finely printed four color calendar pages. The image needed to be graphic and hold up well in two, three, and four-color printing processes. Understanding the printing process was essential in making this project successful. "I knew that the fine lines would disappear on the paper bags, and to compensate for this I worked with very graphical shapes to represent what the company does."

Claesson started by gathering simple clipart into a FreeHand document that reflected what the company sold — scissors, calculators, tapes, pencils, floppies, and so on, as seen on the left (8.42). He then started to work with size, balance, and color as seen on the right. In the final sketch, he experimented with the look and feel of different process colors (8.43).

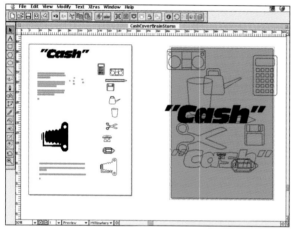

8.42

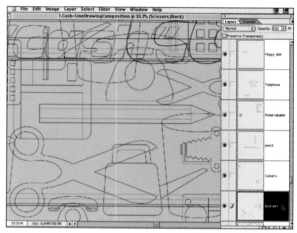

8.44

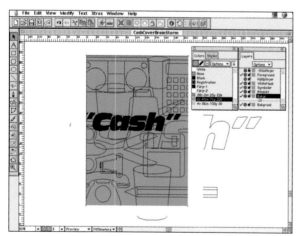

8.43

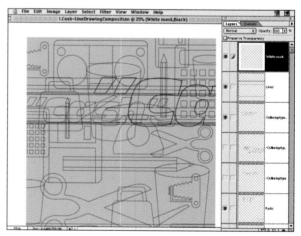

8.45

After finessing the composition in FreeHand, Claesson brought the individual paths into individual layers in a new Photoshop document (8.44) and masked out the edge of the image with a white frame on the top-most layer (8.45), exactly as he does in his personal work to focus the viewer's attention. After flattening the layers (8.46), he separated the negative spaces into separate layers by selecting shapes with the magic wand and copying them onto a new layer and filling with white (8.47). Here is the layered file in progress before Claesson brings in the Pantone color layers (8.48).

Next, Claesson duplicated the work in progress file (8.49) and used careful screening and Gaussian blurring to finish the composition. By manipulating the basic design with the blur and adding distinctive lines (8.50), he reworked the same initial design to achieve different end results (8.51). Once again, rather than using the standard

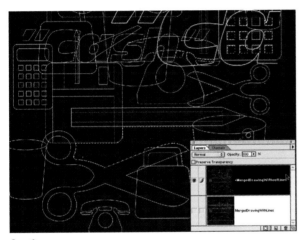

8.46

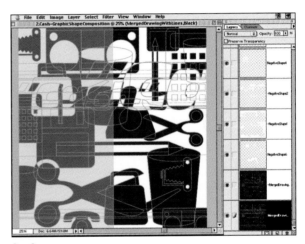

8.48

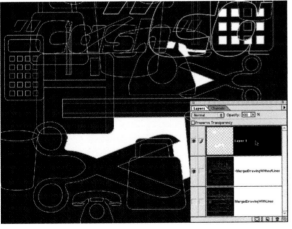

8.47

8.49

blur filters, Claesson created freeform masks (8.52) with very soft edges and used these to control the blur.

Finally, Claesson separated the file into the corresponding printing plates to create these variations on the same theme (8.53 – 8.55).

8.50

8.51

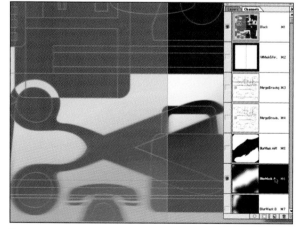

8.52

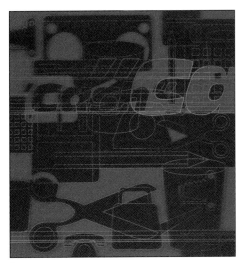

8.53

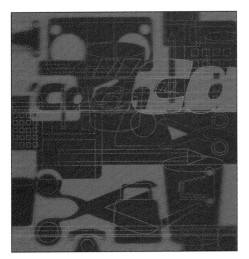

8.54

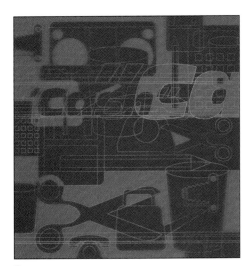

8.55

TYPOGRAPHIC
EFFECTS
Photoshop

CHAPTER 9
SPECIAL TYPE EFFECTS

Whether a picture is really worth a thousand words is a subject for debate. Take a masterwork by Eugène Delacroix and display it within sight of countryman and contemporary Victor Hugo, and you can count on 1,000 words minimum. But flash an Easter card in front of the character Lenny in *Of Mice and Men*, and about the best you can expect is, "Duh, dat's a pretty bunny, George!"

Even so, there's clearly some magic that occurs when you combine pictures and words into a single element. In his cover art for *Sports Illustrated*'s baseball and football calendars (9.1), Brooklyn-based artist Eric Reinfeld proves that text can both tell and show its message. "Photoshop's not the kind of program where you set some type, kern it a little, and say 'gee, nice headline.' I mean, you *can* do that, but if you do, you're not bringing any creativity to bear; you're just plopping words together. Photoshop gives you an opportunity to distort type, add dimension, and hopefully infuse it with a little of your own aesthetic energy."

Reinfeld should know. The artist derives a significant part of his income from turning type into full-fledged artistic elements with genuine form and substance. From the raised lettering of the *Sports Illustrated* cover art (9.1) to the waxy edges of the Marét logo (9.2), Reinfeld gives us the sense that his type is actually made of something. Even the corporate-cool letters in Time-Warner's empire ads (9.3) convey a subtle presence of depth.

In this chapter, Reinfeld shows you how to mold matter into abstraction. After all, when working in

Photoshop gives you an opportunity to distort type, add dimension, and hopefully infuse it with a little of your own aesthetic energy.

ERIC REINFELD

Photoshop, your goal is not so much to create real-world type as it is to build letters from the essence of life. You know the photograph is an image. We can plainly see that the artwork is an image. But lest we forget, the type is every bit an image as well.

THE BASIC APPROACH

Reinfeld uses two programs to make his text. "Photoshop is a heck of a program for stylizing type, but I think everyone agrees that it's not the best program for creating the letters in the first place. There's a plug-in from Extensis called PhotoTools that improves Photoshop's type capabilities. I use it when I'm making quick comps, just to get ideas across and see how they look. But when I start on the final artwork, I create the type in Illustrator and then bring it into Photoshop. The antialiasing is much better that way."

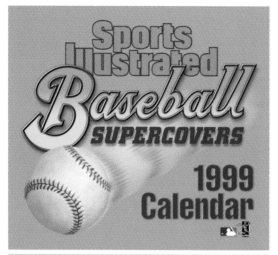

9.2

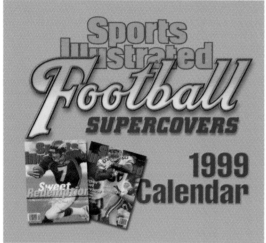

9.3

9.1

Artwork by Eric Reinfeld

ARTIST:

Eric Reinfeld

STUDIO:

87 Seventh Avenue

Brooklyn, New York 11217

718/783-2313

reinfeld1@aol.com

macsushi@earthlink.net

SYSTEM:

SuperMac S900 604e/225 (Umax)

18GB storage (including Quantum Atlas

and Micronet HotSwapable arrays)

RAM:

300MB total

275MB assigned to Photoshop

MONITORS:

Apple 17- and 20-inchers

EXTRAS:

Targa 2000 Pro video-capture board

VERSION USED:

Photoshop 5.0

Reinfeld saves his type in the native Illustrator (ai) format, and then he opens it up in Photoshop. "Note that I don't Place the file (with File ➢ Place), I open it. That way, I can enter the resolution I want to use, specify RGB or CMYK, and so on. Then, I increase the canvas size by an inch or so all the way around to give myself room to work."

At this point, Reinfeld might import a background. "Because I opened the type from an EPS illustration, the background is transparent. Just as an example, I took in a generic stock image of some clouds and dragged it in as a new layer behind the text (9.4)."

"Now, what I'm about to show you is the simplest kind of type treatment you can do in Photoshop — type filled with an image surrounded by a shiny halo. Of course, it could just as easily be a drop shadow or a color fringe or whatever. Try it a couple of times and you'll see that this basic approach works for a dozen different effects. A clipping group here, some expanding and blurring there, and you're done."

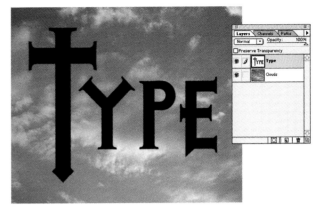

9.4

OTHER APPLICATIONS:
Adobe Illustrator, Adobe After Effects, QuarkXPress, ElectricImage Broadcast, Form·Z

WORK HISTORY:
1985 — Opened up independent branch of father's dry cleaning business.
1987 — Purchased color Mac II system, learned to use PixelPaint and Illustrator.
1990 — Designed belts in Photoshop for New York fashion company.
1992 — Converted *The American Kennel Club Gazette* from traditional to electronic publishing.

1993 — Left job as Senior Desktop Color Technician at high-end service bureau to freelance for Time, Sony, Paramount, and others.
1997 — Authored *Real World After Effects* (Peachpit Press).

FAVORITE COLLECTIBLE:
Antique advertising signs ("If you have old signs in the house, contact me immediately.")

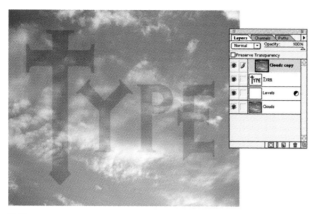

9.5

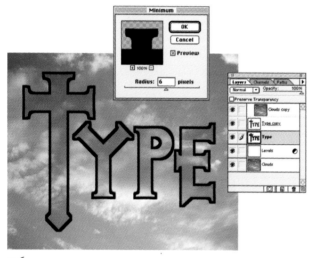

9.6

9.7

CLIPPING IMAGE AGAINST IMAGE

"The clouds were a little muddy, so I went ahead and added a Levels adjustment layer on top of the cloud layer to brighten it up a bit. I didn't apply the Levels command directly, I used an adjustment layer because I still wanted to have access to the original dark clouds. My feeling is, always use adjustment layers when you can. No sense in applying the effect for good until you get everything exactly the way you want it."

Reinfeld's next step was to fill the type with the darker clouds. "I made a copy of the clouds by dragging the layer onto the little page icon. (By the way, I have to say, I hate the way the page and trash icons are right next to each other at the bottom of the Layers palette. I'm constantly throwing away a layer when I mean to copy it.)

"Anyway, I dragged the cloned clouds to the top of the layer stack. Then, I combined the cloud layer with the type below it to make a clipping group." You can do this by pressing ⌘/Ctrl+G. The result is a darker patch of clouds masked by the text (9.5).

EXPANDING THE TYPE FOR THE HALO

"Even though I've got this clipping group, my text is unharmed, same as it ever was. The great thing about this technique is that I can get to my original text any time I need it. Like now."

To make the halo, Reinfeld started by duplicating the text layer. "The weird thing here is that Photoshop makes the duplicated layer part of the clipping group and releases the original. It doesn't matter, of course — it just affects how the layers are named — but I've seen it confuse people."

To make the cloned type thicker, Reinfeld applies Filter ➤ Other ➤ Minimum. "When working with a layer like this, the Minimum filter shrinks the transparency mask and expands the letters. It's a little counterintuitive — seems like Maximum would do the expanding. If you can't keep Minimum and Maximum straight, just try one. If it's wrong, undo and try the other. You've got a 50/50 chance.

"I entered a Radius of 6. But you can do less or more — whatever you want. It just tells Photoshop how far to blow up the text (9.6)." Incidentally, if you create your text directly in Photoshop instead of importing it from Illustrator, make sure you turn off the Preserve Transparency check box before choosing Minimum. Otherwise, the letters are immutable.

BLURRING AND DODGING

"Next, I applied a nice Gaussian Blur so the type spreads out. Some folks like to match the Gaussian Blur radius to the Minimum radius. I usually take it a few notches higher. You just want to get a gradual separation between type and background." At this point, Reinfeld ended up with a drop shadow. To turn it into a halo, he filled the layer with white by pressing ⌘/Ctrl+Shift+Delete (9.7).

  "From here, there are a million different things you can do. Apply blend modes, change the Opacity, modify the other layers. Knock yourself out." To demonstrate, Reinfeld selected Color Dodge from the blend mode pop-up menu in the Layers palette and reduced the Opacity setting to 70 percent. This resulted in a more dramatic halo with hot, glowing edges. Then, he selected the text layer inside the clipping group and applied the Motion Blur filter at a 90 degree angle and a Distance value of 30 pixels. This blurred the halo into the tops and bottoms of the characters without harming the cloud pattern (9.8).

9.8

THE BENEFITS OF LAYERED TYPE

By keeping your effects and text variations on separate layers, you ensure absolute flexibility. "Here's where things become interesting. Try linking the two type layers with that chain icon in the Layers palette. Then, you can move the type mask and halo together. I can even apply Free Transform and flip or distort the two text layers without affecting the cloud patterns at all (9.9). I might also link the top cloud texture with the type to get yet another look."

9.9

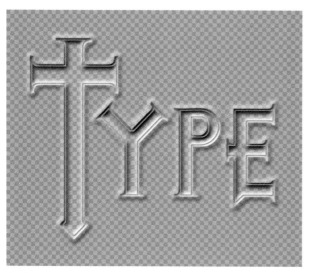

9.10

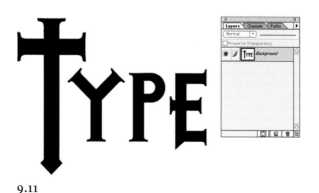

9.11

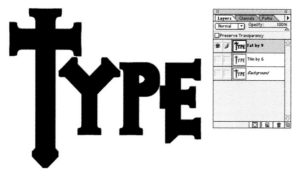

9.12

CREATING SOURCE VARIATIONS

"Okay, that was easy. If you want more sophisticated effects (9.10), you have to do a little more work." Reinfeld marries the old-school approach of building depth via channel operations with some of Photoshop's newer layering functions. "Whenever I create serious type effects, I work in two files. One file is a source file, the other is the target. The source contains the original type and a few layers of simple variations; the target's where I build the actual composition. Then, I use the Apply Image and Calculations commands to bounce back and forth between these two files.

"I start off the source file by opening type I've created in Illustrator and flattening the image so I have one background layer — black type against a white background (9.11). This layer is sacred. I will never, ever, ever touch it, except to duplicate it. Every text effect I create stems from this one background layer."

CHANGING THE WEIGHT

Reinfeld then duplicated the layer twice and created two weight variations using the Minimum and Maximum filters. "Because this is black type against a white background — no transparency — you use Minimum to expand the weight of the type and Maximum to contract it." Reinfeld created a thinner variation with Filter ➢ Other ➢ Maximum set to a radius of 6 pixels, and a fatter version using Minimum and a radius of 9 pixels (9.12). As you'll soon see, these will define the inner and outer edges of his embossed text effects.

MAKING OUTLINES

Next, Reinfeld duplicated his existing base layers — Background, Thin by 6, and Fat by 9 — and applied a trio of effects to each. "First, I apply outline effects. You think, 'Oh, the Find Edges filter,' right? No way, not enough control. I use a layering trick that involves Gaussian Blur and the Difference mode. It's really easy.

"Say I want to start with the original type. I duplicate the background layer and apply the Gaussian Blur set to 1.5 pixels. This gives me a subtle soft edge that will determine the thickness of the outline. Then, I duplicate this new layer, invert it (⌘/Ctrl+I), and apply the Difference blend mode. Then, I do a ⌘/Ctrl+E to merge the two outline layers into one." The result is a soft outline about 3 pixels thick (9.13). Reinfeld repeated this operation on the Thin by 6 and Fat by 9 layers as well.

SOFT EMBOSS EFFECTS

"I use the Emboss filter to give the text depth. But before I can do that, I have to blur the type. Emboss doesn't like hard edges." Reinfeld duplicated the three original type layers — our friends Background, Thin by 6, and Fat by 9 — and applied the Gaussian Blur filter to each with a Radius value of 6. Then, he duplicated each of the blurred layers and applied the Emboss filter. "The settings you use are totally up to you. But you'll probably want to be consistent." For this example, Reinfeld used an Angle value of -60 degrees, a Height of 6 pixels, and an Amount value of 150 percent (9.14).

MOVING THROUGH THE LAYERS

"Whenever you're working in the source file, you're piling on a bunch of opaque layers. So it's never helpful to see more than one layer at a time — you only want to see the layer you're working on. You probably already know to Option/Alt-click on an eyeball icon in the Layers palette to see just one layer. But here's a good one: To switch layers and hide all others, Option/Alt-click on the layer name. You can also use the shortcuts Option/Alt+[and Option/Alt+]."

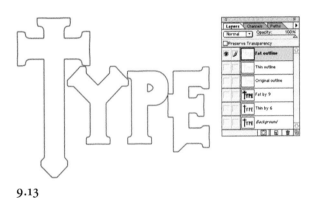

9.13

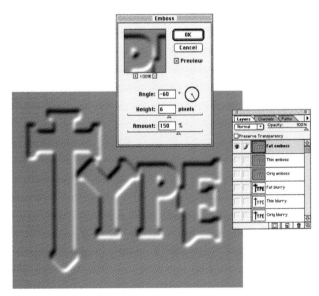

9.14

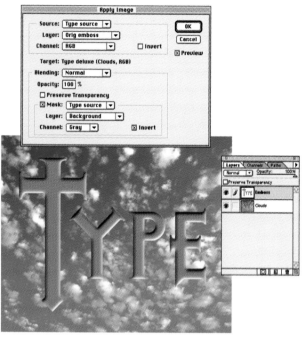

9.15

THE SOLID BLACK LAYER

"Last and certainly least, I create a new layer at the top of the stack and fill it with black. It's nearly always a good idea to have a black layer handy when using channel operations. Many of the layers I've created I'll use as masks, and I'll need to fill the masked areas with black or white. So long as I've got this black layer sitting around, I can make black, white, or any shade of gray."

ASSEMBLING THE ACTUAL COMPOSITION

"When creating your target image, you need to make sure it's the same size as the source." After you choose the New command, select the name of the source file from the Window menu. This ensures a pixel-for-pixel match. "Then, import the image that you want to use as a background for your type. You can use the Place command, or just drag and drop an image from an open file." For this example, Reinfeld used another cloud image.

THE FIRST EMBOSS EFFECT

After dropping in the cloud background, Reinfeld created a new layer for his first emboss effect. "As I mentioned earlier, the Emboss filter works best with blurry edges. But that doesn't mean you want your type to be blurry. The solution is to mask the emboss effect."

Reinfeld chose Image ➤ Apply Image to display the Apply Image dialog box. He selected his source image from the Source pop-up menu, and then selected the standard-weight emboss layer from the Layer pop-up menu. The Blending options were set to Normal and 100 percent. "Be sure to turn the Preview check box on when you're inside this dialog box so you can see what you're doing."

To define the edges of the emboss effect, Reinfeld turned on the Mask check box and again selected the source image from the pop-up menu. This time, however, he selected Background from the Layer pop-up, and turned on the Invert check box. The result is embossed text inside a precise text mask (9.15).

Some may wonder why Reinfeld didn't convert the type to a selection outline and use that to drag and drop the emboss effect. "Hey, try it. It works, but it isn't any easier. You have to hide everything but the background layer and then go to the Channels palette and retrieve the selection. Then, you have to switch to the emboss layer — it's a lot of busy work. I prefer to just send everything through masks, like I did here. The Apply Image dialog box may look tough at first, but once you become familiar with it, it's quite easy to navigate."

9.16

After creating the new emboss layer, Reinfeld applied Hard Light from the blend mode pop-up menu in the Layers palette. This etched the type into the cloudy background (9.16). "See, now that alone is a pretty good type effect. Thank you folks, and have a nice day." But Reinfeld has no intention of stopping there.

THE RED INNER EMBOSS

Reinfeld then set about creating another level of emboss inside the first. Like before, he created a new layer and chose Image ➤ Apply Image. The dialog box came up with the same settings he applied before. All he changed were the two Layers settings. He selected the layer that contains the thin emboss effect from the top Layer pop-up menu. Then, he set the lower Layer pop-up to Thin by 6. This masked the thin emboss effect with the thin type (9.17).

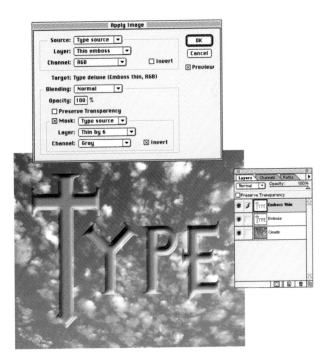

9.17

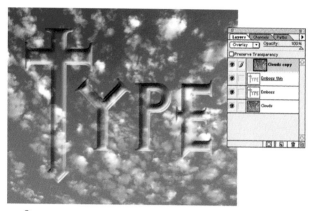

9.18

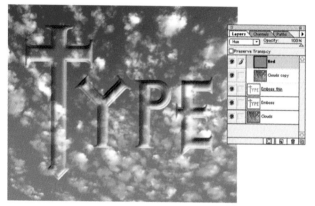

9.19

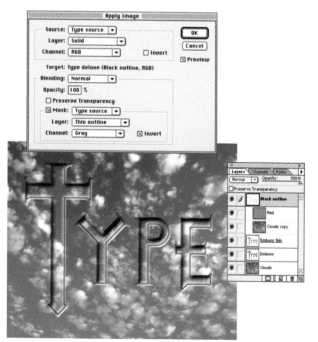

9.20

Reinfeld could have applied the Hard Light mode to this layer as well, but he didn't. "My intention is to give the new emboss layer some additional definition by adding outline effects behind it. This means the new layer has to be opaque." To blend the clouds into this opaque layer, Reinfeld duplicated the cloud layer, dragged it to the top of the Layers palette, and grouped it with the thin emboss effect by pressing ⌘/Ctrl+G. Then, he applied the Overlay mode, which is the exact inverse of Hard Light. As a result, the thin emboss layer appeared to blend in with the clouds exactly like the original emboss effect (9.18).

Just for the heck of it, Reinfeld added a layer to colorize the thin emboss effect with red. After adding yet another new layer, he filled the whole thing with 100 percent red and added it to the clipping group below by pressing ⌘/Ctrl+G. Then, he applied the Hue blend mode. This made the clouds inside the thin embossed type red while leaving both the luminosity and saturation values of the underlying pixels intact (9.19).

"When you have embossed text that's on its own layer and you're using it as the parent of a clipping group, you're ready for anything. If you work much with art directors, you know they like to see stuff really quick. If the art director wants me to try out a new color, I just go to the red layer and press Option/Alt+Delete. Bang, there it is: no work, new color. Everyone can visualize what's going on really easily."

INNER EMBOSS HIGHLIGHTS

Reinfeld's next step was to trace around the red emboss effect using the outline layers from the source file that he had created earlier. Again, he added a new layer, and again he chose the Apply Image command. This time, he switched the top Layer option to the solid black layer, and then he set the bottom Layer option to the thin outline layer. This instructed Photoshop to use the thin outline as a mask and fill it with black (9.20).

Reinfeld moved the new black outline layer to behind the inner emboss clipping group. Then, he pressed ⌘/Ctrl+down arrow and ⌘/Ctrl+right arrow to nudge the outline one pixel down and to the right. He set the Opacity of this layer to 70 percent. This made a subtle black outline underneath the red text.

Naturally, Reinfeld needed a white outline to compliment the black one. So he duplicated the outline layer, inverted it to white by pressing ⌘/Ctrl+I, and nudged the layer two pixels each up and to the left. we've zoomed in on this effect so you can see it in detail (9.21).

THE BIG BACKGROUND EMBOSS

Finally, Reinfeld set about denting the letters into the background sky, as if the type was resting on cloud-patterned fabric. As is his habit, he made a new layer and chose Image ➤ Apply Image. But this time, he did things a little differently. He selected the emboss effect applied to the fat letters from the first Layer pop-up menu. Then, he selected the accompanying Invert check box. The idea here was to switch the highlights and shadows in the emboss effect to better set off the existing emboss layers. For the mask layer, he selected the fat blurry layer from the source image, giving the type soft edges (9.22).

As the *coup de resistance*, Reinfeld dragged the new layer to the bottom of the stack, just above the clouds. He applied the Hard Light blend mode and set the Opacity to 80 percent. The end product is a sight to behold (9.23).

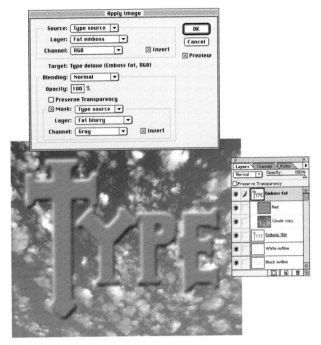

9.22

9.23

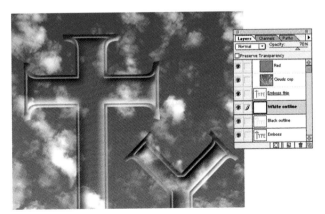

9.21

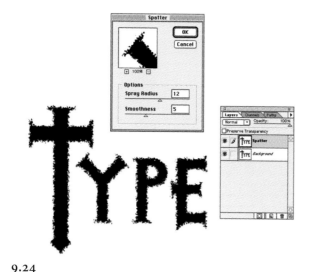

9.24

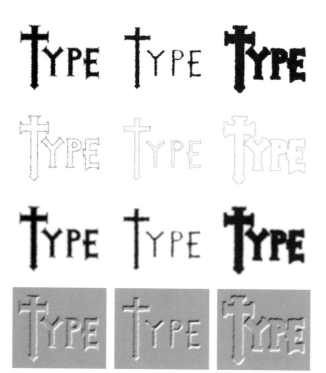

9.25

"What you've got here is an infinitely flexible composition, with a full set of source layers to go along with it. You'll notice, I didn't use all the source layers — hey, that's my prerogative. But later, maybe I will. The point is, I can go back and change my mind any time I want. This leaves me free to learn new effects and explore fresh territory."

ROUGHING IT

"By now, you're probably starting to get an idea of what I do. The specific steps aren't all that important. It's the approach that really matters. Put together a source file full of outline, Gaussian Blur, and Emboss variations, and you can experiment for days."

If you harbor any doubts about this, Reinfeld's next demonstration puts them to rest. Starting with a copy of the same gothic text that he's used in previous examples, Reinfeld applied Filter ➤ Brush Strokes ➤ Spatter. "I don't care for most of the Gallery Effects filters that were added to Photoshop 4, but this one's very handy." The filter roughs up the edges of the type, giving the letters a frayed appearance (9.24).

"That one simple modification makes a tremendous difference. From here on out, it's just a matter of repeating the thin, fat, outline, blur, and emboss stuff that I did earlier (9.25). Then, when you go into your composition file, you can have a field day." Reinfeld isn't exaggerating. The berry images feature three different adaptations of Reinfeld's technique, one of which he created (9.26) and two of which Deke designed (9.27 and 9.28). Every nuance is the result of retrieving outlined, blurred, and embossed layers from a source file and sending them through thin, fat, outlined, and blurred masks. Speaking from personal experience, it's a lot of fun.

ERIC'S CLOSING PEARLS OF WISDOM

"Before you go, I have to pass along a few parting shots here. First, if you decide to work in RGB, that's fine. Just be careful to pick the colors for your type properly. And by that, I mean set your color picker to CMYK. Even in the RGB color space, this ensures that while you may get an ugly color, you won't get a color that won't print.

"Second, the beauty of this whole approach is that you can take a composition you've applied to one background and substitute in a whole different background. For example, in a matter of seconds, I could replace the clouds or the berries with a new image and completely change the look of my type.

"Third, a lot of folks have asked me my impression of Photoshop 5's layer effects. For the most part, I just use them for comping. They help me to add quick lighting effects, toss together some glows and shadows, things like that. But I've also experienced some banding issues. When you use layer effects on their own, you can run into artifacts and weird blends. So when I finish roughing out a layer effect, I'll choose Layer ➤ Effects ➤ Create Layer to break up the effects onto their own layers. Then I'll rebuild the effect by hand, or modify it with an adjustment layer, whatever. The point is, don't just accept the first thing Photoshop spits out. You can edit the effect to get exactly what you want.

"And last, if nothing else, this little exercise proves that text in Photoshop can look awesome. Zoom in on your type and check out how sharp your edges are. Some people say that you can't get sharp type out of Photoshop, but they're wrong. At 300 pixels per inch or better, you can count on your text looking great. Take my word for it — this stuff works."

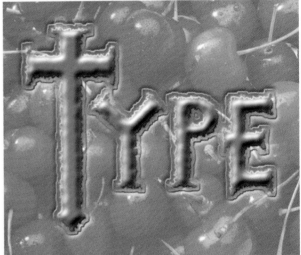

9.26 (TOP), **9.27** (MIDDLE), **9.28** (BOTTOM)

CHAPTER 10
THE TAO OF LAYERING

Greg Vander Houwen is easily one of the most cerebral Photoshop artists we know. To his credit, the guy spends as much time analyzing and reflecting on what he does as he spends doing it. In the eight years he's worked with Photoshop, he's discovered three broad and unifying principles of computer imaging:

"First — and I think everyone has discovered this — computers don't like us for the way we use them, and they pay us back by stealing our time. Probably one out of every ten times I walk up to my machine, there's some new problem that I have to mess with. It's no use fighting; the computer always has the upper hand. It literally owns your data." You have to coax the machine to share its data through attentiveness and patient problem solving.

"Second, Photoshop is a great program, but it's by no means perfect. It's not even intelligent in any conventional sense. So it's up to you to recognize its shortcomings and anticipate them. Photoshop is like a force of nature that you do well to understand and embrace.

"Third, simplicity is key to the way I work. I'm not keen on complex sequences. The bottom line is, even though I'm technically capable, I can't remember long procedures. The best techniques are the simple ones that I can mix and match like jazz licks. If I can quickly recall and 'play' the operation, only then does it become practical."

The net result is an artistic philosophy based on anticipating mistakes and working with as little fanfare as possible. Vander Houwen's primary ally in this

Photoshop is like a force of nature that you do well to understand and embrace.
GREG VANDER HOUWEN

quest is the common layer. "Layers have made my life substantially better. I have clients who perpetually come back to me and say, 'Gee, Greg, that's great, but you know, what we were thinking was *this*.' It always translates to me having to change something. But so long as I stick with virtual compositing — relying on blend modes, layer options, layer masks, and adjustment layers — then I can always go back and retrieve the original data." With layers, Vander Houwen makes it easy and keeps it safe.

BASE CAMPS AND SERIOUS ALTERATIONS

"There are two concepts that are central to the way I think — 'base camps' and 'serious alterations.' A base camp is just a saved version of a file at a certain stage in its development. Back in Photoshop 2.5, before layers came along, I was constantly saving versions so that I could revert back to previous stages of the artwork. Now that I have layers, I still use base camps as an added precaution. I tend to save a base camp

129

whenever my gut says, 'You know, if you lost this, it could be very bad.'

"A serious alteration is a modification that you apply directly to a pixel. For example, applying the Levels command directly to an image is a serious alteration; using an adjustment layer is not. . . . I try not to commit a serious alteration when an alternative is available. But many serious alterations are unavoidable. The trick is, before I commit a serious alteration, I make sure to create a base camp. Then, I'm covered."

Vander Houwen even goes so far as to archive many base camps to CD-ROM on the off-chance he might need it in the future. "On CD, I can go back years and extract bits and pieces from files because I've been working this way. It doesn't happen very often, but I've had situations where the client calls up and says, 'Now, we know this is a big change and we know it was six months ago, but the thing is, we got this deadline. We realize you'll have to work through the night, and this is going to cost us a huge sum of money.' I'm tempted to say, 'Yeah, it is. That's going to hurt a lot. Boy, are you right.' But instead, I pop in the CD, grab the right base camp, and surprise the client with a miracle turnaround."

The figures (10.1, 10.2, 10.3) demonstrate the lengths Vander Houwen goes to in his virtual compositing. "Don't get hung up on the numbers. These are just demonstration composites, but they should give you a good idea of how I work."

10.1 (26 LAYERS, 2 BASE CAMPS)

ROUGHING OUT A COMPOSITION

"I always start off by blocking out the basic composite. I throw things onto their own layers, so as not to damage them. Then, I add layer masks using gradients and brushes. I might play with the Opacity setting, too. The bottom line is, I'm trying to build the roughest, fastest composite I can, so I can make decisions and figure out if there are any problems with the composite. You might have a nice sketch put together, but until you get the images nested, you can't see exactly where things work and where they might go wrong."

ARTIST:
Greg Vander Houwen

ORGANIZATION:
Interact
P.O. Box 498
Issaquah, Washington 98027
(206) 999-2584
gregvh@netcandy.com

SYSTEM:
Power Mac 8100/110
6GB storage

RAM:
110MB total
90MB assigned to Photoshop

MONITOR:
Apple 17-inch

EXTRAS:
Wacom 12 × 12 electrostatic tablet

VERSION USED:
Photoshop 5.0

OTHER APPLICATIONS:
Adobe Illustrator, Fractal Design Painter,
ElectricImage Broadcast

10.2 (16 LAYERS, 3 BASE CAMPS)

10.3 (21 LAYERS, 3 BASE CAMPS)

WORK HISTORY:

<u>1977</u> — Sold photographs for $200 to farming magazine at 14 years old.

<u>1983</u> — Searched around in vain for job in Los Angeles video industry, retreated to home-town computer store and began to pursue computer graphics.

<u>1989</u> — Acquired alpha version of Photoshop, created first published image for *Verbum* magazine.

<u>1991</u> — Started his own design firm, which now includes Apple, Adobe, and Microsoft as clients.

<u>1992</u> — Learned compositing and retouching techniques at Ivey Seright imaging lab.

<u>1997</u> — Helped Microsoft to develop new graphical interface.

FAVORITE CARTOON CHARACTER:

The Tick ("Aside from Buddha, he's the most enlightened intellect I've ever encountered.")

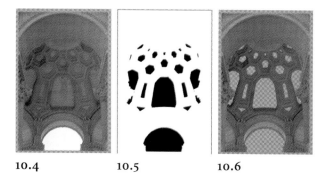

10.4   10.5   10.6

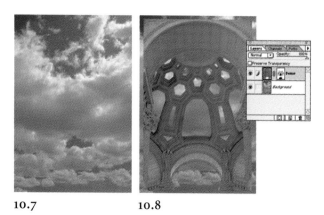

10.7   10.8

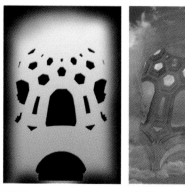

10.9   10.10

CHAIN SAWING A LAYER MASK

As an example, Vander Houwen had an idea to create a dome with transparent windows looking up into a cloudy sky. Up front, there was one obvious problem: the dome didn't have any windows (10.4). But it did have indented panels that could be removed to serve as windows. Rather than deleting these panels, Vander Houwen converted the dome to a floating layer and added a layer mask (10.5).

"I clicked around with the polygon lasso tool until I selected the panels. It's like chain sawing — I just hacked through it in rough slashes. After I got a halfway decent selection, I Option-clicked the layer mask icon at the bottom of the Layers palette to mask away the selected areas. Then, with the layer mask on, I took out my brushes and tweaked it. I used the Shift key and clicked from point to point along the straight edges." The result is a windowed dome, without so much as a pixel in the original image harmed (10.6).

DROPPING THE DOME

Compositing the dome against the sky (10.7) was a simple matter of dragging the dome with the move tool (or ⌘/Ctrl-dragging with some other tool) and dropping it into the sky. By pressing the Shift key during the drop, Vander Houwen center-registered the dome inside the sky (10.8).

The layered image wasn't quite the same size as the sky, so the dome had a harsh rectangular edge around it. Rather than resizing the dome or cropping the sky, Vander Houwen decided to simply brush around the layer mask some more. He applied a black fringe with the paintbrush tool (10.9), starting with a big fuzzy brush and working down to smaller ones. "Begin big and general, then work toward precision," Vander Houwen advises. Although the fringe took just a minute or two to create, it rendered a very serviceable fade (10.10).

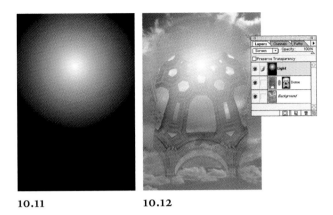

10.11   10.12

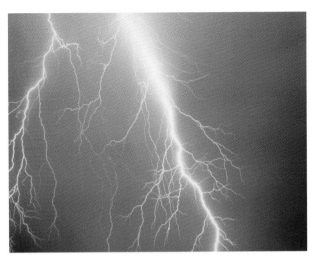

10.13 (TOP), 10.14 (BOTTOM)

THE LIGHT FROM ON HIGH

Finally, the dome needed a bright, glorious light streaming in from the sky. Vander Houwen created a new layer and filled it with a very simple white-to-black radial gradation (10.11). Then, he applied the Screen blend mode from the Layers palette to drop out the black and highlight the layers below (10.12). "I always tell people, Screen and Multiply are 90 percent of what they need to know about blend modes. Screen stacks lightness; Multiply stacks darkness. So I use Screen to keep light stuff like glows, and Multiply to keep dark stuff like shadows."

No special filter, a very simple approach, and not a single serious alteration — it's the ideal composition. "My first goal is always to assemble the rough elements together so I can quickly adapt if needed, or call the art director and say, 'Mayday! This is never going to work!' A rough composite gives you a basis for negotiation and compromise."

USING LAYER OPTIONS

"For another composition, I was asked to layer some lightning (10.13) against some clouds (10.14). Obviously, I wanted to keep the light stuff and make the dark stuff go away. Blend modes and layer options are great for that. You don't need to use the magic wand tool and get those jagged halos around the edges, and you don't need to resort to a complex mask. Let Photoshop do the work for you."

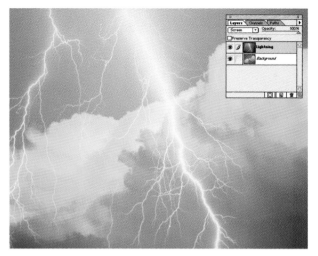

10.15

10.16 (TOP), 10.17 (BOTTOM)

Vander Houwen started by layering the lightning in front of the clouds and applying the Screen blend mode from the Layers palette (10.15). But this resulted in a universal lightening effect that washed out the clouds below. The trick is to keep only the lightest pixels in the lightning layer and make the others invisible. Sounds like a job for layer options.

DROPPING OUT AND FORCING THROUGH

Vander Houwen double-clicked the Lightning layer in the Layers palette to bring up the Layers Options dialog box. Then, he adjusted the black triangle in the slider bar labeled This Layer. This dropped out the original background for the layer. To soften the transition between visible and invisible pixels, he Option/Alt-dragged the triangle to break it in half. The result is lightning that looks like it was photographed with the original image (10.16).

But that wasn't enough. Vander Houwen also wanted to force the lightest colors in the clouds in front of the lightning. So he dragged and then Option/Alt-dragged the white triangle in the Underlying slider bar. This created the effect of the lightning going through the clouds (10.17).

NEVER TRY TO MASK LIGHTNING

"I had a client who said, 'We know how hard it is to knock out lightning because it's got all those fingers. Maybe you could use an alpha channel or something.' And I thought, if I had to create a mask for lightning, it would take me a week and it probably wouldn't look right. The layer options effect takes a few seconds to pull off, it doesn't harm the original image, and it looks better than anything I could accomplish with a mask," as the magnified detail shows (10.18). "And it's not just lightning. It's stars, it's city lights, it's anything light. Or anything dark — for example, layer options are great for compositing scanned logos against different backgrounds. I just move the white slider, and the paper goes away."

"Along with blend modes, layer options are basically your way to control the overlay of light and dark stuff. If you can get your head around that, then you can even control how individual color channels land by editing red, green, and blue separately. For example, blue skies can be made to go away rather easily by tweaking the sliders in the blue component."

TONAL ADJUSTMENTS IN LAYER MASKS

"One of my favorite little techniques to show people that they should care about layer masks is just to put a couple of images together and run gradients across them. If you don't like the way the effect works, you don't need to undo. Just run gradient after gradient after gradient. Each new gradient will obliterate the last one. Or you can run a simple black-to-white gradient. And then use a tonal control like Levels or Curves to manipulate the mask transitions."

GRADIENT LAYER MASKS

For this example, Vander Houwen took a photograph of a woman's face (10.19) and layered it against a sunset (10.20) so the woman's right eye aligned exactly on top of the sun. "I just dragged on the eye and dropped onto the sun. If you know a little about your composition ahead of time, alignment is easy."

Vander Houwen added a layer mask by clicking the left-hand icon at the bottom of the Layers palette. He selected the gradient tool and chose Foreground to Background in the Gradient Tool Options palette (with the foreground and background colors set to their defaults of black and white). Then, he dragged from the lower-right to the upper-left corner in the mask (10.21). The lower-right corner became transparent and faded into opacity (10.22), again without upsetting a pixel in the original images.

10.18

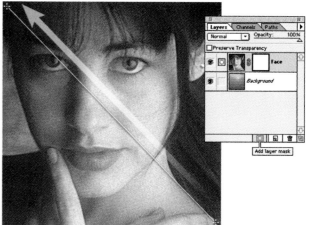

10.21 (TOP), 10.22 (BOTTOM)

10.19 (TOP), 10.20 (BOTTOM)

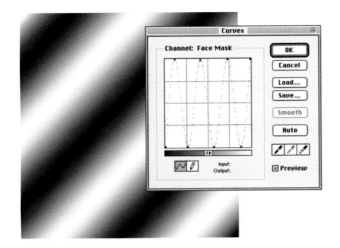

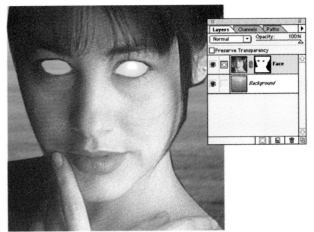

10.23 (TOP), 10.24 (BOTTOM)

10.25 (TOP), 10.26 (BOTTOM)

Using the Curves command, Vander Houwen created a spiky color map that resulted in an alternating series of blacks and whites inside the layer mask (10.23). "A simple black-to-white gradation can yield all kinds of effects with Curves." The upshot is a strobe effect that flashes the face on and off over the course of the image (10.24).

TONAL EDGE ADJUSTMENTS

"I also use this technique to refine selections. I make a hasty selection around an image element that's just roughly in the shape of the thing. Then, I convert the selection to a layer mask (10.25), blur the heck out of it (10.26), and go into Levels or Curves and manipu-

late the edge (10.27). This way, I can draw the layer into the background or draw it away from the background, without a lot of work. In most cases, I have to go back and edit the mask further (10.28), but this simple spreading and choking technique eliminates about 70 percent of the job."

The lasso isn't the only selection tool that can benefit from this technique. "One of the key things I've learned about Photoshop is that if I had to rely exclusively on the magic wand to make a selection, I'd be a sad puppy. So I use the magic wand to get me half the way, and then play with layer masking from there. Suddenly, it's a cool tool that quickly eliminates a large part of my work."

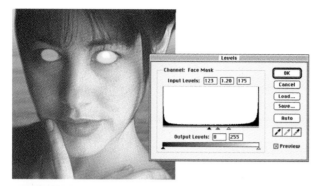

10.27 (TOP), 10.28 (BOTTOM)

QUICK EFFECT MASKS

"A lot of special effects can be achieved with the help of layer masks. For example, Photoshop doesn't offer a unidirectional motion trail filter. That's okay, because you can easily whip one together yourself."

The jet fighter (10.29) is an image that's just begging for a motion trail. Vander Houwen duplicated the image to a new layer and applied a hefty dose of Motion Blur filter. "I matched the Angle value to the angle of the jet, and I changed the Distance to 300 pixels." That's a pretty huge value considering the modest resolution of this image. In fact, the jet is pretty well blown to bits (10.30).

Vander Houwen then added a layer mask and painted in the forward part of the blurred plane to reveal the original underneath. "I start painting with huge brushes — the bigger the brush, the better to start with. I just knock it out at first, then I refine with smaller brushes. I hit the number and bracket keys like a madman to adjust the brush settings on the fly. I never touch the palettes if I can help it — it takes too long and interrupts the flow."

He Shift-clicked along the sides of the wings — with the grain of the motion blur — to get rid of any blurring Photoshop may have applied to the sky. And he filled in a few spots inside the jet with light grays to bring back some of the detail. The finished mask appears in grayscale (10.31) with the resulting motion trail effect shown below it (10.32).

"Sometimes the simplicity of these effects is a little painful. This one in particular makes me flinch a little because, in the past, I did it so badly. I would hand-draw the motion trail with the smudge tool or something equally difficult. But that's the way it is, right? The price of today's success is often yesterday's pain."

WALKING THE VIRTUAL MILE

"This last file includes a bunch of good examples of how you can easily layer image elements using the techniques I explained before, all working together in concert. I started by dragging and dropping all my elements into a single composition. I have to say that I've really embraced drag-and-drop lately because I finally figured out its advantage. Everyone tells you that drag and drop doesn't take up any Clipboard memory. But you know what that means? You aren't leaving the picture of the 5MB duck or whatever up in the Clipboard for two hours while you wait for it to cause an out-of-memory error. Besides, it's easier — you just grab the thing and haul it over."

BUILDING THE LAYERS

Vander Houwen started this particular image by filling a layer with black and adding stars to it (10.33). To make the stars, he applied the Add Noise filter and turned on both the Gaussian and Monochrome options. Then, he applied Gaussian Blur with a Radius of 1.0 and used the Levels command to exaggerate the brightness of the blurred dots.

He next dragged in a sky photo and set the blend mode to Screen so the stars would remain visible (10.34). Then, he introduced two more elements — the Golden Gate bridge and a statue in harsh light (10.35). Both elements consume relatively small chunks of the image window and require blending. Vander Houwen dropped away the sky pixels in the

10.29

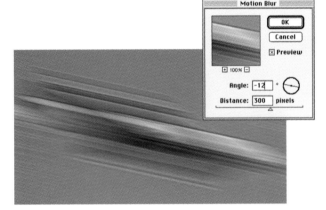

10.30

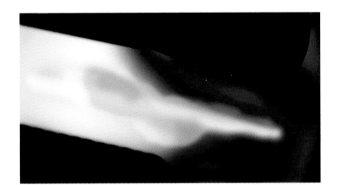

10.31 (TOP), 10.32 (BOTTOM)

10.33 (TOP), 10.34 (BOTTOM)

10.35 (TOP), 10.36 (BOTTOM)

bridge layer using the Layer Options dialog box. He set the Blend If pop-up menu to Blue and adjusted the white This Layer triangle. (Try this on any bright sky image, and you'll quickly see how well it works.) Then, he added gradient layer masks to both layers to create even fades (10.36).

The last image to be tossed on the stack was the rolling fog (10.37). This image completely covered the stuff behind it, so Vander Houwen again relied on his friends, the layer options. By adjusting the black triangle in the This Layer slider bar, he was able to drop the black sky away and melt the fog gracefully into its background (10.38).

10.37 (TOP), 10.38 (BOTTOM)

STRIKING BASE CAMP

"I often modify the position of the elements with the arrow keys and Shift-arrow. It's fast and accurate — whether you have a dirty mouse or what, the arrow keys let you get the layer exactly where you want it. Also, up here in Seattle, my caffeine intake makes it impossible to nudge stuff by any other method.

"When I get it all together and everything's basically in place, I save my base camp. This is a separate file — dot 2 or whatever — so that the previous file remains fixed in time. Of course, I save the base camp in the Photoshop native format; and I can't think of any reason for using another format until my image is 100 percent finished. And even then, I always keep a Photoshop file as backup."

THE FINISHING TOUCHES

The text is Helvetica Compressed, further squished and skewed using the Free Transform command, and then filtered with Motion Blur. Vander Houwen also added a gradient layer mask to fade the text in the corners (10.39). Finally, he added a layer mask to the second-to-bottom sky layer. Then, he airbrushed in black with the airbrush to uncover an area of starry night behind the text (10.40).

"When I was doing 9-to-5 production work, I learned the hard way that you don't worry about the details until the end. You concentrate on the biggest problems — the major composite parts — and work your way down to increasing levels of refinement. Otherwise, you end up blowing away that detail work you did earlier, and you waste a lot of time."

10.39 (TOP), **10.40** (BOTTOM)

GREG KEEPS THE SKETCH HANDY

Vander Houwen likes to scan his original sketch (10.41) and stick it in a mask channel. This way, he can refer to the sketch at any time by clicking the eyeball in front of the mask name in the Channels palette. The sketch channel appears as a color overlay (10.42) without affecting his ability to edit the image file. "This lets me position, rotate, scale, and distort elements with extreme accuracy. But it can also help when explaining images to art directors. When there's an approved sketch, it's hard to argue. The sketch is like a visual contract."

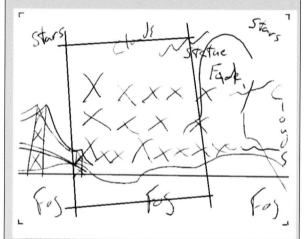

10.41 (TOP), 10.42 (BOTTOM)

Once again, we have an example of a composition in which no scanned image was directly modified. "I messed with the text, but I can redo that in a few seconds. After I get the image finessed to the point I'm more or less happy with it, I save another base camp. Then, I merge some layers or flatten the image and move on. It gives me piece of mind and sheer naked freedom to continue on to the next job without any worries of losing my work."

FOLLOWING THE PATH THAT IS ALWAYS IN MOTION

"Ideally, the goal for me is to play Photoshop like an instrument. Playing jazz Photoshop is where I'd like to be someday. But I figure I need about ten more years — if they'd just quit changing the program. Imagine if you were playing the sax, and they kept moving the buttons on you every couple of years. Not that I don't like the changes — sometimes they're great. But becoming a musician with an instrument that's in constant flux is a challenge.

"Even if the program stood still, I might never master it. Every week it seems like I figure out a better way to do something and realize how hard it was to do it the old way. In fact, I kind of hope I never get it down completely. I hope I always cringe at the way I used to do things because that means I'll be getting better."

PART II
SPECIFIC
APPLICATIONS

High-Resolution Imaging for
   Advertising 167
Fine Art Printing 183
Pixels to Platinum 197
Photographing for
   Photoshop 227
Fashion Photography 241
Creative QuickTime VR 269
The Quick Guide to Digital
   Cameras 297
Photoshop in Motion 311
Inventing Photo-Realistic Worlds
   323
Creating Images for the World
   Wide Web 337
Buttons, Buttons, Buttons 349

CHAPTER 11
HIGH-RESOLUTION IMAGING FOR ADVERTISING

The world of high-end advertising is a world of painstaking illusion and deliberate trickery. The companies who commission these ads are not simply trying to exaggerate the quality and performance of their products. If it were that simple, we'd all own Vegematics and Ronco would be king. A good advertisement misleads with the intent to entertain. It lures you inside it; offers a brief thrill, a smile, or a moment of glamour; and invites you to leave with the promise that more can be had for a price. Purchasing the product pays admission into the illusion. The fact that you receive a physical good in return is often little more than a nostalgic formality paying homage to the old barter-based society.

As one of Manhattan's most respected and admired commercial artists, Robert Bowen understands the role of illusion in advertising. "I've spent a fair amount of time looking at the history of art. I'm particularly interested in an approach called *trompe l'oeil* (pronounced *tromp-loy*) — which is French for 'trick the eye.' Trompe l'oeil images want to look real, like they were arranged and photographed exactly as you see them. But they're actually impossible."

Hollywood is the most conspicuous purveyor of the craft. "The intention of a typical movie — particularly an effects-oriented film — is to convey the look of realism without suggesting that what you're seeing actually happened. Everyone who goes to see a movie such as *Twister* or *Volcano* knows that it's not real. But if it has the appearance of realism, then they can suspend their disbelief and give themselves over to what they see. It's all based on an aesthetic of photorealism, as opposed to a more illustrative look that's grounded in the graphic tradition."

> *Trompe l'oeil images want to look real, like they were arranged and photographed exactly as you see them. But they're actually impossible.*
>
> ROBERT BOWEN

BOB'S EXPLORATION INTO THE UNREAL

Bowen's art expresses roughly as much reverence for the laws of nature as a Lewis Carroll story. He grabs elements from the normal world, flings them down the rabbit's hole, and reassembles them on the other side. Curiously, the view from the bottom of the hole is often better than the one from above.

For example, we are all aware that young girls sometimes wear braces (11.1) and that cows as a rule do not (11.2). And yet, the appearance of a photorealistic cow undergoing dental adjustment is somehow extremely attractive. It amazes because it's peculiar; it amuses because it's so incredibly absurd. Without its accompanying ad copy, we may never understand why AT&T commissioned this artwork to target college students. But chances are good that the image of a "Cheshire Cow" will stick in your head. It's a smiling, ungulate, radioactive aberration.

The same goes for the mouse-headed man Bowen created for the high-tech company SDRC (11.3).

145

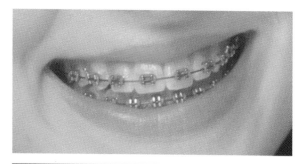

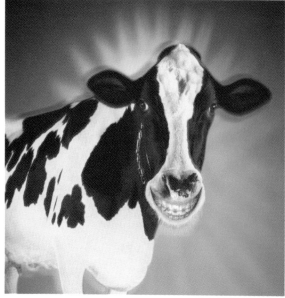

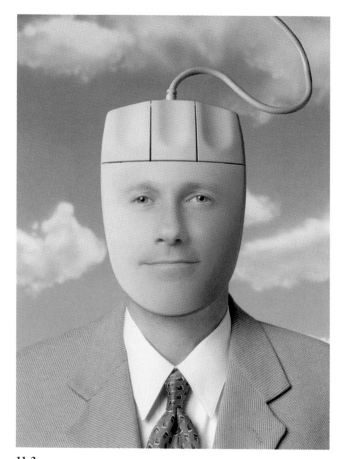

11.1 (TOP), 11.2 (BOTTOM)

Photography by Dennis Gallante

11.3

Photography by Howard Berman

ARTIST:
Robert Bowen

ORGANIZATION:
Robert Bowen Studio
New York City, NY
bowenbob@aol.com

SYSTEMS:
PowerWave 604/150 (Power Computing)
10GB storage
Silicon Graphics Indy 4400

RAM:
212MB total
190MB assigned to Photoshop

MONITOR:
Radius IntelliColor 20e

EXTRAS:
Adaptec Ultra-Wide controller with
2-drive 8GB Barracuda array

VERSION USED:
Photoshop 5.0

OTHER APPLICATIONS:
On Mac: Live Picture, Adobe Illustrator,
QuarkXPress
On SGI: Barco Creator, Alias Power
Animator

This time, inspiration was close at hand. "I find this image kind of haunting. It reminds me of how I feel after a really bad day." But while the image looks a little painful, Bowen claims it was relatively easy to create. "I just painted the colorized mouse layer in and out with the face layer. I also threw in a few adjustment layers to match the highlights and colors."

Not all of Bowen's images are so outrageous. Sometimes he bends reality to soothe it. Several years ago, he worked with photographer Ryszard Horowitz on a series of images for Adobe that featured giant watery slabs hovering in space. "In this case, a slab of green universe pours water into the desert (11.4). It's kind of a pleasant idea — bringing life to a difficult world." Another image Bowen created for Adobe's introduction of Photoshop 5.0 is more fanciful (11.5). "I used lots of channel operations and adjustment layers to get the water ripples. The background was an invention created from chunks of photographic stuff that I shot during my teaching stint at CCI (the Center for Creative Imaging) in Maine."

In addition to his paid work for clients, Bowen devotes a modicum of time to creating stock images and purely personal art. Even then, he plays with what is real and what is not. "When I was in Italy, I took a lot of pictures of Roman ruins and came up with what amounts to a game of spaces (11.6). It's just

11.4

Photography by Ryszard Horowitz

WORK HISTORY:

<u>1979</u> — Graduated from Pratt Institute with MFA, experimented with Polarized light projection.

<u>1984</u> — Studied computer science at Pratt and wrote simple 3-D wireframe animation program.

<u>1986</u> — Designed 3-D animation and TV commercials for Fantastic Animation Machine.

<u>1990</u> — Headed up print division at R/Greenberg Associates, worked on TV commercials and feature films (*Predator II* and *Last Action Hero*).

<u>1994</u> — Started his own company aimed at creating final art for high-end ad campaigns.

FAVORITE OLD MOVIE MAXIM:

"Time flies like an arrow, fruit flies like a banana." (Courtesy of Groucho Marx)

11.5

Photography by Howard Berman

something I did for myself, and this is the first time it's been printed. The whole foreground is tiled from a single arch that's about as tall as it is wide." Bowen cloned bits and pieces of the foreground texture to interrupt the repeating patterns. "If you look closely, you can still find a pattern, but I've worked it until it doesn't annoy me."

The most surprising elements in the image are found inside the archways. What initially appear to be rocky groves are actually distant views of the Roman Colosseum. "Everything about it is a contradiction. I repeated a small fragment to make it large and reduced the large elements to make them small. The overall image has a brooding interior quality, and yet it was all photographed outdoors." Last but not least, out of ruins, Bowen has created an inviolate structure.

"I'm trying to trick the eye without putting one over on anybody. I'm not seeking a photo-journalistic effect, but rather one that is obviously faked with all the hallmarks of realism. In a sense, I'm painting an impossible picture using stuff that you see every day." The most unlikely contradiction of all, however, may be Bowen himself. Soft-spoken and unassuming, widely regarded as one of the easiest people to work with east of the Mississippi, Bowen just so happens to occupy the exact point where reality hits the fan.

11.6

11.7

Photography by Ryszard Horowitz

MANAGING POPULATIONS OF A FEW MILLION PIXELS

Unfortunately, churning out elaborate visual fantasies is not all fun and games. Bowen has to deal with the same grim facts of Photoshop that confront every other professional image editor. Extreme resolutions and color space conversions take their toll.

"Typically, I work at very high resolutions. And much of what I do is poster art, so the images get very large." A piece of art commissioned by The New School, a New York City art school, is a case in point (11.7). Originally measuring 6561 × 4200 pixels (about 78MB), the image was large enough to double as both front and back cover for the summer course catalog and a poster-sized subway advertisement.

"The clear blue Caribbean water against the backdrop of the Manhattan skyline made for a utopian view of New York harbor. Parsons also wanted me to push the concept of hats. Students have to try on different hats to decide what they want to be." In order to get the entire image — water, skyline, hats, and all — to fit on this page, we had to downsample the artwork to a paltry 30 percent of its original size. But never fear, we've also included a detail at full resolution (11.8). Regardless of size, the clarity is impeccable.

11.8

WORKING WITH SUPER-HUGE FILES

Things must get miserably slow when editing such incredibly large images, particularly when you start slapping on the layers. But Bowen knows from experience that today's slowdowns have nothing on the past. "In the old days, we were working with images this size on IIfx machines. That was pitiful. I don't know how I survived. But with a Power Mac, lots of RAM, and a fast disk array, Photoshop is actually pretty fast, even when I'm working in poster-sized images with 10 or 12 layers. I love Barco on the SGI and Live Picture on the Mac, but I still spend most of my time in Photoshop because of the blend modes and other compositing advantages."

Bowen argues that speed buys you more than lost time; it gives you greater freedom to experiment. "Something big happened to me when the Power Macs came out. Suddenly, I could work in real time. Before then, I had to spend a lot of time planning and imagining what it was going to look like. But with faster machines, I can just do stuff and see it happen on screen. You wouldn't believe what a difference that makes in the way I work. The experience is becoming more and more immediate — almost like working with traditional tools, except that these tools are hundreds of times more powerful."

CMYK FILES AND RGB TRANSPARENCIES

Some service bureau technicians will tell you that a guy like Bowen never ventures outside CMYK in his life. But like most Photoshop artists, Bowen spends his creative time in RGB with periodic visits to Photoshop's CMYK preview mode (⌘/Ctrl+Y). And for about half of his jobs, he never converts to CMYK at all. "When I deliver digital files, I always convert to CMYK. I never let anyone do an RGB to CMYK conversion of a Photoshop file on a different computer. That will always be bad. But lots of times, I give the client an RGB transparency. Then, they scan it with a Scitex or other high-end CMYK scanner. Different clients prefer one or the other."

But with transparencies, aren't you effectively printing a digital file, only to have it rescanned again? "Yes and no. When you record to film, you simply match

its full resolution. Unlike printed separations, RGB film resolution is measured in pixels per millimeter, which is called 'rez.' Some film is rez-20, some is rez-40." That's 20 or 40 pixels per millimeter — or the equivalent of 500 to 1,000 pixels per inch — on film that measures 4×5 or 8×10 inches. "A rez-20 transparency is a little soft, a rez-40 transparency is sharper. I stick with rez-40 because I like to deliver a sharper product.

"After that, the transparency is treated like a resolution-independent source, just like photographic film. There's no attempt to scan one pixel in a CMYK file for each pixel in the RGB transparency. It can basically be projected to any size. It's sort of like the difference between 35mm and 70mm film. Both can be projected onto huge screens in a movie theater, but the 70mm film has less grain."

CASE STUDIES AND NONEXISTENT WORLDS

Now that we have all the exposition and technical stuff out of the way, it's time to peek over Bowen's shoulder and see how he creates his artwork. Throughout the remainder of the chapter, we'll pull apart four jobs that have appeared in major magazine ads in recent years. With clients as varied as Panasonic and Johnnie Walker Black, this small collection represents a few of Bowen's best.

STAGING AN ILLUSTRATION

In an ad for Adaptec (11.9), Bowen wanted to create the effect of sudden and dramatic color set against a drab background. "The Adaptec image is one of the best examples of my use of trompe l'oeil. I was inspired by a short story by Jorge Luis Borges called 'The Aleph.' The title refers to a place where you can literally see a whole universe from a single point of view. I turned this idea into a theatrical set. The stage is a loft roof somewhere in Brooklyn on a rainy, dismal day (11.10). But the roof scene is really just a backdrop. The color image of these buildings is leaning up against it, even casting a shadow (11.11). The result is a spatial play."

11.9

Photography by Robert Bowen and Howard Berman

Bowen's construction is extremely simple. Each element — roof, shadow, color buildings, and vent (lower right corner) — appears on its own layer. The shadow required some layer masking, but that's it. "Of course, for this particular ad, the client wanted a lot of color. I started by adding some depth inside the buildings (11.11), but then I substituted the green space instead."

This was an unusual ad in that Bowen actually appeared inside it. Photographer Howard Berman shot Bowen against a plain white backdrop, with the base of his coat elevated to indicate a small breeze (11.12). After scanning himself, Bowen created a rough mask around his body, dragged and dropped the selection into the Adaptec composition, and scaled the layer to match its new surroundings (11.13). He finessed the edges with a layer mask and added a shadow by applying Levels adjustments to the background layers. To make the tie-dye pattern in the shirt, he applied a rainbow gradient to a separate layer, subject to the Color blend mode. He also added small color highlights to the function strip along the top of the Wacom tablet clutched in his right arm (11.14).

11.10 (TOP), 11.11 (BOTTOM)

11.12   **11.13**   **11.14**

"There are three levels here, with the gray city interrupted by the color city which is interrupted by the green country. But the thing that interests me most is that the most drab element in the image — the grunge background — is presented as a total fake. Nothing about the entire image is real, except for me. Even my shirt is a forgery."

DRINKING WITH DOLPHINS

"This next ad is part of a campaign that Johnnie Walker's been running for a couple of years. Each ad shows an individual involved in a creative pursuit set against a natural landscape. There's been a sculptor, an architect, a painter, a filmmaker. One golfer. A jazz bass player. This one is about a computer artist (11.15), a topic that's particularly near and dear to my heart.

11.15

Photography by Eric Meola

"We had lots of pictures for this ad. There were two background shots, both from the California coast." One photograph served as the main background (11.16), with additional waves brought in from the second image (11.17). "The deck and computer stand are both props that we shot inside the studio (11.18). We also had several shots of the computer artist. He's the product of two or three different photos.

TEXTURING GRADIENT SKIES

"The sky in the Johnnie Walker ad is an all-digital creation. If you've ever tried to work with a flat gradient in Photoshop, you know there's always some degree of banding (11.19). The way to get around this is to put the gradient on a separate layer and then apply the Add Noise filter to each color channel independently. For this image, I think I applied an Amount of 8 in the Red channel and 4 in the other two (11.20). I also applied Gaussian Blur separately to each channel at very low values — 0.5 one time, 0.3 another (11.21). In the worst cases, I might create a couple of skies on different layers and then combine them at 50 percent Opacity or so." The inset boxes in the figures show magnified views.

11.19 (TOP), 11.20 (MIDDLE), 11.21 (BOTTOM)

11.16 (TOP), 11.17 (MIDDLE), 11.18 (BOTTOM)

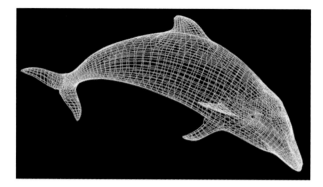

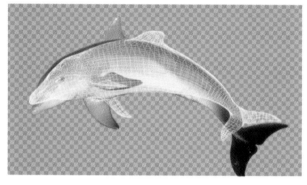

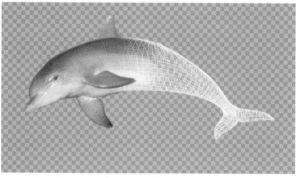

11.22 (TOP), 11.23 (MIDDLE), 11.24 (BOTTOM)

"The dolphin came from two pieces of stock art, including a photograph and a piece of 3-D clip art (11.22). Once we chose the stock image for the front part of the dolphin, I imported the image as a template layer into Alias Power Animator on the SGI machine. Then, I rotated and bent the model into the correct position until the wireframe matched the photo. Then, I anti-aliased the wireframe and imported it into Photoshop." After aligning the wireframe and dolphin on separate layers (11.23), Bowen brushed in layer masks to erase away the left side of the wireframe layer and the right side of the dolphin (11.24). The result was a graceful transition between the physical and digital worlds.

"The wireframe shown on the computer screen in the ad is the same 3-D dolphin model. But it had to be big enough so you could see it easily and make out what it was. So I rotated the model into a different position and magnified it so we see just the tail." The relationship between the onscreen tail and the leaping dolphin in digital transition questions the nature of creativity. Is the artist sketching what he sees, or is the dolphin a product of computer-aided manufacturing? Bowen consciously sprinkles these ambiguities throughout his artwork. "I don't know about you, but I've never seen anyone work with a computer on a pedestal. Where's the keyboard? What's it plugged in to? Little puzzles and contradictions like these invite the viewer to get involved in the artwork."

CRAFTING A SPONTANEOUS SNAPSHOT

"The circus image comes from an ad for a warehouse management product by Computer Associates. The idea was, if your current warehouse management software is like this (11.25), then you need our product."

While the main subject of the image is based on a living, breathing elephant, she wasn't actually caught in the act of dancing the hula. "A trained elephant can manage to sit up, but it sits on a stool with both legs on the ground (11.26). It can also raise its legs up, but at most two at a time. The final elephant is close to an actual pose, but it's an amalgam of two or three pictures (11.27). Not including the hula skirt or the hat, of course."

One of Bowen's early drafts includes a parrot on the monkey's head and a second little dog on the left side of the weight (11.28). What made Bowen cut these elements out and submit such a strangely balanced composition (11.25)? "When you create these complex composites, you start off with the intention of building the whole world. But very often, after working for a few days and zooming in on a few details, you find that a slice of the image is far more dynamic than the whole. It happens so often that I made a decision up front to experiment with the framing on this image.

11.25

Photography by Howard Berman

11.26

11.27

BOB URGES YOU TO GO ALL THE WAY

An off-center image is one thing, but a completely cockeyed composition is another. Isn't it? Bowen suggests that it rarely pays to work in small increments. "Let's say a client says to you, 'I want that elephant moved a little to the left.' If you're a little green, you'll do as you're told and move the elephant just the slightest amount. Then the client looks at it and decides that the elephant has nothing to do with it — some other piece of the artwork needs rethinking. All the while, the first impression was right. It was the elephant, you just didn't take it far enough. My advice is to take things too far. Then, evaluate and come back midway if you need to. But don't take baby steps. Take your risks up front and try to push it all the way out there."

11.28

11.29

Photography by Howard Berman

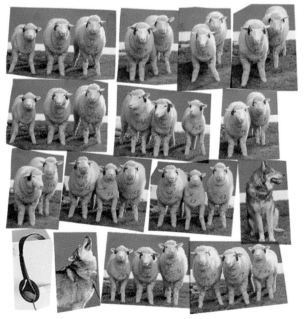

11.30

"I decided to capture the appearance of an instantaneous photograph. The final artwork is off center to suggest that it was captured with a 35mm camera. For one brief moment, all these animals were just in the right place at the right time. That's what I love about working in Photoshop. You can create a scene that says, 'Here's something ridiculous that happened for a split second. We were fortunate enough to record it on film.' But it's really just another trick."

THE PHYSICS OF CLONING SHEEP

One of Bowen's most complex images called for a wolf rising up from a sea of sheep. And just to keep things interesting, the client, Panasonic, wanted to see every animal wearing headphones (11.29). "If you're a farmer, then your eyes are probably pretty accustomed to picking out sheep. You might recognize that there are just three sheep repeated over and over a hundred or so times."

Photographer Howard Berman shot the sheep in his studio, complete with headphones (11.30). But Bowen wasn't satisfied with the results. "There's something I call 'cartoon physics.' It applies to anything nonsensical, like the way headphones look on a sheep. The camera doesn't lie, so it shows headphones on a sheep the way they really are. But if they don't look right, then they don't conform to the laws of cartoon physics. You have no choice but to edit them."

But the real fun came in duplicating the sheep into tidy and infinite rows. "For me, this was a fun perspective problem. Philosophically, we know that the sheep in front should be bigger than the ones in back. But what percentage do you scale down the sheep for each row? The solution of course is to apply some more cartoon physics. Maybe try reducing each row by 10 percent. That works for the first four rows, then you have to try something different. It was a matter of experimenting row by row.

"After I got the sheep arranged in rows, I had to deal with the focal issues. As you can see, there's a depth of field going on here — a nice sharp foreground, getting blurry as we move toward the back. I spent a lot of time applying the Gaussian Blur filter in incremental steps and then painting in shadows."

To us, this job in particular seems like a recipe for aggravation. Photographing sheep, outfitting them with headphones, cloning three sheep into 300, experimenting with depth and perspective, and grappling with some of the more difficult applications of cartoon physics — it takes a while to say, let alone do. "After I put together the rough comp (11.31), I knew right away it was going to be a learning experience. If you compare the rough to the finished piece (11.29), you can see that I had a lot of depth and perspective issues left to work out on the job. Still, I figured it would be interesting, so what the heck? Sure, I probably ended up spending a couple extra days on it, but it didn't kill me."

THE INFINITE DINER

Bowen used a combination of cartoon physics and straight perspective drawing to pull off an ad for IBM servers (11.32). "The idea was that one server could service an infinite number of people." The problem, of course, was rounding up an infinite number of people for a photo shoot. Even hiring 100 or so models — infinitely shy of infinite — is prohibitively expensive. So Bowen again turned to cloning.

"Howard Berman photographed a small group of people — about a dozen — in different locations in the diner (11.33, 11.34). We changed the colors of their clothing, experimented with different camera angles, changed the lighting.

"I finally committed to one camera angle, but we had to use a wide-angle lens, which really distorts space. The center seats had the least amount of distortion, so I built my perspective around them. I ended up repeating a series of seats over and over again, each time scaled to about 50 percent (11.35). I must confess, the finished effect still looks a little wonky, maybe impossible. But it has a consistent vanishing point, which is what you need to create a credible sense of depth.

11.31

"In the end, I spent a lot of time retouching the people and the ceiling. The hardest part was the checkered floor. Luckily, there was an overlay of black text in the final ad, which helped cover up some of the weirdness."

AND NOW FOR SOMETHING COMPLETELY DIFFERENT

Before we said our good-byes, Bowen had the uncommon courtesy to walk us through an image that has nothing whatsoever to do with advertising (11.36). "If you have a pair of 3-D glasses lying around — the kind with the red and blue lenses — take a look at this image. It's called an anaglyph. You've probably seen this kind of effect printed in comic books, but I think you'll find that this might possibly be the best anaglyph you'll ever see. You can really feel the space of the great valley between the buildings. It stretches way, way back.

11.32

Photography by Howard Berman

11.33

11.34

11.35

"As you probably know, a stereo picture is made from a left and right view, one for each eye. So I started by taking photos from the position of the left eye and the right eye — actually a little wider apart. In this case, I was shooting from the offices of Apple Computer here in New York.

"Then, I took the photos into Photoshop and converted them to grayscale. I copied the left-eye view, created a new RGB image, and pasted it into the Red channel. Then, I copied the right-eye view and pasted it into the Green and Blue channels of the new image. Switch back to the RGB view, and the two views converge.

"On top of all that, I've added a very simple warp inside Photoshop. I merely applied Filter ➢ Distort ➢ Shear, which is great for creating vertical waves. For me, it's the Shear filter that really makes the picture. You just don't see buildings roll back and forth like that in real life." Not in New York, anyway. Now, if this were San Francisco . . .

By the way, most 3-D glasses work better for viewing RGB light than printed CMYK colors. If you want to see the image without any ghosting, you can load Bowen's full-resolution original off the CD included at the back of the book. "Open it up in Photoshop and zoom into it. Then, move it around. It'll blow your mind." Honestly, if you don't learn one thing from this book, playing around with this image will make it a worthwhile purchase.

11.36
©1997 Robert Bowen

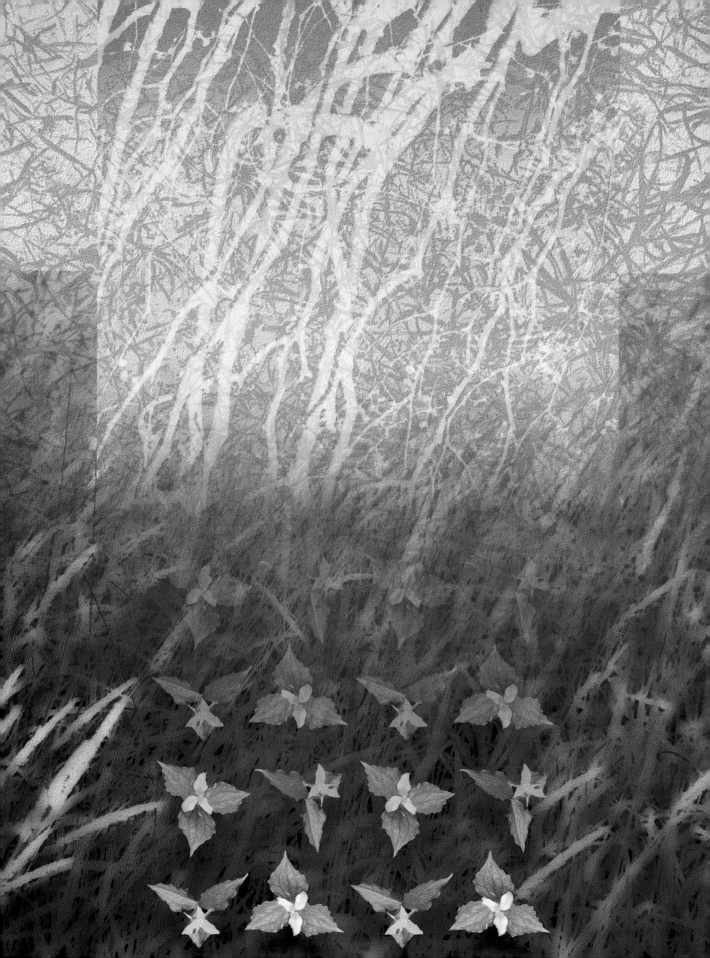

CHAPTER 12
FINE ART PRINTING

For a typical commercial artist working in print media, the goal is to create a piece of artwork that the client can reproduce hundreds, thousands, or even millions of times. Computers are perfect for this purpose, because they permit you to create camera-ready files that include lots of different elements and layers, eliminating the need for fragile mechanicals and expensive stat-camera composites. When the artist hands off the finished Photoshop file to an art director or client, the file includes all elements fully intact. All the production designer has to do is convert the image to CMYK, slap it on a page, and send it to the printer.

But not all artists design for mass-market output. Consider the case of fine artist Karin Schminke, a cofounder of the loose-knit Unique Editions. ("We're really just five independent artists who have come together to form a support group.") As the name of the organization implies, Schminke and her colleagues create one-of-a-kind artwork, suitable for framing and hanging on the wall. For Schminke, the electronic files are just approximations of the effect she wants to achieve. The final physical, tangible paper output is the stuff that really counts.

In Schminke's world, a color ink-jet printer is just another tool in her paint box, one that she can mix freely with other media. Obviously, she can't paint onto the paper while she's printing, nor can she attach a brush to the printer head, so she does the next best thing — she applies her elements in passes. She frequently starts with a layer of acrylics or other media, prints a lightened version of an image over the dried acrylic, paints in a few areas, prints over a few

With Photoshop, you can bring together elements of printmaking, painting, and photography in ways that you couldn't have before.

KARIN SCHMINKE

other areas, and so on until the artwork takes on the look of a finished piece.

"Before I started printing my own art, I looked at what I was getting on the monitor and made decisions based on that. The screen was the determining factor. But once I got involved in the output process, it started to reflect back on the decisions that I made while I was working in the image. There's no longer a break where I'm done creating the artwork and it's time to print. It all blends together. Now the printing reflects on everything I do — down to the way I shoot the original photo. And obviously, everything I do affects the print." For Schminke, the printer is a full-fledged element in the creative process, not just a machine that churns out the finished piece. The result is an interactive continuum that weaves Photoshop so tightly into the fabric of the fine art tradition that it's often impossible to tell a computer was involved at all (12.1).

12.1

ARTIST:
Karin Schminke

ORGANIZATION:
Unique Editions
425/402-8606
http://www.schminke.com
kschminke@schminke.com

SYSTEM:
Intergraph ExtremeZ
13GB storage

RAM:
535MB total
50 percent assigned to Photoshop

MONITOR:
Intergraph 21-inch

EXTRAS:
CalComp Drawing Slate tablet
Epson Expression 836 scanner
CalComp TechJet 175i MX wide-format
printer, Encad NovaJet Pro50

VERSION USED:
Photoshop 5.0

OTHER APPLICATIONS:
Fractal Design Painter, Macromedia xRes,
Adobe Illustrator

THE MESSY WORLD OF MIXED MEDIA

At this moment in time, Schminke's digital tools are an Epson Expression 836 scanner, an Olympus D-600L camera, Photoshop, and a 36-inch-wide CalComp TechJet 175i ink-jet printer. Her printing stock includes watercolor paper, specially prepared ink-jet canvas, and Stonehenge cotton rag paper — all available commercially. She paints with just about any media she can get her hands on, including acrylics, pastels, diluted glue for sizing, and photo-sensitive pigments (12.2).

Schminke contends that by mixing digital and traditional media, she can expand her color gamut and achieve subtle variations in hue and saturation that you simply can't achieve with CMYK inks on their own. She achieves her effects by printing on top of painted media, painting on top of printed ink, and even double-striking — that is, printing the same image twice in a row to burn in the inks and give them greater depth and range.

Obviously, it's a tricky and unscientific process; one that requires repeated inspection, testing, reflection, and a fair amount of old-fashioned creative brooding. Because she's working with traditional media, it's possible to reach a point of no return. Schminke freely admits that she's failed — or at least dead-ended — at an effect that isn't altogether successful and had to start over. It's a risk you take when you work in the real world bereft of an Undo command, but it offers its share of unique rewards. And Schminke for one wouldn't have it any other way.

12.2

WORK HISTORY:

<u>1979</u> — Learned BASIC computer language in University of Iowa graduate MFA program.

<u>1985</u> — Developed and taught first computer graphics course at University of Wisconsin, Eau Claire.

<u>1987</u> — First exhibition of digital artwork at Wisconsin ArtsWest, a juried fine art exhibition.

<u>1994</u> — Switched emphasis to fine art and cofounded Unique Editions.

<u>1997</u> — Participated as artist in residence at Smithsonian's National Museum of American Art.

FAVORITE U.S. NATIONAL PARK:

Olympic National Forest, west of Seattle. ("It's got everything.")

12.3   12.4   12.5

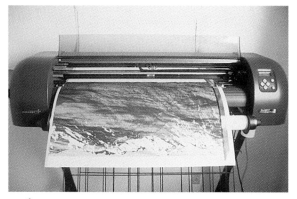

12.6

12.7

PAINTING AND PRINTING, PRINTING AND PAINTING

The best way to get a feel for what Schminke is up to is to watch her work. Through electronic files, process snapshots, and finished artwork, we'll observe Schminke in her studio creating a piece from beginning to end.

CREATING THE SUBIMAGE

For starters, Schminke created the *subimage*, which is the underlying photographic composition that serves as a backdrop and foundation for her piece *Mountain Meadow*. After scanning two of her photographic images to Photo CD — mountains (12.3) and sea foam (12.4) — she layered the second image on top of the first. Then she inverted the sea layer and applied the Overlay blend mode from the Layers palette. Finally, she duplicated the sea layer and reduced the Opacity to exaggerate the color and bring out additional details (12.5). As you can see,

the mountains and trees from the bottom layer are clearer in the composite than they are in the original.

PRINTING THE SUBIMAGE

Schminke decided to create her artwork on rag paper with deckled edges. "It's a rough, natural edge that comes from pulling the paper off the screen during the paper-making process." To bleed all the way beyond the last fibers in the deckled edges, Schminke taped an acetate strip to either side. "I used double-stick tape to paste the acetate to the bottom of the paper. The printer can only print so close to the edges of the media. So the acetate exaggerates the width of the page and allows me to print over the edges."

Schminke ran the 30 × 42 inch paper through the CalComp printer (12.6) to output the completed subimage (12.7). It's interesting to notice the difference in color between the Photoshop file (12.5) and printed image (12.7). Likely the result of calibration issues, the inherent gamut of the printer, and the off-white color of the paper, these are conditions to which every artist has to adapt and work around. "Unexpected color shifts in the prints are just a part of the process. I calibrate enough to control them within an acceptable range, then I make the most of the results."

After stripping the acetate away from the deckled edges (12.8), Schminke applied a layer of protective fixative. "I usually go ahead and apply some kind of spray-on fixative, although I'm not entirely convinced that it works. I put on several coats hoping they'll retard the bleeding of the inks into other media. It helps a little, but it doesn't altogether stop the problem."

CREATING THE INSET IMAGE

Now for the next layer in the traditional media stack — the inset superimage. Schminke created a square composition in Photoshop that features two elks (12.9) layered on top of a leafless tree (12.10). To make the branches work as a framing device, she swapped the left and right halves of the tree. When viewed on its own (12.11), the composition is rather crude, with an obvious seam down the middle. But the seam will disappear when printed onto the final artwork. "With enough experience, you learn what will output and what won't."

A GOLD BACKGROUND FOR THE INSET IMAGE

Schminke wanted the inset image to occupy a square area in the center of the artwork. But if she had simply overprinted the image, it would have blotted out the artwork below it and turned it into a muddy mess. So Schminke applied an underpainting to distinguish the inset image from its background.

After laying down masking tape to block out a square in the artwork, Schminke applied a coating of gold acrylic paint (12.12). "The paint isn't entirely even or opaque. It's kind of a shimmering gold — just enough to set off the inset image from the subimage, so the two mix together while remaining independently identifiable."

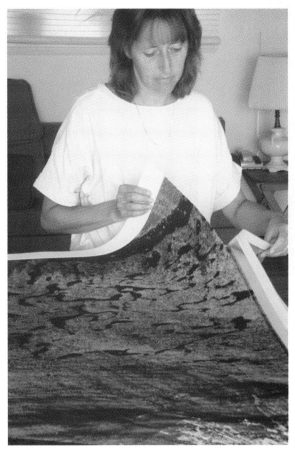

12.8

TESTING THE OVERPRINT WITH ACETATE

"By the time I invest all this effort in the background, I get a little paranoid about printing directly onto the artwork and messing it up. So I'll print onto acetate and use that to mock up the image (12.13). Even though the colors are a lot different than they'll appear in the final artwork, the acetate helps me to determine scale, positioning, and get at least a feel for the color."

The acetate was also helpful for determining the amount of ink to apply to the final overprinting. "I wanted the elk to appear somewhat 'illusionistic.' You have to look just right to see them — look away and they're gone, just like real wildlife." Schminke ended up lightening the image a few notches with the Curves command to get the desired effect.

OVERPRINTING THE INSET IMAGE

When overprinting one image onto another — particularly when a shimmering gold acrylic square is involved — registration has to be right on. Naturally, Schminke uses Photoshop's Canvas Size command to make sure that the images are the same physical size and resolution. But she also has to be careful that the paper is registered properly as it feeds through the printer.

12.9 (TOP), 12.10 (MIDDLE), 12.11 (BOTTOM)   12.12

"Every printer has something that you can use as an alignment marker. On my CalComp, it's the clamps that hold the paper in place. When I put the paper in for the first time, I make sure to draw little pencil marks on the sides of the artwork by the edges of the clamps. Then when I reinsert the paper for a second or third pass, I can make sure that the paper is properly aligned.

"In the case of *Mountain Meadow*, I also had to make sure the inset image filled the gold square. In Photoshop, I sized the inset image so it was about a half-inch taller and wider than the square. And I left the masking tape in place as I printed the image. When I stripped off the masking tape, the registration was perfect (12.14)."

12.14

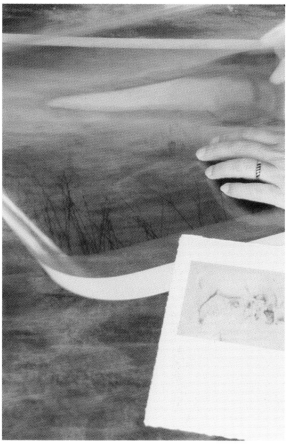

12.13

12.15

12.16

Doesn't Schminke run the risk of peeling off paint and ink as she removes the tape? "I'm pretty careful, so it's not usually a problem. But if I do get a little crack or something, I'm mixing so much media that it's easy to go in and touch up the mistakes." Clearly, there are advantages to having traditional tools lying around.

PRINTING ON BLACK

The vast majority of commercial art is printed on white paper. Every once in a while, you might come across a flier output on some fluorescent parchment, but most designers regard colored stock with about as much enthusiasm as a school teacher grading a writing assignment on purple notebook paper.

Again, fine artists buck the trend. "Recently, I got this idea that I wanted to print on black paper." Offhand, this sounds like a formula for disappointment, particularly given that ink-jet printers apply translucent colors. In other words, the printer can darken the paper, but it can never lighten it. The solution, then, is to create an opaque underpainting and print on top of that.

PAINTING ONTO A PRINTED TEMPLATE

"I started with a photograph of some lily pads that I brushed and combined with two other photos inside Macromedia xRes (12.15). Then I increased the contrast of the image inside Photoshop and printed it onto black rag paper (12.16). The printout wasn't super colorful, of course, but I could see it well enough to use it as a template. Then I painted over the image with acrylics to create the color underpainting (12.17).

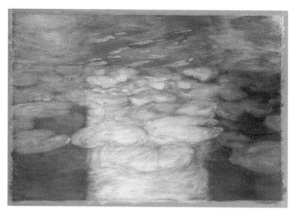

12.17

PRINTING ONTO ACRYLIC

"Now, at this point, I should say that if you're going to print on top of acrylic, you need to put some sort of coating over it. A company called StellaColor makes a precoat that you can paint onto anything, and it provides a surface to accept the ink-jet dot. Without it, the ink would simply smear across the acrylic."

After applying the coating, Schminke ran the paper through the printer again, overprinting the same image she had applied before (12.18). "Painting an image over itself and then printing on top of that — it's obviously a lot of work. But I was able to come up with a much different image while at the same time maintaining a consistent theme. It's a good demonstration of how you can take an image and greatly alter it by experimenting with the output. Better still, I sold the piece immediately, and I was asked to submit another version of the lilies to that same gallery."

12.18

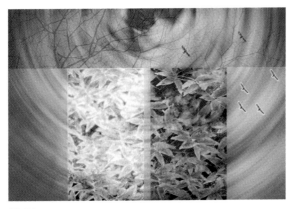

12.19

PRINTING ONTO LIQUID PHOTO EMULSION

"Another media that I use a lot these days is KwikPrint." KwikPrint is a special brand of photo-sensitive emulsion that you can apply with a paint-brush. Where the emulsion is exposed to light, it adheres to the paper. Where it isn't exposed, the KwikPrint washes away.

What good is it? "I use it for backgrounds. For example, *Night Vortex* (12.19) is a piece that I created in Photoshop a while back. I really liked the image, but I had never managed to get an exciting print from it. But when I printed it against the KwikPrint background, it just came together (12.20)." It's easiest to see the light blue KwikPrint in the border around the artwork.

Schminke started by creating the wavy grass-like tex-ture for the KwikPrint layer as a grayscale image inside

12.20

Photoshop. Then she inverted the texture to create a negative (12.21) and printed the negative onto acetate. "Actually, I double-struck the negative. Before I took the acetate out of the printer, I had the printer reload it (a special function of the CalComp). The acetate automatically went right back to where it started, and then ran through again. This made the inks denser, so they would completely block out the light."

Next, Schminke pretreated a sheet of paper with iridescent gold acrylic, and then applied the light blue KwikPrint. She laid the acetate on top of the KwikPrint-coated paper, exposed it for a few minutes to photographic flood lights, removed the acetate, and rinsed off the unexposed emulsion.

"When you apply paint with a brush, the brush-strokes have an inherent texture. But digital output is generally pretty flat, so sometimes it helps to build up a texture with different kinds of paints. The wavy KwikPrint substrate gave this image exactly the kind of texture I had been looking for. It also helps to enhance the color gamut. In *Night Vortex*, I'm getting colors that are brand new to the digital print world."

PROTECTING YOUR INK-JET ARTWORK

High-end color output is notoriously fragile. The ultra-violet (UV) radiation in common sunlight can cause visible bleaching in a matter of months. Schminke recommends, "You should always varnish your ink-jet artwork to protect it. The best product that I know of right now is called MSA Varnish from Golden Artist Colors. It's a mineral spirit-based varnish with high UV protection that comes in three finishes — gloss, satin, and matte. You have to thin it with mineral spirits, not the odorless variety, and you have to apply four coats. The first two have to be the gloss because it absorbs into the paper the best. The next two can be anything, depending on what kind of finish you want. If you apply the matte varnish on top of the gloss, for example, the artwork has a flat finish that's virtually clear."

According to Schminke, the varnish is designed to last. "A guy from Golden varnished pieces we gave him from several different printers. Then he took some untreated watercolors and acrylics, and put them all under the lights. He kept them there for two weeks, long enough to simulate 30 years of museum conditions. The treated ink-jet prints held up as well as the untreated conventional watercolor. It also protects your prints from water — without the varnish, the ink is water soluble.

"Now, this was a company rep, so you have to take his results with a grain of salt. But it goes to show that you should definitely apply some kind of coating. Or hire it out. I've found a local company that applies the varnish for me, because you need good ventilation to use this stuff."

What about UV-protective glass? "When you're shipping art around the country, you can't use glass at all. It breaks too easily and it adds to your shipping costs. But if somebody wants to put UV glass on top of the artwork after they buy it, that's great. They're just adding another layer of protection."

SHOPPING FOR A FINE-ART PRINTER

For the fine artist on a tight budget, is owning a high-quality ink-jet printer a realistic option? "The industry is just now at the point where an independent artist can afford to purchase a high-end color printer. Right now, I have a wide-format CalComp printer that costs about $10,000. But the prices are falling rapidly. The next generation of that printer will cost more like $8,000, making it accessible for schools and groups of artists. The smaller 1,440-dpi Epson StylusColor 3000 is less than $2,000. It's looking very close in quality to an Iris," the $40,000 color proofing device from Scitex.

12.21

12.22

If you happen to be in the market for a high-resolution color printer, one of the most important things to look at is the paper path. "You want the most straight-through paper path you can get, so the paper doesn't have to curl around a lot of rollers. You should be able to feed a stiff paper stock — like an off-the-shelf watercolor paper — without it getting bent or mangled or hitting up against the head. You might even be able to build a collage and feed it through the printer."

As an exservice bureau hack, the idea of printing on a collage struck Deke as a recipe for disaster. "Oh, no, I've cut up paper and put it through several times. Of course, I make sure I don't pile on too many layers. But something like rice paper against a thicker background — that works fine." While technically not a collage, Schminke has also experimented with printing on coarse and inconsistent surface textures. "I've painted on pumice mixed in with acrylic and then printed on top of that (12.22)." The straighter the paper path, the less likelihood the paint and pumice will flake off.

"The second issue is the head clearance. How much room is there between the print head and the surface that you're printing on? All printer manufacturers have approved substrates — papers that they've tested that they know will work. But artists are going to immediately start putting their own paper in." Too little clearance causes paper jams and can damage the print head; too much clearance lowers the clarity. "The ideal solution would be an adjustable clearance. But these printers are just starting to come out.

"Finally, you also want to be able to adjust the position of the paper after you've loaded it into the printer. This facilitates overprinting and other alignment tasks."

As when making any major purchase, it's a good idea to test the printer firsthand. Schminke recommends that you experiment not only with different paper stocks, but also with different artist materials. "In one test, I laid down a layer of oil pastels and then ran it through a Hewlett-Packard 560c (12.23). The girl, the shadow, and the triangle come from a Photoshop file; the background strokes I applied traditionally."

WHY MIX DIGITAL WITH TRADITIONAL

Some digital purists might venture to suggest that Schminke spends so much time outside Photoshop that she might as well not use the program at all. After all, one of the big reasons that artists turn to computers is to get away from the limitations and sheer messiness of conventional tools. What's to be gained by mixing the digital and traditional worlds?

"Photoshop is an extremely enabling tool. It allows you to try out a lot of different ideas and put artwork together in ways that were very difficult before. Superimposing a photograph on top of a painting — there's an example of something that I simply could not have accomplished without a computer. With Photoshop, you can bring together elements of print-making, painting, and photography in ways that you couldn't have before.

"It's such a natural mix that one of the artists in my group, Judith Moncrieff, came up with a name for it. We tell people we create 'tradigital' artwork. It fits, don't you think?"

12.23

CHAPTER 13
PIXELS TO PLATINUM

Everyday, we see hundreds of photographs — on the Web, in magazines, on television, and in this very book. The difference between seeing a photograph reproduced in a magazine and viewing a well-crafted print in a gallery is as eye-opening as seeing an original oil painting for the first time, after only knowing the image from an art history tome. A reproduction of a photograph will of course contain the same subject matter as the print in the gallery, but the well-made photographic print has an intangible luminance and tonality that can only be appreciated by viewing the original. For curators, collectors, and fine-art photographers, the photographic print that is the most revered is the platinum print, which is known "for the delicacy of its tones, its permanence, and its print surfaces, which suggest that the image is a part of the paper."[1]

Today, it is easy to point to the creative and technical advantages of working with digital tools, but many photographers do not have the vision or commitment to adopt the new technologies to improve and expand their creative expression. Dan Burkholder is a fine-art photographer whose talent is matched by his sense of the moment, and whose understanding of traditional photographic processes in combination with his mastery of Photoshop has offered him new creative opportunities to explore his inner vision. He relies on traditional photographic skills (13.1), while investing the time to learn, experiment, and master the digital tools and techniques required to produce compelling and powerful images on finely made

You just know that the first time an early photographer used a slow shutter speed on his camera and discovered the blurred-moving-subject syndrome it was a delightful, though unexpected, revelation! Electronic imaging does the same thing, bringing its own plate of effects and revelations to the photographic smorgasbord.

DAN BURKHOLDER

platinum prints. The images that Burkholder creates are meant to be seen and enjoyed in a gallery setting, where the original prints reveal the subtle transitions and careful attention to detail that is visible in the carefully crafted platinum print (13.2).

> **NOTE**
>
> The reproductions in this chapter have been toned in Photoshop to mimic the color and tone of the platinum print.

---

[1] *Encyclopedia of Photography, 3rd Edition*. Edited by Leslie Strobel and Richard Zakia. Focal Press.

13.1

13.2

ARTIST:
Dan Burkholder

ORGANIZATION:
7003 Forest Meadow
San Antonio, TX 78240
210/523-9913
http://www.danburkholder.com
danphoto@aol.com

SYSTEM, MAC:
Power Computing 240 (Mac clone)
Mac OS 8.1
6GB storage

RAM:
224MB total
180MB assigned to Photoshop

MONITORS:
19-inch Rasterops monitor
15-inch AppleVision Multiscan monitor

EXTRAS:
Wacom ArtPad 6 x 9
Polaroid SprintScan Plus 35
UMAX Astra 1200s flatbed scanner with
transparency adapter
Fisher-Price Fun Photo Maker digital
camera
Pinnacle Micro APEX 4.6GB Magneto-
optical storage

VERSION USED:
Photoshop 5.0

Burkholder is recognized as a pioneer in fine art digital photography. He has developed a technique that combines the beauty and permanence of the platinum print with the visual intrigue and precision of digital imaging (13.3). Making a platinum print differs from making a regular print, in which the photographer uses a darkroom enlarger to blow-up the negative and expose the photo paper. Because of the relative insensitivity of platinum paper, the image needs to be exposed with strong UV light and then contact printed, meaning that the paper is in direct contact with the negative and the image is exactly as large as the negative. The exposures can last up to ten minutes depending on the density of the negative and the strength of the light source. In essence, platinum printing is a hand-done process in which fine art rag paper is coated with ferric oxalate, potassium chloroplatinate, and oxalic acid and is then allowed to dry. After the paper is dry, the artist makes the contact print.

Burkholder has been printing in platinum for the past 15 years. Before that, he had printed with the standard silver paper that you can buy in any photo supply store. "But, I found myself torturing the silver gelatin emulsion with bleaching and toning to achieve a certain feel in the final print. My first attempts at platinum, though far from perfect, made me realize that the warmth and texture of the platinum print was the voice I wanted in my images."

OTHER APPLICATIONS:

QuarkXPress 4.0, KPT 2.0, Microsoft Office 98

WORK HISTORY:

1970 — Used $60.00 from birthday money to buy first 35mm rangefinder camera.

1973 — Bought first serious camera, a Nikon F2.

1980 — Received BA degree from Brooks Institute of Photography.

1981 — First one-person show.

1983 — Attended platinum printing workshop, "where I discovered the right voice for my photography."

1984 — Moved away from shooting large format (read static) subjects.

1990 — Received MS degree from Brooks Institute of Photography.

1992 — Saw full-color image on a 24-bit monitor, emptied all pockets, and bought a Macintosh IIci. Sold 11x14-inch View Camera and used proceeds to purchase more RAM.

1995 — Published the book *Making Digital Negatives for Contact Printing*.

1998 — Represented by 20 galleries throughout the US.

FAVORITE STUPID PET TRICKS:

They're all stupid at Dan's house. "Our two dogs have learned to wear glasses!"

13.3

EUREKA!

In 1992, Burkholder visited a friend who had recently bought into a graphic service bureau. As he explains, "Watching the big halftone negatives crank out of the imagesetter was a revelation. There just had to be a way to exploit this inexpensive medium for making enlarged digital negatives and apply it to contact print processes like platinum, palladium, or cyanotype prints." For fine artists, working with enlarged negatives from imagesetter output is ideal for making prints on standard silver halide photographic paper from digital files that look like classic black-and-white photos.

So Burkholder began the testing, cursing, and more testing, that finally enabled him to make 16×20-inch negatives from digital files — all without getting his hands wet or having to stand in the darkroom wondering if he had used the right exposure or if the image was in focus. "So off I went, learning about offset printing, imagesetters, line-screens, bitmaps,

and lots of other alien stuff." Once the testing was complete, which included throwing gobs of lithographic film in the trash, Burkholder could make 8×10-inch negatives for under $8 each or a 16×20-inch negative for about $30 and use these negatives to produce beautiful platinum prints that have the tonality and richness that underline his aesthetics. An additional advantage to working in platinum is that the prints are archival and will easily outlast any silver-based traditional photographic print.

In the process, Burkholder realized that to make great negatives on an imagesetter, he had to tackle the sensitometry issue and find a way to get the imagesetter output to look more like traditional film. "To a photographer, standard imagesetter output looks flat, as if it were underexposed and underdeveloped. To make an enlarged negative that I could use for contact printing, I had to experiment with applying extreme curves to increase contrast and to open up the entire image. Once I understood the difference between imagesetter output and photographically enlarged negatives, I could produce negatives that work for either platinum printing, other alternative processes, or with traditional photo paper."

CALIBRATE OR DO NOT PASS GO!

Burkholder uses Photoshop to refine single exposures, create composites, and convert grayscale images to bitmap files. These bitmaps are completely random arrangements of dots: Where the dots on the negative are denser, the print will be lighter and, conversely, where the dots on the negative are few, the print will be darker. But before he starts scanning, compositing, or outputting a file, he calibrates his monitor with the much-improved monitor calibration utility, Adobe Gamma, that comes with Photoshop 5. "Calibration is the most important step in all computer-imaging processes. Sadly, few take it as seriously as they should."

Even after Burkholder calibrates his monitor, he still doesn't trust it! "I always have the Info Palette open and use it like an on-screen densitometer to measure tonal values numerically (objectively) rather than visually (subjectively). As one who is constantly fooled by the on-screen image, I take that advice seriously. You'll never catch me Photoshopping without the Info palette! But going a step further, I like to have more objective and visual help when I print the final negative on platinum. By including a step tablet [or step wedge] with the image, I can assess the tonal values, and make adjustments if necessary." A step wedge is a test target that goes from black to white in specific increments. Photographers and printers have used these for years when testing exposure and making prints to see how the dark, middle, and light tones translate when printed.

To make your own 13-step wedge, follow these steps:

1. Create a new grayscale Photoshop file 10" × 1" at 300 ppi.

2. Press D to reset the foreground and background colors to black and white.

3. Double-click on the gradient tool to open up the gradient tool's options, set the blend to go foreground to background, and deselect Dither (13.4).

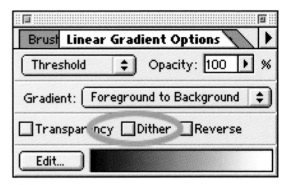

13.4

4. While holding down the Shift key (which forces the blend to be perfectly straight), draw the blend from left to right along the long end of the image.

5. Choose Go ➢ Image ➢ Adjust ➢ Posterize and use a setting of 11.

> **NOTE**
>
> In Photoshop 4.0 you will get exact 10 percent step wedges, but in version 5.0 you will *not* get 11 evenly sized steps. The gradient tool has been changed in 5.0, so the transitions near the ends of a gradient are smoother. This means they are actually larger (more pixels) than other steps closer to the middle. So although the 50 percent gray wedge exactly straddles the 1500 pixel mark, the white and the black steps will be larger. To compensate for this and to add more information to the lightest and darkest steps, follow Step 6.

6. To add tonal distinction in the highlights and shadows, add two additional tones: one at 5 percent and the next at 95 percent dot. With the marquee tool select a rectangular area between the 0 percent and 10 percent area and fill it with a 5 percent white. This will yield finer steps to evaluate the highlights (13.5).

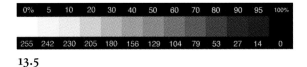

13.5

7. With the marquee tool select a rectangular area between the 90 percent and 100 percent area and fill with a 95 percent black.

Pasting this step wedge next to your image before sending the file to an imagesetter gives you a visual reference to check and control the tones in the image. For example, it is easier to see if the highlights are getting blown-out or the shadows are blocking up

with a step wedge than trying to judge an image where the actual image content can distract you from making important contrast evaluations and tonal corrections. For critical images, Burkholder creates a step wedge that has 1 percent density steps in the highlights and shadows (13.6). The final image carries tone beautifully in both the highlights and shadow areas (13.7).

13.6

13.7

THE CAMERA AS NOTEBOOK

"I use my 35mm cameras as visual notebooks — I take pictures of whatever intrigues me or is simply beautiful. I don't go out shooting with a specific image in mind that I want to construct. Using the camera as a visual notetaker frees me up from having to complete the image when the shutter is fired. In fact, sometimes hitting the Enter key on the Mac is the final step."

Burkholder's subject matter can be as banal as traffic seen from an overpass on a gray day (13.8), but the way he interprets the final image allows the viewer to see the scene completely differently (13.9). "If I can build the image so that people can be launched on their own emotional journey when they view my prints, then I've done my job. As an artist, I have to control the design and tonality on that piece of paper so the viewer's eyes will move about the image properly."

13.8

13.9

INPUT

Burkholder scans his own 35mm film with a Polaroid SprintScan 35Plus. With a wink he explains, "I live by the rule of thumb that you should gather enough pixels to provide 300 ppi at the final image size. Then, when that rule is no longer convenient, I violate it with a passion! Since the Polaroid SprintScan 35Plus film scanner can capture 2,700 pixels across the 1" dimension of the negative, that would limit me to making 9×14-inch prints. Some of my prints are 12×18-inches, so I have to do a good bit of resampling to get to that desired dimension. Now I'm not saying my larger prints look like they were shot with an 8×10-inch view camera; they don't. I am saying that with judicious sharpening and retouching, there is no evidence of aliasing or pixelization."

Burkholder shoots both conventional black-and-white films, such as Kodak T-Max 3200 (rated at 800 ASA), and chromogenic films (color-processed films that produce a monochromatic, dye structure negative), such as Kodak T400CN or Ilford XP2. Interestingly enough, although his final output will be in black and white, Burkholder scans in RGB. "When I scan in a chromogenic negative, I scan it in as RGB and then look through the three channels to select the best one. Crazy as it sounds, the best channel can vary, apparently because of dye colors that vary between film batches or chemistry changes during processing."

To extract the best grayscale image from his originals, Burkholder uses the new Channel Mixer feature (Image ➤ Adjust ➤ Channel Mixer). By moving the Red, Green, and Blue sliders, he controls how much each color channel will contribute to the final grayscale image. "First, I check Monochrome at the bottom of the Channel Mixer dialog box. This makes the Channel Mixer create a color image with just gray values, ideal for my purposes! I ignore the Constant slider. It can get you in trouble with its linear quality, much as Brightness and Contrast can clip important data from your image. If I were scanning a bunch of negatives from the same emulsion batch that had been processed at the same lab, I'd be able to recall these Channel Mixer settings by clicking Save and giving the setting a name like T400CN, Pro Photo Lab. For the next scan, I'd simply click the Load button, short-cutting the need to experiment with the sliders again."

The best aspect about using the Channel Mixer is the added tonal richness (13.10) that comes completely from the original scan data — no Levels or Curves have been used to alter the image tonality. That means the image is not being degraded at all, something that all conventional tonal adjustment will do to some extent. "Working from chromogenic films, the Channel Mixer control is just one more step I use to grab the best image information from my $1^{1}/_{2}$ square inches of film real estate. Photographers who need to create grayscale images from color originals will see even more dramatic improvements in their final grayscale images." As you can see, the first image (13.10) was created with the Channel Mixer and the second was a straight scan with the scanner set to grayscale (13.11) — not very attractive is it?

13.10

13.11

HIGH-TECH BACKLASH

One of Burkholder's current projects is working with the Fisher-Price Fun Photo Maker, which is a $45 digital camera that plays a tune as it spools the image from the video chip to the print head and then prints onto fax paper. The prints are crude and full of artifacts, which also means they can be beautiful and charming (13.12 and 13.13). "The computer is an incredible intoxicant for photographers. After almost seven years of steep learning curve fatigue, I've found the Fisher-Price work to be a welcomed departure. In fact, there is no manipulation whatsoever on the images. I simply shoot, let the camera produce the fax-paper print, scan the print with a PaperPort scanner, and make the negative for platinum contact printing right on the desktop with an Epson Photo ink-jet printer. This combination has brought back an element of simplicity and playfulness that was getting buried under too many software manuals!"

13.12

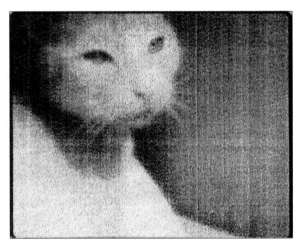

13.13

THE DIGITAL DARKROOM

Burkholder uses Photoshop to emulate the traditional darkroom to crop, lighten, darken, and so on, a single exposure. "Many times I'll just work with one image rather than combine several image parts. *Flatiron in Spring, New York* is a good example (13.14). I shot the original with a Contax T rangefinder camera that had a fixed wide angle lens, so I didn't have many options on filling the frame, and I used Photoshop to crop the image. The one filter I love to use is the Gaussian Glow filter in Kai's Power Tools. It diffuses the mid and upper values but protects deep shadow detail from the diffusion (13.15). I'm still using version 2.0 of KPT; I just can't get a handle on those organic interfaces of the newer MetaCreations products."

13.14

13.15

Taking the idea of interpreting a single image further, in the original photograph of *Mary Lou Mourning at Our Mother's Death Bed*, there is distracting medical hardware and household items that have nothing to do with the collision of life and death that had just taken place (13.16).

The first thing Burkholder did was edit out those areas with the clone tool. To cover up the sink on the right, he selected a section of curtain and, using the move tool, pressed Option/Alt and dragged the selection over the sink (13.17 and 13.18). In Photoshop 5.0, drag-duplicating a selected area does not automatically create a new layer. To create a new layer from the duplicated material, choose Layer ➤ New ➤ Layer Via Cut or Layer ➤ New ➤ Layer Via Copy immediately after duplicating (13.19 and 13.20). "This was easier than massive cloning and only required a bit of clone tool touch-up to look right."

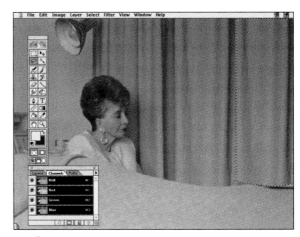

13.18

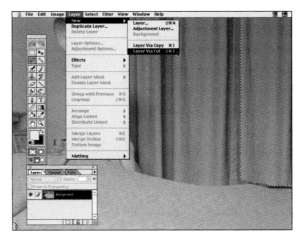

13.19

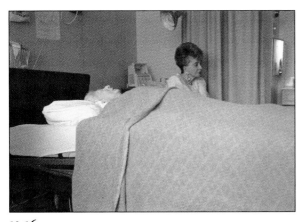

13.16

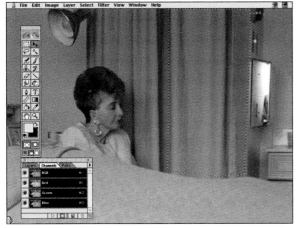

13.17

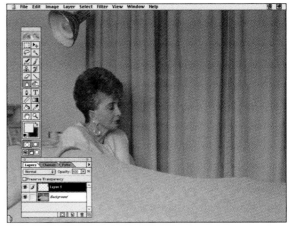

13.20

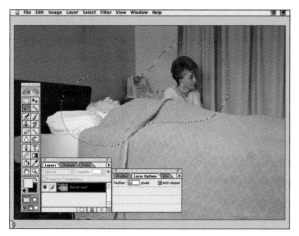

13.21

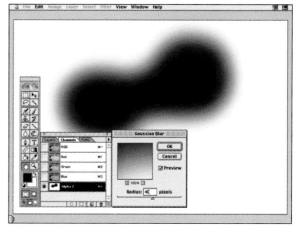

13.22

Finally, Burkholder used an Alpha channel (13.21 and 13.22) to softly select both his mother's and sister's heads to protect them as he applied an image adjustment layer with Curves to darken the edges of the image (13.23). "This focuses the viewer's eyes on what is essential in the image rather than having their

eyes wander around the picture. For me, there is no doubt that the final image is much more emotionally honest (13.24). This is what photography can do better than any other medium! It doesn't really matter whether the tools are digital or conventional."

13.23

13.24

MATCHING THE FILM GRAIN

Burkholder's composite work is surreal and part of that surrealism comes from the fact that the qualities of the images that he combines have a similar tone and grain structure. "Since I shoot exclusively with 35mm, I have to be careful about combining small parts of images that will reveal film grain if I oversample them or make them too large in the composite."

The composite image *Man Lifting Rock* is a good example of how Burkholder circumnavigated the grain clash problem. The *Rock Lifter* was exposed on T-Max 3200 film (shot at EI 800) (13.25). This film has a beautiful, sharp grain texture, but if the grain collided with that of the background, the image would fail. By comparison, the background image of the water and moss-covered rocks (13.26) was shot on a tripod with T-Max 100 film, which is a super-fine grain film. Some neutral density filtration was added to permit a slower shutter speed that would give the water some movement softness. The background was cloned symmetrically, but notice the subtle movement of moss detail that helps break up the Rorschach effect.

13.25

13.26

Relative size to the rescue! Notice the size difference of the two image parts: the fine-grain background is printed practically full frame, whereas the rock lifter himself is relatively small in the frame. The courser grain of the high-speed film is functionally compressed to match that of the fine-grain background (13.26).

CREATING THE LIGHT

The image *Rodential Resurrection* is made up of two images: the background alleyway and the picture of a dead squirrel (13.27). By using image adjustment layers and a soft drop shadow, Burkholder created a whimsical image with a richer sense of light than the original images. He started by opening up the tonal value of the background layer with Curves, which gives the cobblestones a shimmery quality that belies their humble origins. After separating the squirrel with Extensis Mask Pro and dragging it onto the Alleyway file, Burkholder added another image adjustment layer, but he grouped this Curve with the squirrel in order to clip the Curves adjustment to affect just the pixels in the squirrel layer (13.28).

13.27

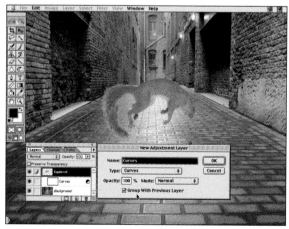

13.28

NOTE

Extensis Mask Pro is a Photoshop plug-in for creating complex masks and clipping paths. It works with color matching technology and enables you to choose which colors to keep and which colors to drop to make fine masks.

13.29

To apply the finishing touch to the image, Burkholder wanted to add a soft drop shadow under the squirrel. Here's how he did it:

1. First he added a new layer, by pressing Option/Alt and clicking on the new layer icon to bring up the New Layer dialog box. This allows the user to select a blend mode while creating the layer.

2. He selected Softlight to activate the option to fill that layer with softlight-neutral gray (13.29). By selecting this option, the layer is filled with a 50 percent fill that is "invisible," as the blend mode Softlight has no affect at exactly 50 percent gray.

3. Burkholder pressed ⌘/Ctrl and clicked the squirrel layer to load the squirrel's transparency as a selection.

4. He added a curve image adjustment layer, making sure to select Group With Previous Layer (13.30).

5. Using Curves, Burkholder darkened down the shadow and immediately noticed that the shadow was directly on top of the squirrel (13.31).

6. He used the move tool to position the shadow on the ground.

13.30

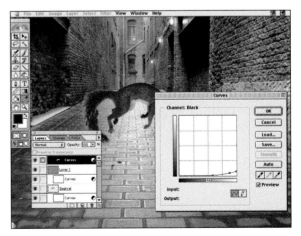

13.31

7. Using the Transform command (⌘/Ctrl+T), he rotated the shadow and, more importantly, matched the shadow's perspective with the vanishing point apparent in the receding cobblestones (13.32).

8. Finally, Burkholder used a Gaussian Blur of 8 to soften the shadow (13.33).

> **TIP**
>
> To access the Transform options quickly, use the Control key on a Mac or the right mouse button on a PC and click any handle point of the transform bounding box (13.34).

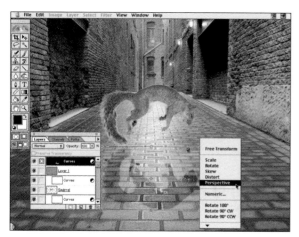

13.32

13.34

13.33

FROM GRAYSCALE TO BITMAP

After Burkholder has created an image, the last step is to prepare the file for final output. This includes adding the step wedge to the file, altering the contrast of the image to compensate for the inherent flatness of imagesetter output, and finalizing the size of the image. "The important thing to remember when working with bitmaps is to honor the all-important 1:2 ratio. For negatives that will be used for platinum, palladium, or cyanotype printing, scan in at 300 ppi, do all digital darkroom work, flatten, and then size up to 600 ppi with Image Size. Then carefully use Unsharp Masking and choose Image ➢ Mode ➢ Bitmap, making sure to use a diffusion dither at 1200 dpi. Take the file to the service bureau where they'll run the imagesetter at 2400 dpi. If you are planning on contact printing with silver halide materials (that is, standard photo paper), I recommend "upsampling" your grayscale to 900 ppi, making an 1800 dpi bitmap, and then running the imagesetter at 3600 ppi. That way your highlights will hold tonal detail." Just follow these steps:

1. Increase the canvas size of the image and paste the 13-step wedge onto the edge of the image (13.35).

2. Apply a radical contrast adjustment with Curves to the grayscale image (13.36). "This is necessary because a normal halftone negative will have very weak separation in the shadow areas, owing to the different contrast needs of the ink-on-paper printing industry. Remember, these negatives were meant to burn printing plates, not to expose conventional silver or platinum photographic papers." (See the CD-ROM at the back of the book for examples of Burkholder's Curves.)

3. Use Image Size to size the files up from 300 ppi to 600 ppi (13.37).

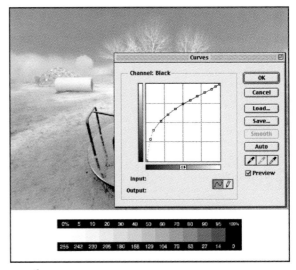

13.36

13.35

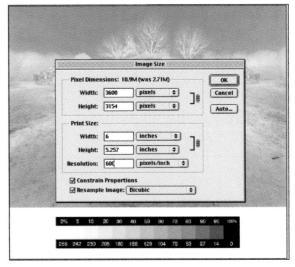

13.37

4. Apply careful Unsharp Mask to offset any softness that sizing the image up may have added to the image (13.38).

5. Convert the file from grayscale to bitmap (13.39), making sure to double the output size to 1200 ppi, using a Diffusion Dither (13.40).

Grayscale files contain 256 subtle gray tones from pure black to bright white (13.41). Bitmap files are made up of black and white dots, without any gray values (13.42). As Dan explains, "Bitmaps have a beautiful, photographic quality that just isn't realized with the standard 'soldiers in a row' line-screen look. Before Photoshop 4.0, bitmaps were rendered terribly on screen. You'd have never guessed that a wonderful negative would result. At higher resolutions, you won't be able to see the dot on a rougher print medium like platinum (13.43), though you might on traditional silver gelatin paper due to it's harder, more revealing gelatin surface."

13.38

13.40

13.39

13.41

13.42

13.43

WORKING WITH THE SERVICE BUREAU

To find a service bureau, look in the Yellow Pages or your local phone book under Typesetting and Printing or Desktop Services. "I've devoted a section in my book (*Making Digital Negatives for Contact Printing*) to communicating with service bureaus. Photographers and printing industry people still talk different languages, so I took pains to eliminate the 'Tower of Babel' effect. Most importantly, you have to remember that service bureaus crank out hundreds of files for offset film everyday and they are used to seeing low contrast film that is ideal to burn printing plates. Let them know that your film will look different and that you don't want them to change anything."

Service bureaus will have you fill out a job order form. The most important things to remember are

- The resolution of the imagesetter output will be either 2400 ppi or 3600 ppi, as discussed earlier in this chapter.
- The final output will be negative film, with the emulsion side down.
- For line screen, check "bitmap" and that the image has been "prescreened." Some service bureaus will ask you to specify a line screen. If so, Burkholder suggests 150 lpi, and it shouldn't affect the EPS file either way.

THE FILM IS DONE!

You can use these enlarged negatives to make beautiful contact prints with alternative processes or conventional silver paper. Remember to use the step wedge to evaluate the print. If the tones are not printing accurately, return to the original file, adjust the contrast curve, and rerun the film to get negatives that print well. For example, if you make a print and the highlights in the step wedge are darker than they should be, you can either visually estimate what the tones are printing as or use a densitometer to measure the film and then adjust the tones accordingly by altering the Transfer Function.

13.44

As seen in this test print (13.44), the highlights are printing too dark, and Burkholder has estimated and noted what those values are. To compensate for the highlights printing too dark, subtract the printed value from the target value to reduce the values in order to compensate for the imagesetter. To correct for values, in this case the shadows, add the missing value to the target number to compensate.

To fine-tune how your file is translated to film by the imagesetter, you can either tweak the final Curve applied to the image before converting the file to bitmap, or you can alter the transfer function of the file. Burkholder refers to this as creating your own PAC (Personal Adjustment Curve). Follow the steps below to create a PAC and optimize your files for output.

1. After noting the values that need correction, choose Page Set-up (13.45) and click Transfer (13.46).

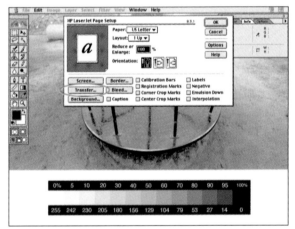

13.45

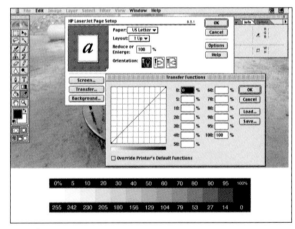

13.46

2. In this example, the highlights are printing too dark, so Burkholder compensates by reducing the values. The 10 percent dot is printing as 16, so he subtracts 10 from 16 and enters the resulting value of 6 at the 10 percent point (13.47). Continuing up the curve, Burkholder compensates the light values that are printing too lightly by adding the missing difference to the dark transfer points. In this example, the 80 percent dot is printing as 75, so he enters 85 to compensate for the missing 5 percent.

3. When saving the file as a Photoshop EPS, make sure to select the Include Transfer Function option (13.48).

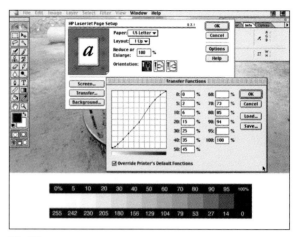

13.47

ADDITIONAL FINESSE

"In my personal work, I'm now doing much more duotone printing. That is, I make two enlarged negatives that I pin register and print sequentially on the same sheet of platinum-sensitized paper. One negative is made to expose the highlight and midtones, while the other prints the shadows. The added control is wonderful and the pluses of the process are readily apparent with incredible image control — I can hold subtle highlights and still print rich blacks with detail."

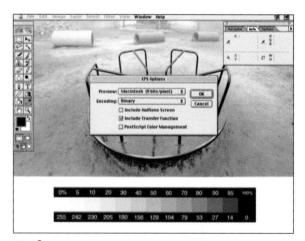

13.48

When addressing the aesthetic aspects of imaging, the technical side of Burkholder recedes and the artist that is working to create compelling and meaningful images emerges. "I think all photographers are striving for control of the medium to one degree or another. The issues of truth and integrity, while so important in other areas of the medium (photojournalism comes to mind), are generally misplaced in fine art photography. My personal concern is with emotional honesty, trying my hardest to orchestrate an emotional response in the viewer that mirrors (or at least suggests) my own feelings about the subject."

A beautiful example of Dan's personal philosophy is reflected in the image *In the Turtle in Church, Alice, Texas*. The print is successful because it brings together the three elements (13.49–13.52) in a unified, serene, and even reverential way. That expression of purpose on the turtle's face helps guide the viewer's response in a way that a less serious subject would have failed to do.

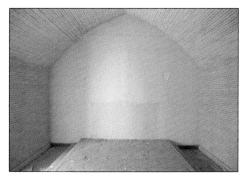

13.49

13.50

13.51

13.52

WORKING WITH A GALLERY

Burkholder's work is represented by a number of galleries, and his platinum prints are popular with collectors because platinum prints are among the most archival prints possible. When asked why he doesn't make Iris prints that could easily be made to mimic the tones of a platinum print, he responds, "First of all, the permanence of Iris prints has not been established and secondly, although I work on the computer, I still love to work with my hands. I enjoy hand-coating the fine-art rag paper and working in the darkroom. The mechanically produced print will never completely replace the hand-made art object."

Burkholder works to develop a partnership with his galleries. "I don't let them dictate how many prints I will produce or how large an edition will be. In fact, any gallery that tries to limit the number of prints is confusing photography with lithography, and I prefer not to work with them." More interesting is how Burkholder prices his prints. "When I release a new print for sale, the price starts low, and as the image becomes more popular, the price rises. This gives buyers the incentive to purchase new work since it is less expensive and will only be more expensive if they delay. I also like to think that this policy allows younger collectors that may have less disposable income to collect artwork without breaking the bank."

DISCOVERING STYLE

Burkholder learns from his mistakes and incorporates what he's learned into his work. "I like to think of the digital darkroom as just one more arena in which I'm free (and prone) to screw-up and discover new visual phenomena. You just know that the first time an early photographer used a slow shutter speed on his camera and discovered the blurred-moving-subject syndrome it was a delightful, though unexpected, revelation! The camera had revealed something that the human eye could never have captured. Electronic imaging does the same thing, bringing it's own plate of effects and revelations to the photographic smorgasbord." The *Speckled Vulture in Pine Forest* (13.53) is one of those "happy mistake" images. The negative of the bird in the tree was shot with a long telephoto against a bald, bright, hazy sky. It was a thin negative, practically clear film except for the tree branches and bird. Dan was trying desperately to amplify the minute detail in Photoshop with Curves and the Unsharp Mask filter. As he watched the monitor, he found, "I was getting the equivalent of electronic *noise* in the image. I was simply dialing in too much gain, much like turning a radio's volume up to hear a very faint station. My first thought was 'Well Dan, you've screwed up another image,' but then I pushed back the chair and looked at the monitor again and thought, 'Hey, this is neat. This is a feeling of texture that neither the camera nor I would have imagined!' These are the happy mistakes that add to the magic of the medium.

"I just have to propose that the quest for style is best left as an issue of joyful discovery (inevitable if the artistic spirit is truly present), rather than the fruit of intention. If you have something unique to say, you'll eventually find you are saying it uniquely and that will become your artistic style."

13.53

CHAPTER 14
PHOTOGRAPHING FOR PHOTOSHOP

P rior to the advent of computer imaging, photographers' choices were relatively limited. Compositing was by no means impossible, but the costs were high and the results were frequently crude. More often than not, the ideal solution was to set up a shot as commissioned and steer clear of special effects.

For example, if a client asked you to come up with a picture of a pig wearing a baseball cap and tennis shoes, your most efficient approach may have involved calling a few local animal trainers and asking if by chance they handle porkers who enjoy playing dress-up. If such a ham could be hired, the real fun would begin. The fact that clothes are generally designed to fit humans presents a few costuming challenges. How do you keep tapering hooves inside shoes? How do you attach a hat to an animal whose neck is higher than its forehead? And if by chance the beast is not as enthusiastic about fashion as advertised, how much time is wasted as the trainer pulls the battling bacon off the photographer's flattened form?

Chicago-based photographer Jeff Schewe has little doubt that the new ways for creating such images are an improvement over the old ways. Having graduated from the prestigious Rochester Institute of Technology more than a decade before anyone had even heard of Photoshop, Schewe is steeped in the traditional studio experience. He continues to use traditional tools, and his conventional training is every bit as applicable now as it was 20 years ago. The difference is that these days, he sets up his shots with an eye toward editing them in Photoshop.

So, if the need arises for Schewe to put clothes on a pig — as indeed it did — he photographs animal and clothing separately and combines them digitally.

Each time I start a job, I establish one strategy that encompasses both the photography and the imaging. I can shoot exactly what I need and put it together exactly the way I want.

JEFF SCHEWE

Schewe explains, "Each time I start a job, I establish one strategy that encompasses both the photography and the imaging. I can shoot exactly what I need and put it together exactly the way I want." Together, camera and computer give you absolute control over the creative process.

HOW EXACTLY DO YOU DRESS UP A PIG

"The Chicago Board of Trade commissioned me to do a piece that promoted trading in pork bellies. The headline was, 'Hogs are hipper than you think.' So we got this hog in the studio. He was someone's 4-H pet — his name was Pork Chop — and he came in a large dog carrier. I shot him on a white background (14.1). At first, it freaked him out because he couldn't see anything to stand on. Then, shortly after we got that problem resolved, he got this really relaxed look on his face; then he peed.

14.1

14.2

"Any time you photograph animals, you have to operate inside the framework of what they'll do. The art director wanted the pig's head up, but pigs are made to keep their noses in the dirt. We went through half a dozen types of food to see which one would get him to lift his head. The one he liked best was whole wheat bread. After a lot of messing around, we got fifty or so shots off. And out of those fifty, the art director and I got it down to three or four where he looked like he was smiling.

"After we selected the pig picture we wanted, I bought two pairs of kid's sneakers and positioned them very carefully to match the location and angle of the pig's feet. Then, I flew in a scrim to cast a pig-like shadow (14.2). And I put the hat up on a balloon."

We've gone ahead and composited the pig against his clothes to show how well they line up (14.3). The alignment isn't exact, but it's close enough to make the lighting consistent and keep the compositing time in Photoshop to an absolute minimum. How does Schewe line up his shots? "Back in the early days, I used to do complicated tracings. Now, I just hold up the transparency and eyeball it."

The final composition (14.4) involved more than nudging the shoes and hats into place and slapping them onto the pig. "It's very unusual to find an old pig with a curly tail. Their tails are typically docked,

ARTIST:
Jeff Schewe

ORGANIZATION:
Schewe Photography
624 West Willow
Chicago, Illinois 60614
312/951-6334
schewe@aol.com

SYSTEM:
Genesis 720 (DayStar, four 180MHz 604e CPUs)
16GB storage (two 8GB Seagate arrays with JackHammers SCSI accelerators)

RAM:
1GB total
925MB assigned to Photoshop

MONITOR:
Radius 17- and 21-inch PrecisionViews

EXTRAS:
Wacom 12 x 12 tablet, Light Source Colortron color sampler, Leaf 45 slider scanner, Shinko ColorStream II

VERSION USED:
Photoshop 5.0.

and this guy was no exception. So I had to curl the tail by cloning it inside Photoshop. I used the Spherize filter to distort his body and give him an extra 50 pounds. I think pigs look a little happier when they're fattened up." Then, there's that bizarre concern that never fails to pop up in commercial mammal photography. "The art director wasn't terribly comfortable with the exact state of the genitalia, so I more or less unisexed him."

MATCHING BACKGROUNDS

When photographing his raw images, Schewe is always careful to match the position of his elements and the lighting conditions. But he's equally careful to match backgrounds. "According to the old wisdom — prior to computer imaging — you used a white background whenever you wanted to composite something, so the printer could make a knockout litho. In this day and age, unless you want white as your final background, it's the worst color to shoot against. Your edges become overly hot, making compositing very difficult.

"So, I try to make sure that I photograph all elements against a background that matches or is at least appropriate to the final background. For example, the Fruit of the Loom ad shows a bull's head

14.3

14.4

OTHER APPLICATIONS:
Adobe Illustrator, QuarkXPress, Valis MetaFlow, Live Picture, Fractal Design Painter, Specular Collage

WORK HISTORY:
1978 — Received B.S. in Commercial Photography from Rochester Institute of Technology, graduated with highest honors.

1981 — Opened commercial advertising studio, specializing in large negative compositing and multiple-exposure work.

1984 — Bought first Mac out of back of semi, created first computer imaging job on proprietary system.

1991 — Created first job in Photoshop, structured Photoshop course at Center for Creative Imaging.

1993 — Bought into early adopter program for Live Picture, later brought in as alpha tester for the likes of xRes and Photoshop.

FAVORITE MOTORCYCLE:
BMW R1100GS ("After sitting in a darkened room for hours on end, I like to sit outside for a few hours on end.")

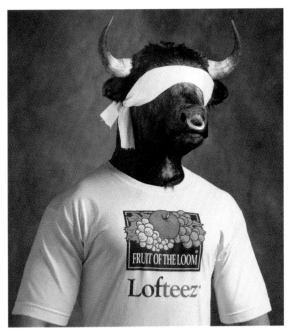

14.5

14.6

coming out of a muscular guy's body (14.5). I shot the live human element first (14.6) because the live element requires the most care. The art director and I had to figure out the pose, adjust the appearance of the lighting on the T-shirt, play with the body language, and make all the little decisions that come into play when setting up a shot.

"After we picked out a shot we were both happy with, I photographed the bull's head under the same light and against the same background (14.7). I positioned it so that the angle of the head and neck pretty much matched the body." With several days between the shots, Schewe must occasionally strike and repitch his backdrops. Doesn't that make it difficult to get everything exactly right? "I don't spend any time trying to register the background for one element to the background of another. I care about the density and the hue, so that the darkness is similar and the colors are approximately the same.

"Finally, I almost always shoot the background by itself. This gives me the option of working with the background as a separate element. So in this case, I masked the body, masked the head, put the head and the body together, and then put them both against the empty background. Because the backgrounds are consistent, I don't have any problems with haloing or weird edge artifacts. I have a little bit of latitude with my masks, and yet my edges appear completely nat-

14.7

ural, as if I had shot everything exactly as you see it."

Just out of curiosity, where in the world did Schewe come across such a photogenic bull's head? "One of the advantages of working in a big city is that there's no end to the weird stuff a photo-stylist can find. You wouldn't believe the junk you can find if you search long enough. As I recall, we rented two bull's heads for this job, one black and one brown. I think it cost me around $100." Decapitated bulls at $50 a head — there's an offer you can't refuse.

MIXING MULTIPLE LIVE ELEMENTS

When Schewe combines living and inanimate elements, he always starts off by shooting the less predictable living item. Then, he sets up the more obedient inanimate objects based on the position and lighting of the live ones. By starting with the most chaotic element in a composition, he can achieve higher levels of control and order as he works through the job.

But how does it work when he has to shoot two or more live elements? "One job I did called for a centaur — in this case, half woman, half Shetland pony (14.8). Even in Chicago, you can't rent one of those, so I had to merge a woman and a pony together. Any time I work with two live elements, I start with the less intelligent and less versatile of the two. So I had to shoot the pony first and work within the limitations of what he could do.

"After taking a lot of shots, we managed to get an attentive pose with the head high up (14.9). I'm imagining the woman taking the place of the pony's head, so I need the neck nice and vertical. Once I got the transparency back from the lab, I was able to position the woman so she stood at the same three-quarter angle as the animal's head (14.10). We also outfitted her in a wig that was more or less the same color as the pony's mane."

14.8

14.9

14.10

14.11   14.12   14.13

14.14

METICULOUS PATHS FOR INTRICATE EDGES

Obviously, Schewe's compositions involve some complex masking. But he works a little bit differently from other artists. "I use paths to create about 80 percent of my selections (14.11). I usually draw the paths at 200 percent view size so that I can clearly see the line of demarcation between the subject and the background (14.12). I can literally decide while I'm creating the path exactly where I'm going to clip something. If I see a piece of material that looks goofy, no problem; I just clip it away."

Schewe acknowledges that paths can be exasperating and time consuming, particularly when taken to these extremes. "But I've found that if you spend the time up front making a really excellent selection, you spend far less time fixing problems in your final composition."

After Schewe completes his paths, he converts them to a selection, saves the selection as a mask, and adds soft edges where needed using filters such as Median and Gaussian Blur (14.13). "One of my strategies is to mimic the photographic resolution of an image as accurately as possible. If something is critically sharp in the photograph, I'll make sure it's critically sharp in the selection. If it's slightly soft in the photo, it'll be slightly soft in the selection. Again, it takes a while to get it just right, but it's worth it in the end."

ALL AGAINST A GRADIENT BACKGROUND

Here again, Schewe layered his elements against an empty version of the background. "But this time I lit the background more dramatically, so that it was dark at the top and lighter at the bottom. Then, I played with the gradation and lighting inside Photoshop to get the final effect I was looking for (14.14)."

Merging the elements together was mostly a matter of blending the horse's neck into the woman's torso. "I selected the horse from the neck down and the woman from the waist up, then I layered them against my empty background with the woman in front (14.15). I added a layer mask to the front layer to fade out the woman's torso (14.16). I also had to distort the pony's mane to send it flowing into her hair, and I lightened her hair to match the mane. There's always a lot of back and forth work in an image like this, even when the original elements are so painstakingly matched."

14.15   14.16

PLAYING WITH SCALE

If a shot involves strictly inanimate objects, you might expect Schewe to set up the scene exactly as he wants it and steer clear of Photoshop. But that's rarely the case. "There are all kinds of reasons to shoot inanimate elements in groups and composite them in Photoshop." A good example is the spud family portrait that Schewe created for a potato fungicide ad (14.17), which toys with the notion of relative scale. "I've got three different levels of scale going on here. A potato isn't really big enough to wear a hat or jewelry. And both the potatoes and their accessories would have been dwarfed by the TV if they were really seated as close as they're pictured in the ad. So I had to shoot each of the three groups of items separately.

"The main background shot is the TV against a plain wall with this kind of skylight lighting (14.18). That's relatively a straight shot — I may have gone in there and experimented a little bit with the gradations. Then, I propped the potatoes against a little model of a sofa (14.19). The pattern on the sofa is even miniaturized so that the flowers look the same relative size as they would on a real sofa.

14.17

14.18

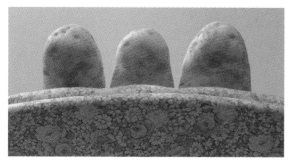

14.19

"I had to play with the light so that the potatoes cast the same shadows as the TV, despite their smaller size. This was largely a matter of bringing the lights in closer and adjusting the intensity. I also included a little blue light down in front so it looked like a glow was coming from the TV. You can see that the blue glow doesn't exactly match the blue from the TV screen — it's a little more purple — but I was able to correct that when I composited the images in Photoshop (14.20). The light was really just a color cue so I could see how a cool glow would reflect off the potato bodies.

"Then, I needed the beanie for the baby spud, the pearls for Mom, and the glasses and pipe for Dad (14.21). I shot two pipes because the art director couldn't decide which one he wanted to use. There was also a discussion about whether we should add earrings to the side of Mom, so the mannequin actually has a couple of earrings stuck to her head. As usual, I had to adjust the lighting, including bringing the blue glow in from the left side. That sheet next to the mannequin is there to reflect the glow onto the beanie. Then, I shot it all to a single piece of film to keep the scanning to a minimum.

"The one element that's strictly digital is the smoke coming off the pipe (14.22). I added the smoke inside Photoshop by airbrushing with a small brush and light Exposure settings. I believe I split the pipe and glasses onto separate layers and then added the smoke on another layer in between the two. That way, I could erase the smoke and adjust the Opacity without harming any of my original elements.

"My one big conceptual contribution was to put a bowl of potato chips on top of the TV (14.23). The art director loved that. But then, somebody actually wrote the company to complain about the suggestion of cannibalism." Either it's a tuber-based homage to *Soylent Green*, or these are some very sick taters.

14.20

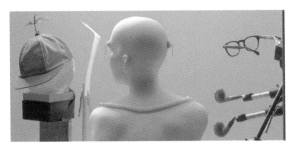

14.21

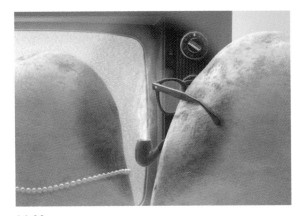

14.22

14.23

14.24

14.25

14.26

REFLECTIONS AND REFRACTIONS

According to Schewe, glass and water are some of the hardest substances to photograph. "Because of the way they reflect and refract the elements around them, you have to be very careful with your lighting." Things become even more complicated in the compositing phase. Any time you position an element near glass or water, you duplicate and distort the element to account for reflecting and refracting.

Schewe's snowglobe artwork is an example of just how difficult the process can get. "The concept was to take a snowglobe filled with a little snowy golf scene and then composite it against a stock photo of a golf course (14.24). Again, we have an issue of scale — an enlarged globe against a reduced background — but the more complex task is the globe itself. I guess I could have built a little golf scene inside the globe, kind of like a ship in a bottle. But I doubt that would have given me enough control over the lighting and refraction. For me, it was easier to photograph the pieces and glue them together inside Photoshop."

WITH AND WITHOUT FLAKES

"I started by shooting a snowglobe on a stand, under what appeared to be hard outdoor light (14.25). I set the globe against a green background with a blue overhead to simulate the general appearance of grass and sky. The globe had a rubber stopper at the bottom of it so I could empty the water and fill it up again. After shooting it empty, I took several shots of the globe with the snow floating around inside it (14.26). Interestingly enough, to get the amount of snow I wanted, I had to break open three small Jesus snowglobes and steal the snowflakes from them."

Schewe modeled the contents of the globe from scratch (14.27). "I contoured the base out of foam and coated it with fake snow. The miniature trees came from a model train set. I painted a long thin dowel to make the flagpole, then I added a piece of red tape for the flag."

INNER AND OUTER REFRACTIONS

Having photographed his raw materials, Schewe began to assemble them in a layered Photoshop file. "I started by masking away the background behind my snowy golf scene. Then, I used Filter ➤ Distort ➤ Spherize to warp the scene around the globe (14.28)." Schewe spent some time examining the way a globe refracts light to get his layers just right. "A glass ball is a curious thing. It bulges elements inside it, but it flips and pinches the stuff behind it. If you look at the original globe shot (14.25), you'll notice a layer of blue along the bottom of the glass. That blue is actually hovering a few feet above the frame." Peering through two surfaces of curved glass — one concave, the other convex — turns the world upside-down.

"To get this effect, I selected a portion of the stock photo background, rotated it 180 degrees, and then applied Filter ➤ Distort ➤ Pinch two or three times in a row (14.29). I think I also used Spherize with a negative setting a couple of times to give it some roundness. After that, I added my spherized golf scene (14.30). Since it's just behind one layer of glass, it appears rightside up."

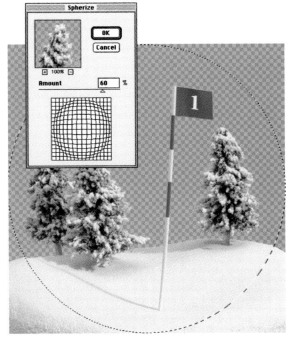

14.28

14.29   **14.30**

14.27

REINSTATING THE REFLECTIONS

By this point, Schewe had covered up the reflections from the original globe, which diminished much of the realism of the image. To restore the reflections, he selected some of the highlights from the base globe layer and duplicated them onto a new layer.

"The best selection tool for this purpose is Select ➤ Color Range. The Color Range command has a great inclusion/exclusion capability, but it's global — that is, it selects colors from all over the image that fall inside the range. So, when I use Color Range, I make three passes. With the same colors selected, I'll run high, medium, and low Fuzziness values. I'll save each selection to a separate channel. Then, I'll combine elements from each of those channels to create the final mask."

After arriving at a satisfactory mask, Schewe selected the highlights — which we've set against black to make them easier to see (14.31) — and copied them to a new layer, which he dragged to the top of the stack. Then, he selected Lighten from the blend mode pop-up menu in the Layers palette, which instructed Photoshop to hide any pixels in the reflection layer that were darker than the pixels below. The result was a universally lightening effect (14.32).

SPRINKLING THE SNOWFLAKES

The last step was to add the floating snowflakes. "The snowflakes needed to be in front of the trees and pinched background, so I had to select them from the snowflake shot and composite them on top." Again, Schewe selected the flakes with the Color Range command (14.33). Then, he pasted the flakes on top of the composition (14.34). "The interesting thing here is that the flakes already had reflections built into them, because I photographed them inside the globe. So it didn't matter if I stacked them on top of the reflection layer or underneath; either way, it looked the same."

MERGING PASSION AND PROFIT

In the periodic skirmishes between photographers and digital artists, Schewe manages to occupy both fronts. It's a lucky thing, too, because his photography gives him a clear advantage over artists who depend on stock images. "One of the things I try to emphasize is that you just can't take disparate images, jam them together in Photoshop, and expect them to be convincing. You can be really skilled and create an interesting montage, but you'll never achieve realism. It's the difference between a photographic marriage and a digital relationship."

Schewe manages to marry image capture and image manipulation so seamlessly (14.35, 14.36) that you'd swear there was never any doubt in his mind that he wanted to be a digital artist. But in truth, his transition to computers had as much to do with maintaining his livelihood as following his creative passions. At the risk of sounding crass, Photoshop is where the money is.

"Right about the time Photoshop came out, I had a couple of jobs where the computer imaging paid twice as much as I made for the photography. It was immediately clear to me that these computer people were taking a big chunk of the overall production pie."

Schewe did what any enterprising photographer would do. After quickly assessing that there was no beating 'em, he joined 'em. "I rented a Macintosh IIci (roughly equivalent to a 386 PC) and spent the weekend doing a job and learning Photoshop at the same time. I picked up the computer Friday night, and I

14.31

14.32

14.33

14.34

had the job done Monday morning. My wife came in and found me asleep at the keyboard.

"The final piece was output to 4 × 5 film, and the client was tickled to death. At that time, I charged just about what it cost me to rent the computer for the imaging. It was definitely a valuable way to start out." Schewe has been evolving his craft on the job ever since.

14.36

14.35

CHAPTER 15
FASHION PHOTOGRAPHY

Many photography students dream of being a famous fashion photographer — travel, beautiful models, great clothes, working with an international clientele. Does it get any better than that? We asked fashion photographer Werner Pawlok. "After twenty years, I am finally able to do the jobs that I dreamed about at the start of my career. When I first started out, I learned about lighting, design, darkroom processes, and special effects from the ground up. It seems that a lot of photographers are dabbling in digital imaging. But for me, learning traditional photo-compositing with in-camera masking and registration easels first helped me to understand and work with digital imaging tools and techniques. Most importantly, I can decide when to solve a visual problem traditionally and when it is better to work with Photoshop to get the effect that I want."

Equally at home shooting in Barcelona (15.1) or Manhattan, Pawlok is an award-winning photographer whose fashion, editorial, and personal projects have literally spanned the globe through exhibitions and magazine assignments. He is a sought-after professional who works with an awe-inspiring client list: Mercedes-Benz, Kodak (15.2), Nike (15.3), Jockey, Colgate, Palmolive, Sony (15.4), Absolut, and BMW, to name a few. "Our clients come to us because they like our work and want us to create a complete look for them. We do everything from concept development to selecting the art director, casting the models, finding locations, testing film stock, digital compositing, retouching, page layout, and going to press. I like to think of myself as a communications mediator, someone who is comfortable working in both still and motion imaging from concept to finished product — it's all exciting to me!"

Our work is divided into three parts — concept, photography, and digital imaging — and the three parts have an equal impact on the success of a job.

WERNER PAWLOK

15.1

213

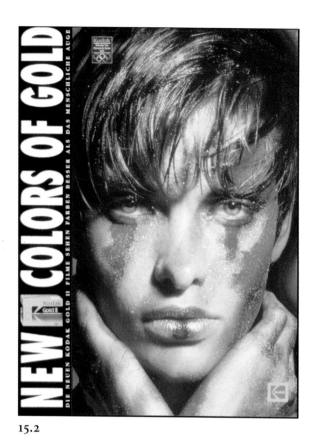

15.2

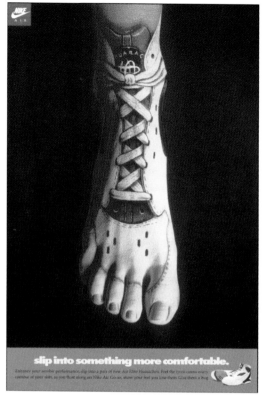

15.3

ARTIST:

Werner Pawlok

ORGANIZATION:

Studio Werner Pawlok
Neue Weinsteige 67A
D-70180 Stuttgart, Germany
(phone) 01149/711 16 49 970
(fax) 01149/711 16 49 975
http://www.pawlok.com
werner@pawlok.com

SYSTEM:

PowerPC 300 G3
Mac OS 8.1
6GB storage

RAM:

192MB total
160MB assigned to Photoshop

MONITOR:

Sony 21-inch

EXTRAS:

Microtech ScanMaker III, Epson Stylus
Color 1520, Polaroid PCD 2000 digital
camera, Leonardo Card for ISDN file
transfer

VERSION USED:

Photoshop 5.0

15.4

CONCEPT, PHOTOGRAPHY, DIGITAL IMAGING

"Our work is divided into three parts — concept, photography, and digital imaging — and the three parts have an equal impact on the success of a job. We plan the photo shoot knowing that the image will be digitally manipulated later on. For example, when we plan a shot with digital in mind, we pay close attention to the selection of film stock and lighting and how that will look when the image is scanned, enhanced, and printed. Making those fundamental decisions at the start of a photo shoot really makes the digital part of the work a lot easier. The more that we take the digital part of the job into consideration, the less redos we will have and the better the final product will be."

Pawlok has been working with digital imaging since the mid '80s when images were enhanced on dedicated, high-end work stations such as the Kodak Premier System. "As photography becomes more entwined with digital technology, being a good photographer, managing a successful studio, and being a digital imaging expert is nearly impossible. Although I do have quite a bit of experience with digital imaging and Photoshop, I also work with a local company named RECOM that does a lot of the high-resolution imaging that is required for our fashion spreads, as seen in *Vogue*, *Mademoiselle*, *Details*, and *GQ* magazines. Collaborating with RECOM allows me to concentrate on concept, photographic execution, and directing. I collaborate very closely with them in both my professional and personal work."

NAILING THE CONCEPT

Developing the concept for a new advertisement campaign can be a sleepless endeavor, as client wishes and budget realities often don't agree. "For example, one of our fashion clients, Otto Kern, wanted to launch a new line of clothing with an

---

OTHER APPLICATIONS:
QuarkXPress 4.0, DV Tools PPC, Adobe Premiere 5.0

WORK HISTORY:
1977 — First photography studio complete with E-6 and Cibachrome processing.
1978 — Taught photography at the Stuttgart Art Academy.
1980 — Opened an in-house photography gallery.
1984 — Moved to Stuttgart and opened a new modern photography studio.
1984–89 — Clients included Philip Morris, Nike, Eastman Kodak, Mercedes Benz, and numerous fashion companies.
1989 — Polaroid transfer work featured on the cover and inside *Stern Magazine* (1.2 million circulation).
1990s — Exhibitions in New York, Tokyo, Geneva, Frankfurt, and so on. Offers "concept to photography to print" services as a collaborative partner to ad agencies.

FAVORITE GOOD FORTUNE:
"When my luggage is the first off of the plane — guess I've been traveling a bit too much!"

attention-getting series of images. The only problem was their budget was limited and the clothes weren't exactly attention-getting. We had to make the images look modern and the series stand out, so as readers flipped through the magazine pages they would immediately recognize the Otto Kern line of clothing." To solve this problem, Pawlok used a combination of casting, photography, and Photoshop to create an attention-getting fashion campaign. Casting a young urban male model with classically chiseled cheekbones and contrasting feminine lips and hair allowed Pawlok to create different looks with the same person (15.5 and 15.6).

15.5

15.6

CHOOSING THE FILM

"While my studio lined up the models, art director, make-up, and hair stylist, I tested the film and lighting. I wanted to shoot black and white for the entire series and add color with Photoshop to some of the images. Each film type has a certain look and feel that can carry an image if used appropriately. It's much better to get the look and feel (how the film handles contrast and tonal rendition) right during the shoot rather than trying to add film grain or rework lighting later with Photoshop. I always test the lighting, film exposure, and processing, through to the final scan and proof before making my decision about film stock. Once I've decided on a film type, I stick with it. I don't shoot a scene in black and white only to pick up another camera and shoot the scene over again with a different type film. It's all about 'seeing' the final image when I'm still shooting it." For the Otto Kern fashion spread, Pawlok decided to use medium format Agfa Pan 25 black-and-white film with butterfly lighting to mimic the classic Hollywood photography of the '40s (15.7 – 15.10).

SHOOTING FOR DIGITAL

During the photo shoot Pawlok is very aware of the needs of the digital process (15.11). He makes sure that the lighting isn't too "contrasty." If he needs to composite images together, he locks down the camera and the lighting to ensure that both camera position and lighting arrangements remain consistent shot to shot. "When shooting for digital, you have to avoid the temptation to randomly switch your point of view or play around with different lenses, thinking that you can fix anything in Photoshop. I bet that with enough time you probably could fix most mistakes, but the point is that this way of thinking doesn't make any business sense. It's easier to make a good photograph than spend hours in Photoshop making up for sloppy studio work."

15.7

15.8

15.9

15.10

15.11

15.12

15.13

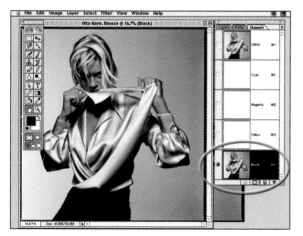

15.14

AFTER THE SHOOT

Once Pawlok is done with the shoot and the film is processed, he does the first edit, which culls out mistakes such as eyes being closed. Simultaneously he does a rough edit for the best images. Then the client or art director does an edit. This leaves Pawlok with approximately 60–80 individual negatives to scan in for digital enhancement and layout. In the studio he uses a Microtech ScanMaker III to do FPO scans. The original film is then sent out to be professionally drum-scanned.

FASHIONABLE PHOTOSHOP

To add color to the black-and-white photos (15.12), Pawlok has developed an intriguing technique that draws the figure out away from the background and makes the final magazine spread seem to jump off the page. Working on the grayscale file, he creates a precise path around the figure, making sure to make a path for any open spaces — for example, between the model's fingers and hair (15.13). He copies the file to the clipboard. Then, he chooses File ≻ New to make a new CMYK image. "As you know, when you copy anything into Photoshop's clipboard, Photoshop will make a new file the exact same size. The detail to pay attention to is that the new file needs to have a white background rather than be transparent." Pawlok pastes the file into the black (K) channel (15.14). When adding color to an image using this method, he works in CMYK in order to keep all the color within the prescribed printer gamut.

Pawlok then drags the path from the original grayscale image to the new CMYK file with the pen tool while pressing ⌘/Ctrl+Option/Alt. This brings the path pieces into the new file in perfect registration. After making the path into a selection, he inverses the selection to select the exact opposite of the model, adds a new layer, and fills this with white (15.15). "By adding the white layer, I am eliminating the film grain from the background, and this will help me to keep the edges clean and abstract the image a bit more without being glaringly obvious."

To create a glowing edge, Pawlok begins by using the Minimum filter to contract the black areas of the layer mask (15.16). He then loads the path as a selection to protect the figure and applies a Gaussian Blur (15.17). "By blurring the edge, I am giving the next filter more tonal information to work with. In this case, I used Alien Skin's Motion Trail filter on the magenta channel to create the yellow glow (15.18)."

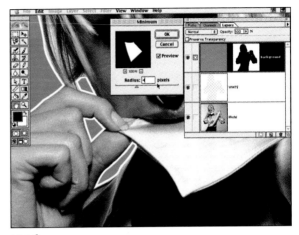

15.16

15.17

15.15

15.18

15.19

15.20

Pawlok had to use the Motion Trail filter twice, in opposite directions, so that the glow was visible on both sides of the model. "Once I have the basic glow down (15.19), I go into the image and add texture to the edges with brushes and the rubber stamp." The final step is to crop the image to the page layout. By adding a slight rotation to the crop, Pawlok makes the image even more dynamic (15.20).

BEAUTY IS PIXEL DEEP

Fashion models are by nature (usually) thin, attractive, and young. Okay, it's not fair that they get three out of three! But even fashion models have their moles, scars, and other slight imperfections — justice is served. Pawlok always works with professional models, hair stylists, and make-up artists, but sometimes even that isn't enough to make the beautiful perfect. "Photoshop lets me take out those slight imperfections that just detract from the image. I don't do a lot of retouching, but every scan needs some clean-up. At the same time I'll take out the mole or scar to give the image the final polish." As seen in this original scan, dust is a problem and the model has a mole on his chest and finger (15.21). The second figure shows the image after color correction, blemish removal, and dust busting (15.22).

15.21

15.22

THE PLEXIGLAS TUNNEL

Pawlok explains a photo session. "We built a Plexiglas tunnel and illuminated it with eight lights from the outside. The models were inside the tunnel or just behind it. One problem with working with Plexi is that it picks up reflections and dust like a magnet. To clean up the whites, I used the pen tool to select the Plexiglas (15.23), made a selection, and added an image adjustment layer with Levels to tighten up the whites (15.24)."

After Pawlok whitened the Plexiglas, he needed to color balance the rest of the image. He loaded the image adjustment mask by ⌘/Ctrl-clicking on the Levels image adjustment layer, inversed the selection, added a new image adjustment layer, and used Selective Color to fine-tune the color. In this case, Pawlok wasn't trying to make the model's skin-tones perfectly neutral. Rather he was balancing the skin tones to the yellow light used in the shot.

15.23

15.24

15.25

15.26

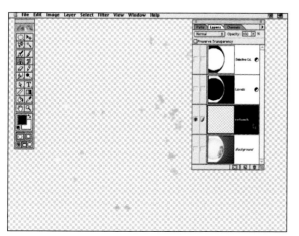

15.27

To retouch blemishes and dust out of an image, Pawlok uses the rubber stamp. More importantly, he does all of the retouching work on a new layer, thereby keeping the retouching separate from the image. "I never work on the original background layer. Also, by keeping the retouching separate, I have more control. If I make a mistake, I can just erase that area and start over." Notice the rubber stamp options are set to Use All Layers (15.25) so that the rubber stamp samples from the layer beneath the empty new layer (15.26). The retouching layer (15.27) shows how Pawlok clones small areas onto a new layer that you will never see once the image is flattened (15.28).

15.28

15.29

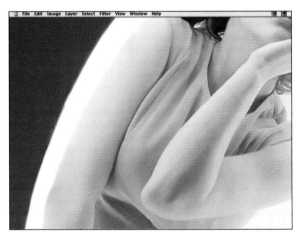

15.30

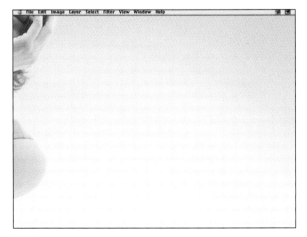

15.31

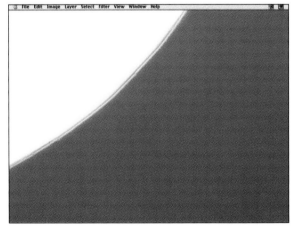

15.32

PHOTOSHOP 5.0 NAVIGATION SHORTCUTS

Photoshop 5.0 has new keyboard shortcuts that move the file exactly one screen at a time, which is very helpful when retouching or dust-busting a file at 100% view. Here are some tips for navigating using an extended keyboard:

- Press the Home key to go to the upper-left corner of the image (15.29).

- Press the Page Down key to go down one screen (15.30).

- Press ⌘/Ctrl+Page Down to move one screen to the right (15.31).

- Press ⌘/Ctrl+Page Up to move one screen to the left.

- Press the End key to go to the bottom righthand corner of the image (15.32).

IMAGE TO LAYOUT

By changing the color gel on the background flash of the Plexiglas tunnel (15.33), Pawlok achieved different colors for each model. He used channel masks to make final color corrections to the skin tones (15.34 and 15.35) and clothing (15.36 and 15.37) as needed. And by rotating the image slightly, he added a dynamic twist to the images that makes them appear to defy gravity ever so slightly (15.38 and 15.39). In

15.35

15.33

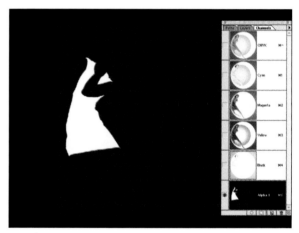

15.36

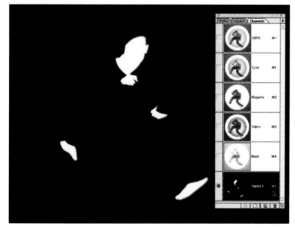

15.34

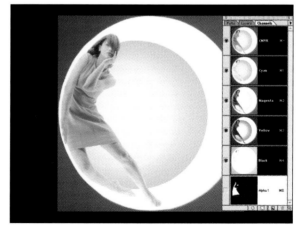

15.37

15.38

15.39

closing Pawlok adds, "I like this series of images a lot. It looks as if the models were dropped in digitally when in reality we photographed them that way. I like to leave the viewer wondering how we achieved a certain effect." The final layout (15.40) is a convoluted journey into the season's fashions that carries the images very well.

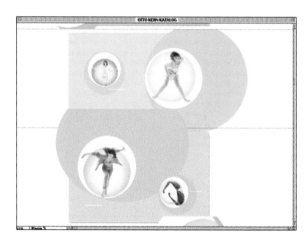

15.40

15.41

PHOTOSHOP OR REALITY?

Some of Pawlok's most attractive work is the seamless compositing he does when the same model appears twice in the image (15.41). "When we do this type of composite work, I can see how my traditional compositing skills and experiences are influencing my digital work. Let me digress for a moment. I've seen a number of photographers become lazy or sloppy in their shooting because they think that they can fix any problem with the computer. In fact, when shooting images that will be composited, it is tremendously important to shoot the images very carefully (15.42 and 15.43) to ensure that the pieces will fit together without having to do a lot of Photoshop manipulation."

15.42

15.43

Planning the shoot is essential. The positions of the models are rehearsed and the set is prepped to mimic the final image (15.44). In this example, Pawlok propped up the model's hand with a cylinder (15.45). In this shot, he rested the model's head on pillows, which will be replaced by the model's own knee in the final composited image (15.46). After finishing the

first shot, he sketched the position of the model onto a piece of acetate attached to the view camera ground glass. Then he locked down the camera stand and lights and used the exact same setup to shoot the second image with the same model in a different piece of clothing.

15.44

15.45

15.46

MASK THIS!

After the shoot the digital compositing work begins. As you can see, the model has very stylized hair with a lot of edge detail. The challenge is to mask out the hair while maintaining the detail. The standard selection tools, such as the magic wand and marquee, rarely allow you to create the transitions required when compositing complex images because they work on edges rather than on transitions. In the following example, Pawlok uses a slick technique to create a hair mask with little effort and, more importantly, without losing the fine hair detail. This technique works best when the hair and background are of contrasting values; for example, dark hair on a light background or blonde hair on a dark background.

PAWLOK'S HAIR MASK TECHNIQUE

Pawlok duplicates the original background layer and fills the background layer with white (15.47). "This gives me a neutral background to view the mask and composite effects later on in the process." Next, he uses the eyedropper to sample a representative color of the background. "If I was working with a light-haired model on a dark background, I would sample the hair — in other words, sample the lighter of the two entities." He adds a new layer on top of the model layer. Then he Option/Alt+Deletes the empty layer with the selected color and sets the layer blend mode to Difference. When using the Difference blend mode, everything that is identical to the layer below turns black and the values that don't match are inversed, relative to their difference (15.48).

15.47

15.48

To accentuate the contrast of the mask to be, Pawlok uses an image adjustment layer with Levels and boosts the contrast slightly — all the time watching that he isn't losing any hair detail (15.49). He then adds a new layer, selects large areas, such as the face, and force fills them with white. He also uses the paint tools to fine-tune the edges of the mask (15.50). Areas that have crisply defined edges, such as the models hands and clothing, are ideal for the pen tool. Did we mention that the pen tool is Pawlok's favorite selection tool (15.51)?

Pawlok loads the path as a selection and then inverses it (15.52), which allows him to paint on the mask with a large black airbrush to clean-up any imperfections. "I don't just force fill with black since this will eat into the edges of the hair."

The challenge is to get the layered mask-in-progress into a layer mask. Pawlok uses a nice workaround to

15.49

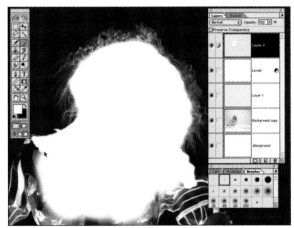

15.50

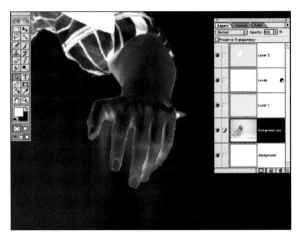

15.51

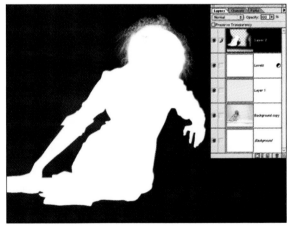

15.52

do just that. First, he selects all and defines the mask-in-progress as a pattern by choosing Edit ➤ Define Pattern (15.53). He then drops down to the layer with the model, adds a layer mask, and fills this with a pattern by choosing Edit ➤ Fill (15.54). Too cool! But wait — Pawlok can't see a change until he turns off the three top production layers to reveal the model against a perfectly white background (15.55). We recommend that you purge the pattern buffer (Edit ➤ Purge ➤ Pattern) after using this technique on large images.

Next, Pawlok drags the new background into the image (15.56). He then fine-tunes the layer mask with a slight Gaussian Blur and Levels (15.57) in order to finesse the edges of the hair to his liking.

15.55

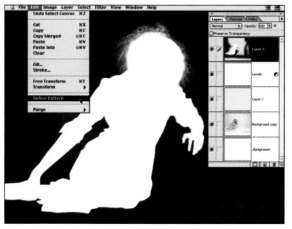

15.53

15.56

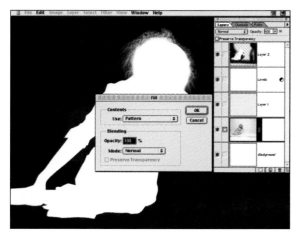

15.54

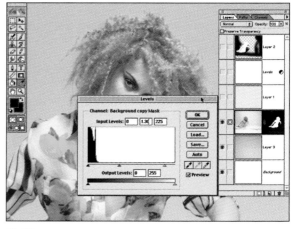

15.57

Here's a close-up of the final image (15.58). Then, Pawlok repeats this masking procedure for the second shot of the model (15.59) and brings her into the image (15.60).

Now the second model's head rests on the first model's knee, making the first model's top hand disappear behind the second model's shoulder. To bring the hand back up front, Pawlok uses the path from the sitting model as a selection (15.61) and creates a layer mask for the lying model with the selection (15.62). By blocking the hand area out with black on

15.60

15.58

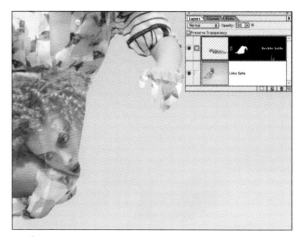

15.61

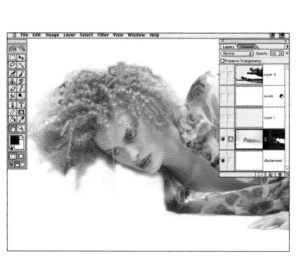

15.59

15.62

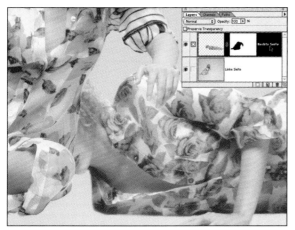

15.63

15.64

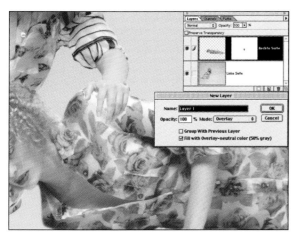

15.65

the layer mask, Pawlok is able to place the disappearing hand on top of the model's shoulder (15.63).

To create subtle shadows, Pawlok adds a layer filled with 50 percent neutral gray and set to Overlay (15.64). He can then dodge or burn on this layer without affecting the image information of the layer below (15.65). Once again, working on a separate layer gives Pawlok much more control in fine-tuning the tonal value of the image (15.66).

A BEAUTIFUL CHALLENGE

Working with the beauty, fashion, and cosmetic industries is one of the most challenging fields in photography today, and Pawlok faces those challenges everyday all around the world. "As I said, I am doing the dream jobs that kept me up late at night twenty years ago. Working with beauty and fashion is exciting and exhausting at the same time. To balance out this demanding and precise work, I work with Polaroid transfers, projections, and painting on prints in my personal work. It is completely different and I need that juxtaposition to stay sharp and interested in the studio's professional work."

15.66

CHAPTER 16
CREATIVE QUICKTIME VR

The physics of photography use optics and light-sensitive materials to fix the three-dimensional world onto a two-dimensional surface that reflects a fixed point of view at a specific moment in time. But wait, photography is more than a physical reaction of light hitting silver. The art of photography includes the photographer's interpretation and the craftsmanship that polishes the initial exposure into a final piece. How does a photographer decide when to take a picture that reflects the mood of a scene? Is one picture enough to convey the atmosphere or to tell the whole story? Many times it isn't, and if you have ever looked at a photograph and wanted to see more or wondered what was just outside of the frame, then QuickTime Virtual Reality (QTVR) photography will intrigue you, as you view a scene with a 360-degree point of view, zooming in on details or moving back to see the bigger picture.

Developed by Apple Computer and released in 1995, QuickTime VR enables photographers, artists, Web designers, museum directors, real estate professionals, forensic experts, and others to take pictures with standard 35mm cameras or digital cameras and then stitch the images to create panoramic scenes that place the viewer in the middle of a 360-degree image. But isn't this book about Photoshop and not about dry definitions of photography and the history of Apple Computer software development? Yes, and this is exactly where Janie Fitzgerald enters the scene. Fitzgerald is a photographer and digital imaging artist who has been working with QTVR since before Apple launched it to the public in May of 1995. In fact, her tutor was an Apple engineer who helped

Now that QTVR is cross-platform and the files are small enough to be used on the Web, the only limitations are the ones that we give ourselves.

JANIE FITZGERALD

develop the technology, and she helped show the engineers what an artist could do with the tools. As Fitzgerald explains, "When I saw QTVR for the first time I was excited and intrigued. I went to every presentation that Apple gave, trying to figure out how they did it and how I could shoot VR photography. When Apple Computer finally gave me the specifications for how to shoot for QTVR, I went to Louisiana and shot dozens of scenes without even knowing what the next step was going to be. When I came back, I showed them my prints that I had taped together and soon after this, the QTVR software was released. I've been shooting QTVR photography ever since."

QTVR AND THE PHOTOGRAPHER

"I have always loved taking pictures. Working with QTVR photography is interesting because I can show the viewer much more of the scene. QTVR is a blend of still imagery and motion pictures. The uniqueness is that it's nonlinear, suspending the sensation of time. It does this by giving viewers the choice to look not only where they want but when they want." An excellent example of how working with and viewing QTVR adds to the art of photography is one of Fitzgerald's early pieces. The opening scene of a New Orleans dress shop window (16.1) is reminiscent of Jean Atget's (1857–1927) body of work, which documents the empty streets, shop windows, and parks of Paris at the turn of the century. Fitzgerald's store window reminds viewers of earlier, idealized times. As you pan to the right you see more information (16.2),

and the meaning and interpretation of the image changes dramatically as you zoom in on the art that is for sale (16.3 and 16.4).

FITZGERALD'S COMMERCIAL WORK

Fitzgerald specializes in panoramic and interactive panoramic QTVR. Her commercial clients include Apple Computer, Eastman Kodak, Dodger Stadium (16.5), and the *Los Angeles Times*, for whom she recently shot the QTVR to accompany an article about the Catholic Missions near Los Angeles.

16.1

16.2

ARTIST:
Janie Fitzgerald

ORGANIZATION:
Axis Images
P.O. Box 381195
Los Angeles, California 90038
http://www.axisimages.com
janie@axisimages.com

SYSTEM:
Power Mac 8500/180
Mac OS 8.1
8GB storage

RAM:
112MB total
60MB assigned to Photoshop

MONITOR:
Apple 21-inch

EXTRAS:
Wacom 6 x 9 ArtPad
CD Writer
QS-8 Audio Synthesizer
Epson Stylus Photo EX printer

**PHOTOGRAPHY EQUIPMENT
FOR QTVR:**
Nikon 35mm with 15mm, 18mm, 20mm, 24mm, and 28mm lenses

16.3

16.4

> **NOTE**
>
> All of the QTVR movies in this chapter are included on the CD-ROM at the back of this book.

16.5

PeaceRiver 360 Panhead
Kaidan Magellan 2000 Object Rig
Kodak DC210 digital camera

VERSION USED:
Photoshop 5.0

OTHER APPLICATIONS:
Apple QTVR Authoring Studio, Sumware ConVRter shareware

WORK HISTORY:
1980s — Worked in a 3D animation studio.
1987 — Branched off into photography.
1992 — Opened portrait studio in Los Angeles.

1994 — Went to a party at the American Film Institute for the launch of Apple QuickTime 2.0, "where I saw the first QTVR movies and I knew that this was exactly what I wanted to do."
1995 — QTVR 1.0 released. Shot first QTVR photographs in the swamps of Louisiana. Shot and made QTVR movies of Yosemite National Park and Bath, England.
1996 — Shot and made QTVR movies for the television programs "ER," "Lois & Clark," "Friends," and "Babylon 5."

1996 — Shot and made multinode QTVR for the Hardrock Café, Las Vegas, for Web and CD-ROM distribution.
1997 — Photographed "Batman & Robin" movie set for Warner Brothers and Apple Computer. Launched *www.vrview.com*, a site dedicated to the artistic uses of QTVR, sponsored by Apple Computer and the Eastman Kodak Company.

Notice that you have the choice to view a high-resolution (400K) or a low-resolution (100K) version, depending on your connection, patience, and need for quality (16.6). With a 28.8 modem the high-resolution QTVR files take approximately 2½ minutes to fully download into browser cache and the low-resolution version comes in well under a minute. Interestingly enough, the entire file doesn't need to download before the you can begin to pan around the image. You can choose to see the inside (16.7 and 16.8) or the outside of the Mission (16.9 and 16.10). For the Hard Rock Café, Fitzgerald shot dozens of

16.6

16.8

16.7

16.9

16.10

scenes and created a multinode QTVR movie. By clicking on hot spots linked to additional QTVR movies, the viewer can move from scene to scene (16.11–16.14).

16.11

16.13

16.12

16.14

16.15

16.16

16.17

FITZGERALD'S PERSONAL WORK

Some of Fitzgerald's personal work reflects a sharp sense of humor and interpretation that takes the viewer by surprise as huge bugs come into the scene. In the QTVR movie *Island*, a collaborative project with artist Robert West, the artists hot-glued plastic bugs to flowers that Fitzgerald photographed in her studio with blue screen to assist in the masking and selection process. The background image is the "bug's eye" view of a gas station. Fitzgerald used Photoshop (16.15) to layout the images against one another and Apple QTVR Authoring Studio to make the final movie (16.16 and 16.17).

In some of Fitzgerald's other personal work, the image becomes so abstract that you feel as if you are seeing into her mind's eye (16.18 and 16.19).

16.18

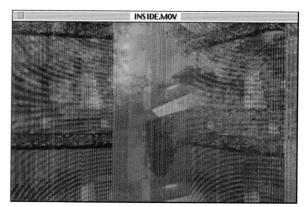

16.19

"Most people think that you have to shoot original photography to make a QTVR movie, but I love to rework my older photographs with Photoshop to create new images for QTVR." In this example, Fitzgerald reworked an original collage (16.20) into a QTVR movie to create an image that is more effective with motion than the still image was alone (16.21 and 16.22).

THE VRVIEW WEB SITE

In addition to doing commercial work and developing a large body of personal work, Fitzgerald also designed and maintains *www.vrview.com*, a Web site dedicated to the artistic exploration of QTVR, featuring the work of numerous international artists (16.23–16.28).

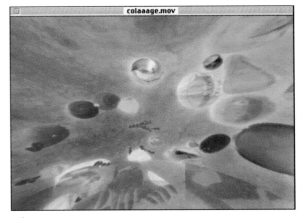

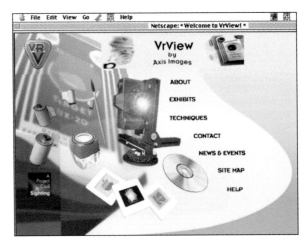

16.22

16.20

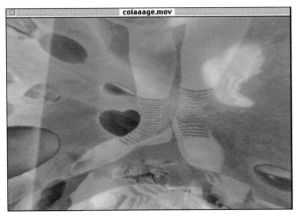

16.21

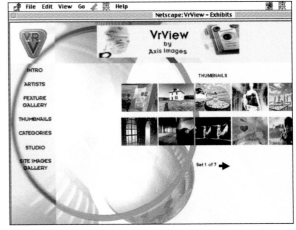

16.23

16.24

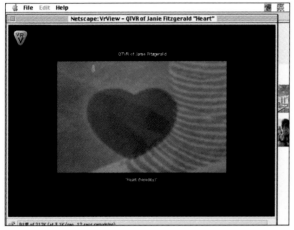

16.25

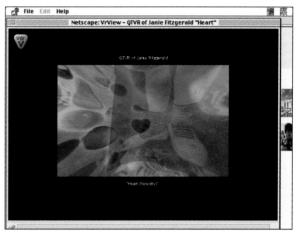

16.26

16.27

16.28

QTVR IN A NUTSHELL

A QTVR panoramic movie begins with the photographer in the center of the environment taking a full set of photos in a 360-degree circle. "Depending on how wide your lens is, you take 12–18 pictures, that overlap by 25–40 percent to complete the 360-degree circle of view." After the film is processed, scanned, and prepped in Photoshop, the individual PICT files (16.29) are brought into Apple QTVR Authoring Studio (16.30) and stitched together to create a single 360-degree image (16.31)." The resulting QTVR

16.29

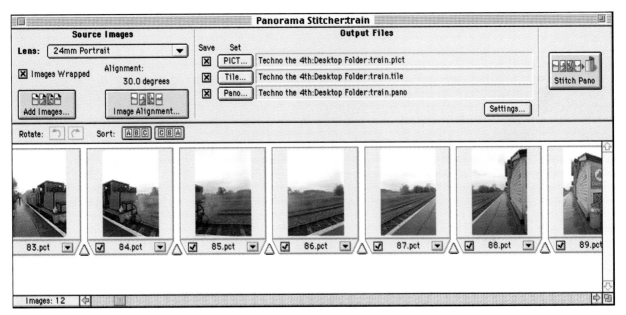

16.30

16.31

16.32

16.33

movie (16.32 and 16.33) makes you feel as if you are standing on the train platform waiting for the train to pull out of the station.

PHOTOGRAPHY FOR QTVR

Shooting photographs for QTVR on location takes a lot of concentration. Fitzgerald does the following things to ensure that she captures the best images:

- Find the best image composition and check that the camera placement, height, and orientation are optimal for the scene. "Shooting in a portrait orientation will give the image better visual height."

- Examine the entire 360-degree scene through the viewfinder and with the lens that will be used for the shoot, concentrating on the foreground to background relationships. QTVR images that have something in the foreground are more interesting and give the viewer a feeling of being in the scene.

- Study the light in the scene. "When working on location with a 15mm lens, it is practically impossible to use flash to light a scene since the lens is so wide. If there are existing lights in a scene, I may exchange the light bulbs for stronger ones and sometimes I use a specialized helium balloon that floats above the camera and holds a light that illuminates the entire room evenly."

- "I use a light meter and work with the camera on manual exposure with the lens stopped down to insure greater depth of field." If the light range varies a lot, Fitzgerald shoots the entire scene once and then with the camera still on the tripod, she pans back and brackets the exposures to take a set of images for the light parts of the image and a set for the dark parts of the image. "I work with color negative film because of its greater exposure latitude in regard to lighting and exposure." After the shoot, the bracketed images are merged in Photoshop to create one set of images that are well exposed for both the highlights and shadows.

■ "It is so easy to forget where you started or if you missed an exposure or not, so concentrating on the task is essential. I can't just go back to a location and reshoot a frame or two if I missed it the first time."

■ Fitzgerald tends to overshoot. It is better to shoot an extra set of exposures or redo a set if there is any doubt that you missed a frame. All professional photographers overshoot because using an extra roll of film is much more efficient (read cheaper) than having to go back to a location and redo an entire shoot because you missed an exposure.

Here are some additional considerations for capturing the best images for stitching:

■ "I work with a panoramic tripod head that can be moved in exact increments, which ensures that each exposure will have the same amount of overlap."

■ Allow for 25–40% overlap between images. This enables the stitching software to create seamless images.

■ Rotate the camera on the nodal point of the lens. The nodal point of the lens is the specific point where light rays intersect on the image plane and the image flips. Aligning the camera on the nodal point will minimize parallax errors that make elements look as if they are sliding in the image when the viewer pans.

■ Photographing the correct number of frames will simplify the stitching process. Tables 16.1 and 16.2 list the most common lens formats for 35mm cameras and digital cameras and how many images to take.

TABLE 16.1 NUMBER OF PHOTOGRAPHS FOR 35MM LENSES

LENS FOCAL LENGTH	PORTRAIT	LANDSCAPE
14mm	12	6
15mm	12	6
16mm	12	6
16mm fisheye	12	4
18mm	12	8
20mm	12	8
24mm	12	8
28mm	18	10
35mm	18	12

TABLE 16.2 NUMBER OF PHOTOGRAPHS FOR CONSUMER DIGITAL CAMERAS

CAMERA	PORTRAIT	LANDSCAPE
Apple QuickTake 200	18	12
Canon PowerShot 600N	12	8
Epson PhotoPC 500	18	14
Fuji DC 300	16	10
Kodak DC-50	18	12
Kodak DC-120	18	12
Kodak DC-210	14	8
Olympus D-200L or D-300L	16	12
Polaroid PCD-2000	18	12

PHOTOSHOP PRODUCTION FOR QTVR

As mentioned earlier, Fitzgerald works with 35mm color negative film. When she has the film processed she does not have prints made and, most importantly, she doesn't have the film cut into strips. "It is much easier to evaluate and find the beginning and end of a panoramic shoot if the film is left intact." After the film is processed, she has the required files scanned onto a Kodak Photo CD Master disk. A Photo CD scan comes in five different resolutions. Fitzgerald uses the 768 × 512 or 1536 × 1024 files for her QTVR work. "I like working with the larger files, since they have more image information and I can do finer retouching and correction with them." The wider your lens, the fewer pictures you have to take and the fewer images you will be stitching together, which will be reflected in a smaller stitched file, as seen in Table 16.3.

TABLE 16.3 PHOTO CD RESOLUTION CHOICES

RESOLUTION	INDIVIDUAL FILE SIZE	STITCHED FILE	MOVIE SIZE
768 x 512 (medium resolution)	1.1MB	5–7MB	500–600K
1536 x 1024 (high resolution)	4.5MB	20–25MB	1–2MB

After acquiring the individual files in Photoshop, Fitzgerald retouches the files and matches the exposures using image adjustment layers. "The stitching software can balance out slight differences of exposure, but prepping the files in Photoshop before stitching helps the stitching software to build scenes that don't have obvious seams."

After bringing the individual files into Apple QTVR Authoring Studio, Fitzgerald stitches the files to produce a movie and a PICT file (16.34). She opens the

PICT file in Photoshop and fine-tunes the color balance with an image adjustment layer (16.35) and masking (16.36). She then imports the improved PICT file back into Apple QTVR Authoring Studio's Panorama Maker and stitches a new panoramic

16.34

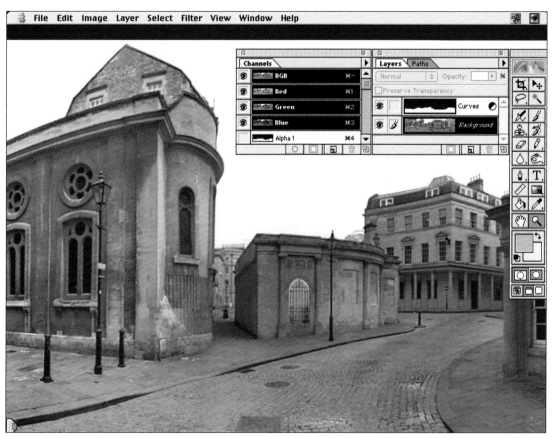

16.35

QTVR movie. Fitzgerald also reworks straightforward PICT files, as seen in this example of the Salk Institute (16.37 and 16.38) and the resulting movie (16.39 and 16.40).

16.36

16.37

16.38

16.39

16.40

PROPORTION AND COLOR

In some of her work, Fitzgerald uses Photoshop to build QTVR spaces that seem familiar yet have an unsettling perspective. "I have a lot of photographs that I shot before QTVR and I use Photoshop to rework them to build QTVR movies." In *Chained Home*, Fitzgerald started with an accidental double-exposure (16.41) and used Photoshop to stretch and tone the image before stitching it.

The most important thing to remember when creating original files for QTVR or when resizing existing files is to make sure the file's pixel width is divisible by 24 and the pixel height dimension is divisible by 96 (16.42 and 16.43). "The stitching process actually slices the image into 12 or 24 tiles, so making sure that the file's width and height follows the 24/96 rule will prevent any problems in the final part of the process.

16.41

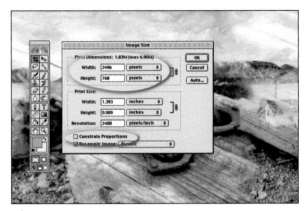

16.42

16.43

"When experimenting with the KPT 3.0 filters, I work on an empty new layer until I find a combination that I like. By keeping the effects on a separate layer I can experiment without affecting the original background layer (16.44)." The curvature of the final movie adds to the sense of space and distance in the scene (16.45).

To add color to black and white and/or infrared photography (16.46), Fitzgerald also uses the duotone feature in Photoshop. In Photoshop 5.0, duotones can be previewed. Fitzgerald experiments with tritones and quadtones to give her infrared images

16.44

16.45

16.46

subtle color palettes that look like finely toned black-and-white gallery prints (16.47). "I don't have to worry about ink sets or if the image will reproduce on paper since my final output is the monitor."

To add the finishing touches to the infrared scenes, Fitzgerald uses QTVR Authoring Studio to determine where a viewer will start when he or she opens the

QTVR file for the first time. When working with an individual PICT file, she imports the image into the Panorama Maker in QTVR Authoring Studio (16.48). After clicking on Make Pano, a preview window appears that enables her to visually determine where the movie will open to in the image (16.49). By having the opening scene zoomed in on the cross,

16.47

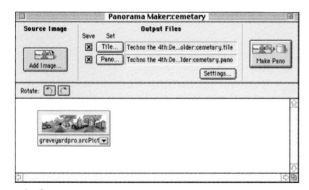

16.48

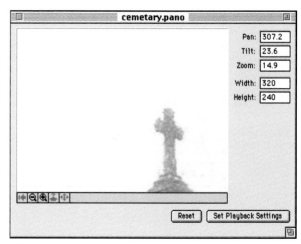

16.49

the viewer is taken by surprise and needs to take a moment to zoom out of the image to become oriented and see that they are "standing" in a graveyard (16.50 – 16.52).

Fitzgerald explains, "I work with QTVR because it is a fascinating way to look at an environment or to tell a story. I hope that my images inspire a sense of wonder." In these desert scenes, the use of infrared film and heavy toning add to the oppressive yet seductive atmosphere in the image (16.53). The fact that the movie opens right on top of a cactus adds to the discomfort portrayed in the scene (16.54).

16.52

16.50

16.53

16.54

16.51

IMAGINARY SPACES

QTVR is often used to document the real world, but Fitzgerald likes to create unusual worlds that don't exist anywhere in reality. In one example, she took beautiful macro shots of roses and used Photoshop to combine them into a long PICT file (16.55) that, when stitched, gives the viewer a decadent bug's eye view of a lush rose garden (16.56 and 16.57). "Everyone thinks

16.55

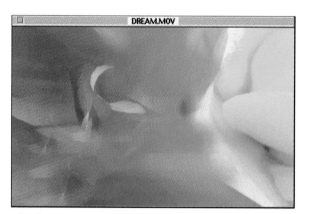

16.56

16.57

that you have to start with a set number of photographs to do QTVR, but I love to experiment with disparate images just to see what I'm going to get."

In the *Malibu* piece (16.58), Fitzgerald combined dozens of images together to create a final PICT file that is 384 x 11,136 pixels. When you pan through the image, there's no discernable beginning or end. "I wanted that effect since this piece is a combination of some of my memories of Malibu and as the images go in and out of focus, you can feel how memories differ yet fit together as they fade in and out (16.59 – 16.61)."

16.58

16.59

16.60

16.61

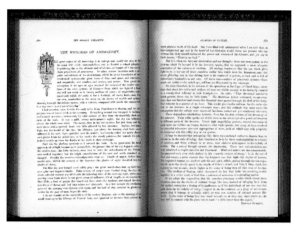

16.62

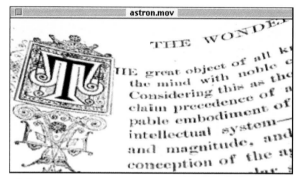

16.63

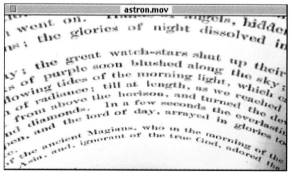

16.64

NOT JUST PHOTOGRAPHS

Fitzgerald creates QTVR from photographs, sketches, direct scans, and even corrupted files. For the Ingrid project, she scanned in an antique book about astronomy (16.62) and then output the file into a QTVR movie. "In the authoring software, I can determine where the viewer will start the movie. And by zooming all the way into the text, it seems as if the viewer is very small, like Alice in Wonderland, and the book is huge (16.63 and 16.64)."

Another great example of experimenting and learning from what went wrong is the QTVR movie *The Maze*. As Janie explains, "I was batch-processing a number of VR files and when I came back, they were all garbled. I backtracked and found that I had accidentally allocated ten times more memory to the stitching software than was physically in the machine. Rather than throwing all the files away, I used them to build images that have an optical illusion that I find fascinating (16.65–16.67)."

16.65

16.66

16.67

VIRTUAL GALLERIES

To create imaginary galleries for her work, Fitzgerald often starts with existing VR movies and uses them as templates to create an abstract gallery. "I shot a VR (16.68) of my studio and traced the lines of the walls and placement of the window to create a space that is architecturally correct, yet abstract." By using the Offset filter (16.69), she can position the window and see if the stitching process is going to leave an unseemly seam (16.70). "By using the offset filter to check how an image is going to wrap, I can prevent any problems with some cloning before stitching the file."

16.68

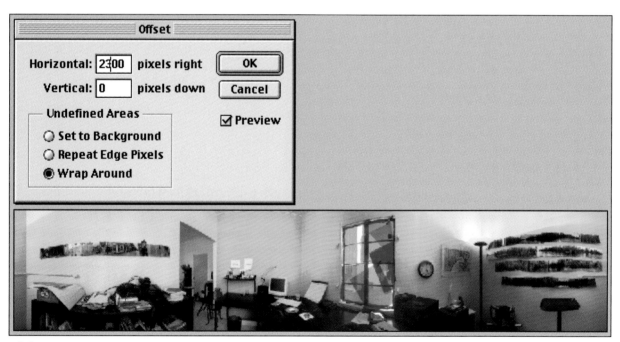

16.69

16.70

Fitzgerald built a gallery for the photo-journalistic work that she did after the Los Angeles riots in 1992. "I created a blank white PICT file that was 3936 × 768 pixels in size and pasted the individual files into it. I like the way that the images are warped since it really gives the sense of being in a round room (16.71–16.73)."

FULL CIRCLE

What inspires Fitzgerald's work? "Since working with QTVR, I find myself experiencing environments much differently. I used to be inspired visually either by details, or interesting landscapes, or an image that was hard but cool. But in each case it was always looking in just one direction, which was forward. Now that has changed. I am much more aware of what is all around me, not just what is in front of me. Now that QTVR is cross-platform and the files are small enough to be used on the Web, the only limitations are the ones that we give ourselves."

16.71

16.72

16.73

CHAPTER 17

THE QUICK GUIDE TO DIGITAL CAMERAS

W hether you're a photographer, a commercial artist, or a weekend Photoshop enthusiast, you've probably heard the siren call of direct-to-disk photography. The very idea that you snap an RGB photograph and download it to a hard disk in less time than it takes to drive to your local film developer and ask, "Are my prints ready?" has a certain universal appeal.

In fact, according to electronic photographer and consultant Katrin Eismann, those photographers who haven't yet gone digital can look forward to a complete transformation of their craft. "In the next five years, 80 percent of professional photographers will be involved in some form of digital imaging. That's up from about 30 percent now. Conventional photography as we know it will be a thing of the past very, very soon."

But while the long-term forecast for digital cameras is sunny, the current state of technology is a bit rough and tumble. As with any new and emerging technology, digital cameras are expensive and every device ships with its own laundry list of rewards and penalties. It's no easy matter to decide whether you should bite the bullet and buy now, or wait for things to settle down and hope that you can make a successful transition when the moment is right.

In this chapter, Eismann walks us through the three prevalent issues of digital photography: when to buy, what to look for, and how to edit images in Photoshop once you start snapping pictures. Much as we'd like to think that if you've seen one Photoshop image you've seen them all, digital photography presents its own share of special concerns.

My advice is always: Get the image right in front of the lens and fix as little as possible in Photoshop.

KATRIN EISMANN

IS A DIGITAL CAMERA RIGHT FOR YOU?

Naturally, no photographer wants to trade in a tried-and-true film camera for something that isn't capable of producing at least the same level of quality. So it's important that the new technology measure up to the old. Eismann insists that it does. "If you just want a quick yes or no, then rest assured — the quality is there. Professional-level digital cameras are every bit as good as film, in some cases better."

Eismann photographed this cat (17.1) with a $10,000 Kodak DCS420, one of the least expensive of the professional models. In the magnified view (17.2), you can clearly see individual hairs around the eye and capillaries in the iris. You can even make out a reflection of a house with a silhouette of Eismann shooting the picture.

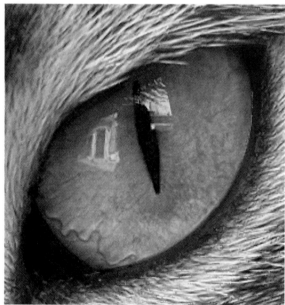

17.1 (TOP), 17.2 (BOTTOM)

The salt shaker (17.3) is the work of a $30,000 Leaf Digital Camera Back II affixed to a Hasselblad ELX camera body. Even when printed at 300 pixels per inch, the image manages to fill the page — and this is just a detail from the full 12MB file. "If I take a 12MB drum scan off a professional piece of film and compare it to a 12MB image shot with the Leaf DCB II, I'll be able to blow up the Leaf image more because there's no grain to get in the way (17.4)."

But while the quality is dreamy, the costs are enough to shock you wide awake. "Granted, you no longer have to pay for film or developing. But a digital camera costs anywhere from a few hundred bucks for a consumer model to $55,000 at the very high end. And that's not including the $10,000 or more for a desktop system required to process these 5MB to 150MB files. I mean, you're not borrowing your kid's IIci. We're talking about enough money to make a down payment on a very nice home."

So the real question is not whether digital measures up to film, but whether it warrants your personal investment. "For every kind of photography, you're going to get a different answer. First you have to determine what photographic niche you fit in, and then you can decide if a digital camera will work for you."

Eismann has identified three major niche criteria — time, quality, and budget. The amount of emphasis you place on each criterion determines what kind of digital camera — if any — will best satisfy your needs.

17.3 (TOP), **17.4** (BOTTOM)

TIME WAITS FOR NO ONE

"As soon as time is an important factor, digital cameras win hands down," Eismann explains. This includes folks who work in news, medicine, government, or any other arena where pictures need to travel quickly. "At the major news services and USA Today, the typical picture deadline for digital files is an hour and a half later than for the guy who's shooting to film. And in the news business, an hour and a half is a major chunk of time."

Just out of curiosity, how do these roving digital journalists transfer their images? "If you're lucky, you have a land line and you use a modem. But most of these guys work with cell phones, which allow them to transmit from buses and even airplanes, as high as 6,000 feet. And in really remote situations, you might find a guy schlepping around a 40-pound satellite dish. But the payoff is that you can transfer 500K in about six to eight minutes."

A MATTER OF QUALITY

A few digital cameras in the $20,000 range can capture more information than film, upward of 35 million pixels. But for the moment, these are scanning cameras which require long exposures — 30 seconds to 12 minutes — and continuous light. "So if you're doing high-quality, display-format photography with live models, you're not going to be working with a scanning camera. In the cosmetic industry, for example, forget it — the model would have to be dead." The exception may be the $55,000 Dicomed BigShot, which quickly captures millions of pixels with an area array. But Eismann isn't prepared to endorse this model. "I'm still hearing very mixed reviews."

But for less demanding product shots — where you can stick inanimate objects under hot lights without anyone complaining — digital cameras can't be beat. "Digital cameras are really taking over the catalog business. Sharper Image, LL Bean, Bon Marché — they're all digital. Ninety percent of catalog images are printed smaller than 8 × 10 inches. So with something like the $22,000 Kodak DCS460 (17.5), you've got it made. The catalogs are produced electronically anyway, so there's just no reason to shoot film."

ARTIST:
Katrin Eismann

COMPANY:
PRAXIS. Digital Solutions
450 7th Street, 4B
Hoboken, NJ 07030
201/659-7378
praxis1@earthlink.net

SYSTEM:
Power Mac 9500/180MP
8GB storage

RAM:
348MB total
300MB assigned to Photoshop

MONITOR:
Mitsubishi Diamond Pro 17TX

OTHER STUFF:
Ergonomic MacTable ("You have to consider your working environment. I've seen people with $15,000 systems using tables from Wal-Mart.")
6 × 9 inch Wacom tablet, and Kodak 8600 Thermal Dye-Sublimation printer

17.5

VERSION USED:
Photoshop 5.0

OTHER APPLICATIONS:
Live Picture, QuarkXPress

WORK HISTORY:
1987 — Following 10-year break after high school, studied fine-art photography at Rochester Institute of Technology.
1991 — First intern at Kodak Center for Creative Imaging in Camden, Maine.

1993 — One of 16 invited artists to participate in international digital imaging show, Montage '93.
1995 — Sponsored by Kodak for eight-country photoimaging tour of Asia.
1999 — Coauthored *Real World Digital Photography*, Peachpit Press.

FAVORITE ROLE MODEL:
Amanda from *Melrose Place* ("She's true to herself . . . well, only herself.")

17.6 (TOP), **17.7** (BOTTOM)

Another quality-related issue to keep in mind is the difference between competing three-shot and one-shot technologies. Both permit you to shoot flash pictures (something the scanning backs don't permit). But where a three-shot camera back captures an image using multiple exposures with red, green, and blue filters, the one-shot camera embeds the filters onto the individual CCD cells. (Incidentally, a CCD is basically the electronic equivalent of film in a digital camera. A huge array of CCD cells — one for each pixel — makes up the imaging surface.) As a result, three-shots are studio cameras ill-suited to moving objects, while the more prevalent one-shots are portable and work like conventional 35mm devices.

But one-shots are not without their failings. "Because you have the RGB filter right on the CCD, you'll often encounter little rainbow patterns in reflective areas and in finely patterned areas such as cloth or hair (17.6). One filtered cell is seeing something that its immediate neighbor does not. With a three-shot, you don't get the rainbows because you're taking full advantage of the resolution of the monochrome array (17.7)." Eismann tells us how to eliminate the one-shot rainbows in Photoshop in the section "Fixing Rainbows" later in this chapter.

If quality isn't important, then you can get by for considerably less money. "For folks who work in documentation, real estate, or insurance (17.8), color and clarity aren't big concerns. If you intend to print the photo on inexpensive paper or post it on the Web, then why even bother with the quality film can offer you?" For these folks, the midrange "megapixel" cameras are ideal. Virtually every major imaging company — Kodak, Olympus, Nikon, Fuji — sells a digital camera that takes pictures with 1024×768 pixels or more for less than $1,000.

THE COST OF DOING BUSINESS

Assessing your financial niche helps you decide if a digital camera fits in your budget. "At the professional level, this is a major business decision. You have to ask yourself, 'What am I saving by investing in this camera?' The obvious answers are film, Polaroid, processing. But more importantly, you're creating a more efficient environment. You're eliminating that delay between shooting the picture and confirming that the job is done so you can move on to another shoot."

So a digital camera may help you squeeze a few additional shoots into your schedule, or it may prevent another business from encroaching on your territory. "You know who's buying the $10,000 cameras right now? The service bureaus, the prepress houses, the professional color labs. They're offering digital photography as an added value." Therefore, the ambitious photographer will need to pay to play. "You ultimately want to get into the digital workflow and start offering retouching and compositing services. The longer you can stay with your image — shoot it, retouch it, composite it, and submit the final image file in CMYK — the longer you will literally be in business."

FILM STILL HAS ITS MERITS

But surely, even a photographer who fits perfectly into a digital niche is going to experience some separation pangs from film. "Oh, there's no doubt. Give me a conventional camera — be it a Nikon or a Hasselblad — and 10 rolls of film, and I can shoot landscapes, portraits, still life, underwater photography — I've got the whole breadth. No digital camera can beat the versatility of conventional film. That's why finding your niche is so important. If you can identify a narrow range of requirements, you're more likely to find a digital camera that suits your needs."

17.8

17.9 (TOP), 17.10 (BOTTOM)

17.11

SELECTING THE BEST CAMERA

Digital cameras are in a rapid state of flux. There are several examples of a vendor introducing and discontinuing a specific model within the same year. So there's no way to create a buyer's guide within the context of this chapter. Computer magazines such as *Macworld, Publish,* and *Digital PhotoWorld* routinely print camera roundups and are better suited to releasing timely recommendations.

That said, Eismann can offer a few general guidelines for evaluating cameras on your own. "Whenever people look at digital cameras, they always ask, 'How big is the file?' The problem is, that's just one of the issues. The other issues — what does the image look like and how does the camera handle — are ultimately more important. If you have to spend too much time editing the images and you don't like working with a camera, then I don't care how big the images are, you're not going to use it. Your investment is just going to sit around and molder on a shelf."

So how do you make sure you'll enjoy using a camera? "When buying a point-and-shoot device, you want to look at the viewfinder." Eismann shot some pictures comparing one of the least expensive cameras ever produced, the $200 Kodak DC20 (17.9), with one of the most expensive rangefinder models, the $3,000 Polaroid PDC-2000 (17.10). She framed both pictures identically, and yet the DC20 shot is mostly hay. "Its viewfinder is just a hole — it's not accurate at all. Here's an example of a camera that's cheap, but what good is it if you can't frame a picture? This is parallax at its worst."

Most rangefinder devices are now adopting color LCD screens (17.11), which can serve as excellent framing aids. But refresh rates vary anywhere from a few frames per second (terrible) to 30 fps (TV quality) or better. And if you're going to use an LCD for live preview, you need lots of juice. "The batteries have to be rechargeable. Some people think this is nit-picking, but wait till you go out in the field and run out of power after half an hour. It can be devastating."

Another consideration is reaction speed. "If you're working with children or animals, having a delay — even one or two seconds — just isn't acceptable." The Polaroid PDC-2000 is an offender here. The camera spends so much time charging its flash that the shutter release may be temporarily inoperable.

"Removable storage is a definite must. This one fellow told me that his camera got digitally constipated. I was like, 'Excuse me, have we met?' But he was right. You have to be able to switch out media when the memory gets full."

For those of you in the market for a professional level camera, there's no substitute for a hands-on inspection. "Before you sink $5,000 or more into a device, make sure to give it the full digital test drive. Most reputable resellers will be happy to visit you in your studio so you can see how the camera performs on your home turf."

SHOOTING AND EDITING YOUR PHOTOS

Much as Eismann appreciates Photoshop, she doesn't recommend it as a panacea for framing and compositional errors. "What I've seen happen when some people get digital cameras is that they'll get lazy. I was out shooting with this one guy and he takes a picture of a model so she looks like she has a telephone pole coming out of her head. He told me, 'Oh, I'll fix that with the rubber stamp.' I was like, 'Wouldn't it be easier to just move over three feet?' My advice is always: Get the image right in front of the lens and fix as little as possible in Photoshop.

"Another thing: When using the low-end cameras, you should make an effort to shoot really graphic subjects. And get in close — no, I mean closer, no I mean *really* close." The chickens bear out Eismann's advice. Deke shot the top group of hens (17.12) with an Olympus D200L, a very good low-end camera in its time. But he made a total mess of the subject by standing five miles away. The two close-up hens (17.13) are much more successful, even though he used a Casio QV-10A, possibly the worst digital camera ever made in terms of picture quality.

17.12 (TOP), **17.13** (BOTTOM)

KATRIN'S LOW-END TIPS

Low-end cameras suffer from pixel shortages, and they spoil what few pixels they have with an excessive dose of compression. So you have to make the best of what little you have to work with when taking the picture. Eismann recommends:

- Get in close so your subject fills the frame.
- Beware of parallax when shooting closer than 3 feet. (If you anticipate doing a lot of close-up work, get a camera with an LCD preview.)
- Avoid fine detail, like leaves, cloth patterns, and so on.
- Avoid high-contrast light. "Don't shoot someone at noon, or he'll have dark shadows on his face like a raccoon."
- If the sunlight does create shadows on your subject, there's an easy way to fix it. "Just turn on the flash. A daylight flash is called a 'fill flash' because it opens up the dark shadows."

ADJUSTING LIGHTING IRREGULARITIES

But even with the best of precautions, pictures will go awry. Eismann shot her fountain boys (17.14) at dusk with a Polaroid PDC-2000 — which despite its shutter release problem, produces excellent midrange images. The subject is close, the detail is smooth, and the lighting is soft. But when Eismann opened the image in Photoshop, she was surprised to see a curious vertical shaft of light running down the middle of the image.

She added a Levels adjustment layer (by ⌘/Ctrl-clicking the page icon at the bottom of the Layers palette). But in lightening the fountain boys, she managed to overlighten the bright shaft. Luckily, every adjustment layer permits a layer mask which you can use to paint away portions of the color correction. Eismann used the gradient tool to create a mask in which the black area mimicked the shaft of light in the photograph (17.15). This involved two strokes of the gradient tool — first white to black and then white to transparent in the opposite direction. (Incidentally, you don't normally see the layer mask;

17.14 (TOP), 17.15 (MIDDLE), 17.16 (BOTTOM)

to make the figure, Deke Option/Alt-clicked the layer mask thumbnail in the Layers palette.)

Finally, Eismann set the blend mode to Screen and set the Opacity to 70 percent (17.16). The effect isn't perfect because the shaft of light is not precisely vertical. But it comes awfully close, especially given how fast you can reproduce these steps. And if you were feeling particular, you could perfect the layer mask by painting in highlights with the airbrush tool.

FIXING RAINBOWS

Earlier, we explained how one-shot cameras can capture unwanted rainbows along the edge of reflective surfaces. The rainbows appear in full bloom in the chrome Marina logo (17.17), which Eismann shot with a Kodak DCS420. Luckily, you can remedy this problem with little effort inside Photoshop.

17.17 (TOP), **17.18** (BOTTOM)

The rainbow is caused by disparity between neighboring pixels. So the solution is to blur the colors slightly and then sharpen the detail, both of which you can accomplish in the Lab mode.

First choose Image ➤ Mode ➤ Lab Color to convert the RGB image to Lab. Then go to the Channels palette and click on the *a* channel. (If you want to preview the effect in color, click in the eyeball column in front of the Lab composite.) Apply the Gaussian Blur filter with a Radius of about 1 pixel for every 1MB of image data. In the case of the 4.5MB Marina logo, Eismann applied a Radius of 3. Then switch to the *b* channel and press ⌘/Ctrl+F to reapply the filter.

So far, all you've affected is the color; the detail is still saved in the luminosity (L) channel. Press ⌘/Ctrl+1 to go to the L channel and choose the Unsharp Mask filter. "I tend to raise the Amount value to 175 percent. And I play with my Radius. Usually it's between 0.75 and 1.5.

"The blurring gets rid of the color artifacting; the sharpening brings out the detail (17.18). Nowadays, I apply this technique to just about every picture I shoot; often there's artifacting that's much more subtle than the rainbows but equally harmful to the appearance of the image. And you can even script this operation from the Actions palette to apply it with a single keystroke in the future."

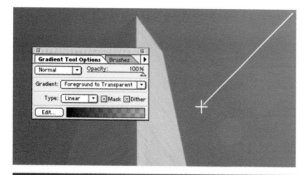

17.19 (TOP), 17.20 (BOTTOM)

SIMPLE BUT SPECIAL EFFECTS

"Every photographer occasionally wants to darken edges or burn down corners, where the edges fade in from black, to help frame the image. To do this, I go into the Layers palette and make an empty layer. I select the gradient tool and set it to Foreground to Transparent. The foreground color is black. Then I drag from a corner about a fifth of the way into the image and let go (17.19). I do that in all four corners. Now, it looks like the image has just gotten ruined. But if I set the blend mode in the Layers palette to Soft Light, I can really control how much I want to burn down those edges. Then I experiment with the Opacity until I get the effect I want (17.20).

"Another way to focus the viewer's attention on the foreground image is to blur the background. In the case of the forks (17.21), the background is a light box with gumdrops on it. I used the pen tool to select the forks and the big gumdrops, then I inversed the selection and applied the Motion Blur filter — not much, maybe 7 or 8 pixels — to give the background a little more dynamic appeal. This also enhances the depth of field, forcing the forks more into the foreground."

KEEPING YOUR PHOTOS SAFE

Eismann offers one last word of advice to photographers making the transition from film. "Archiving may be the most important issue of all for digital photographers. Once again, look at film — it's your capture device, and it's your storage device." There's a good chance that film lasts longer than magnetic media, too. The only electronic media that come close are CDs and MOs (magneto opticals), both of which may endure several decades of use. "I even archive my film shots to Photo CD, because that way, I know I'll use them." What about SyQuest, Zip, or Jaz? "I just use that stuff to transfer files."

17.21

What exactly should you save? "Media is too cheap to cut corners. So save everything. For example, a lot of the high-end cameras will automatically shoot into an archived format, with compressed files arranged neatly in folders. You then acquire the images for editing in Photoshop one picture at a time. I always save back the entire archive. As Leaf, Kodak, and other manufacturers improve their software, I can go back and reacquire the images. It's like reprocessing the images with fresh chemicals."

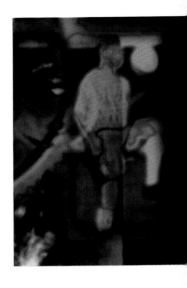

CHAPTER 18
PHOTOSHOP IN MOTION

Nearly everyone who uses Photo-shop dabbles at least occasionally in print media. Many of us also use Photoshop to produce artwork for the Web. But relatively few folks use Photoshop to create images for television or movies. Photoshop is, after all, a still image editor.

Or is it? According to Will Hyde, creative director for some of the most engaging commercials to pop out of your TV set (18.1), Photoshop is an essential ingredient in designing animated text effects and alpha channels for broadcast work. Of course, Photoshop is just one player in a large and expensive game. Products roll and pan with the help of motion-control cameras; compositions render to QuickTime from dedicated editing systems; special effects snap and crackle in Adobe After Effects. But the words and masks emanate from Photoshop. "It's a weird situation. Photoshop isn't the primary program because this is video. But none of it could happen without Photoshop."

If you have a little experience with digital movie editing, you might imagine that Hyde adds frame-by-frame effects by editing Filmstrip files inside Photoshop. Or perhaps he sets up text effects and sends them whizzing across the screen. But as a rule, Hyde's work is more subtle and less predictable. For Nike's rollout for Monica Seles's Air Haze tennis shoe, for example, Hyde assembled layers of text variations inside Photoshop, and then applied moving alpha channels that faded between one layer and the next using After Effects.

It's a weird situation. Photoshop isn't the primary program because this is video. But none of it could happen without Photoshop.

WILL HYDE

Hyde recalls, "Seles is a big Jimi Hendrix fan, so the designers put a guitar on the bottom of the shoe. We used a motion-control camera to shoot the shoe against a green screen. It starts with the guitar in frame (18.2), then the shoe spins away (18.3). Our assignment was to tie Seles to Hendrix. We decided 'Fire' was the common element — the fire of passion."

Inside After Effects, Hyde replaced the green backdrop with scarlet smoke using the Particle Systems filter from KPT Final Effects (18.4). "To emphasize the theme, I wanted to incorporate the fiery, boiling behavior of the smoke into the type itself. It was important that the type wasn't just static but actually morphed into the background. The letters had to look like they're rising from the primordial depths beyond the fire (18.5)." The result is type that flashes and bursts onscreen, like hot gas bubbling through lava. Photoshop provides the gas; After Effects makes it bubble.

18.1

VIDEO IMAGING 101

To get a feel for how Hyde works, it helps to understand a few fundamentals of broadcast design. Not surprisingly, television has different demands than print media. The images don't have to be nearly as big, but there are many more of them. So, where a typical print media artist might struggle with editing and printing a 300-ppi magazine cover, Hyde and other broadcast artists are trying to move that much data every second. It calls for specialized hardware and an equally specialized approach.

PIXELS PER FRAME

A typical video frame contains slightly more pixels than a 13-inch monitor. "Up until fairly recently, we worked at 640 × 480 pixels. Since then, we've moved up to 720 × 540, which is compatible with the D-1 professional broadcast standard."

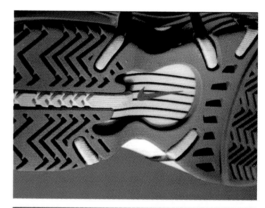

18.2(TOP), 18.3(BOTTOM)

But technically, NTSC handles only 648 × 486 pixels. What's the point of working larger? "First of all, in the D-1 environment, the pixels aren't square, they're rectangular — tall and thin — so you actually have more pixels to work with. Second, when you go from square screen pixels to rectangular D-1 pixels, you never want to get into a position where you're stretching something bigger; you always want to go smaller." Just as in the print world, it's better to start large and sample down.

Hyde is really resolving down to 720 × 486 pixels, which is effectively a compromise between the worlds of computer and TV. "When I work on a 720 × 540 sequence in After Effects, a square is a square and a circle is a circle (18.6). But then, I render out to a QuickTime movie at 720 × 486 pixels, which crunches the height. A square turns into a rectangle and a circle turns into an oval (18.7). The Avid Media Composer doesn't work with QuickTime, so it translates the movie into a native Media file, which uses a resolution called AVR-77. It's still 720 × 486 pixels, but the pixels are a little bit thinner. You're seeing all 720 pixels across the width of the frame, but they fit within the space of 648 pixels (18.8)."

18.4(TOP), 18.5(BOTTOM)

18.6

Artwork by Terry Wakayama

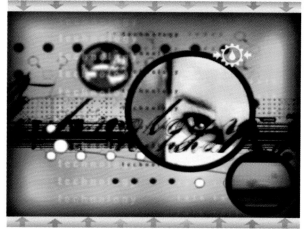

18.7

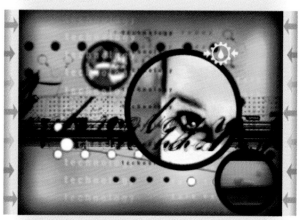

18.8

ARTIST:
Will Hyde

ORGANIZATION:
Pinnacle Post
2334 Elliot Avenue
Seattle, WA 98121
206/443-1000
whyde@pinnaclestudios.com

SYSTEM:
Genesis MP 800 (four 200 MHz processors)
8GB storage (four-drive SledgeHammer array)

RAM:
128MB total
24MB assigned to Photoshop

MONITOR:
Mitsubishi 21-inch

EXTRAS:
Avid Media Composer 1000 nonlinear online editing system

VERSION USED:
Photoshop 4.0

OTHER APPLICATIONS:
Adobe After Effects, Adobe Illustrator, Macromedia FreeHand

REAL-TIME EDITING

Where hardware is concerned, a program such as After Effects makes Photoshop look like the kind of snappy little program you'd stick in a Game Boy. Video editors need hordes of RAM, gobs of hard disk space, and volumes of removable storage. But mostly, they need real-time acceleration.

Think about it — 648 × 486 by 30 frames per second adds up to 27MB of data. You probably think nothing of the fact that Photoshop takes 30 seconds or more to open a 27MB image. But with video, you're asking your hardware to decompress and display 27MB of data one second and get cracking on another 27MB the next. It's enough to make your motherboard shrink in horror.

"Unless you have a specialized set of hardware boards — like the Targa 2000 or the ones that come with the Avid — you can't play back a movie at full resolution and 30 frames per second, even with the fastest machine on earth. I've got a Genesis MP 800 with four CPUs, and I still have to preview my movies at low resolution to see what they look like before I render them at high-res.

"With the Avid, all dissolves, transitions, special effects, and playbacks happen in real time. Say that you're doing a 30-frame dissolve. In a program like Adobe Premiere, that's actually 30 different images with varying levels of transparency. It has to go through and calculate every single frame. With Media Composer, you can perform the effect on the fly. Just tell it, 'I want a 30-frame dissolve' and, bang, it's done."

The Media Composer 1000 is clearly powerful, but it costs about $50,000. What does the video artist on a budget do? "These days, you can get into desktop video with a $5,000 to $10,000 commitment. Anything I'm talking about can be accomplished with a Targa board. You'll have to spend some time rendering, but you'll be able to play and record sequences in real time."

SETTING UP TEXT EFFECTS IN PHOTOSHOP

After Effects is widely regarded as a special effects package, the program you launch after the basic composition is completed. But according to Hyde, it really takes two programs — After Effects and Photoshop — working in tandem. One is the moving extension of the other. "I can switch between Photoshop and After Effects almost effortlessly. File transfer is a cinch, and they both subscribe to many of the same metaphors. The fundamental difference between the two programs is the element of time."

WORK HISTORY:

<u>1988</u> — Used Illustrator to create content for Virginia-based fantasy and science fiction game company.

<u>1991</u> — Graduated from college; hired as art director for *The Stranger*, Seattle's largest weekly newspaper.

<u>1992</u> — Headed up electronic prepress department at commercial printing firm.

<u>1994</u> — Hired as art director at prominent west-coast advertising agency.

<u>1995</u> — Spun off Digital Kitchen, a broadcast design firm.

FAVORITE GROCERY STORE CHAIN:

Piggly Wiggly ("They have the largest selection of chicken gizzards in the continental United States, and no one likes chicken gizzards more than me.")

Photoshop becomes an especially important ingredient when you add type to a movie. "After Effects provides some rudimentary text functions, but they're pretty lame. Sometimes I use Illustrator to create the type, other times I create it in Photoshop. But I always use Photoshop to refine the type and set up the effects."

18.9(TOP), **18.10**(MIDDLE), **18.11**(BOTTOM)

CONVEYING TRANSPARENCY TO AFTER EFFECTS

"In After Effects, you're dealing with a heavily layered image, just as you are in Photoshop. So, your primary concern is the management of transparency. When you take something from Photoshop to After Effects, you need some method to convey transparency. That way, you can layer the Photoshop image on top of moving video and get the two to interact. You can specify transparency in one of two ways: One is to save a flat PICT file with an alpha channel. The other is to create a layered Photoshop file."

The alpha channel is a fourth channel that contains a grayscale mask. Black in the alpha channel represents transparency, white is opaque, and gray represents varying degrees of translucency. "For example, one way to make type is to fill the entire RGB file with the color that you want the type to be (18.9). Then, create your type in the alpha channel (18.10). When you composite the image in After Effects, the actual image content only shows through where there is white in the alpha channel (18.11)."

The alternative is to create your text on an independent layer. This is not only a more intuitive way to work, but it also provides added flexibility. "Every single layer in Photoshop is like a file that has an alpha channel already built into it. It's just that instead of having to create a fourth channel to determine transparency, Photoshop creates the transparency for you. When you bring the native Photoshop file into After Effects, the layers retain the transparency."

It goes even farther than that. The layers you create in Photoshop (18.12) translate intact to After Effects (18.13). "After Effects imports a Photoshop file as a 'composition' element. If you open the composition, you can animate each of the independent layers. Everything's just like it was in Photoshop, including the transfer modes — Normal, Multiply, Overlay, and the rest — whether the eyeball is on or off, and the Opacity setting for the various layers. This means you can do a considerable amount of your design work directly inside Photoshop."

This is not to say that After Effects and Photoshop are 100 percent compatible. "After Effects 3 doesn't support some of the blend modes that were introduced in Photoshop 4. It changes the Color Dodge,

Color Burn, and Exclusion modes to Normal, and it ignores adjustment layers." Adobe claims this problem will be fixed in After Effects 4.0.

"But there is one cool thing about Photoshop 4 that helps a lot. You can have information on a layer that sticks out well beyond the confines of the canvas size. That's great for After Effects because you can import a long string of text inside a narrow image and then pan across it." Even though this "limitless layers" feature — which Adobe calls "big data" — didn't hit Photoshop until version 4, After Effects 3 supports it.

HYDE PREPARES THE HAZE

"The nature of smoke is random and tumbling. To mimic this behavior with type, I set up a layered Photoshop file that contained different iterations of the word 'Air' (18.14), and two others that contained variations on 'Haze' (18.15 and 18.16)." Hyde created the bold and outline effects by stroking the letters in Illustrator. He created the blur effects using the Gaussian Blur and Motion Blur filters in Photoshop. Incidentally, the figures show the words in rows merely so you can distinguish them; in Hyde's original files, each layer was stacked directly in front of another.

18.14

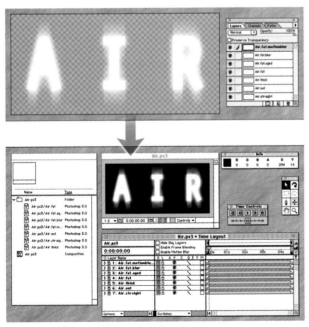

18.12(TOP), **18.13**(BOTTOM)

18.15

18.16

"The next trick was to make the type undulate in and out of the smoky soup. I wanted each layer to appear and disappear almost randomly, like letters in a fog. So, I created a series of fuzzy masks that would move around the type and reveal one layer and hide another, causing the type to pulse."

To accomplish this, Hyde created a series of fuzzy, gelatinous masks (18.17). He made each blob in Photoshop by painting with white inside a black alpha channel. To accommodate After Effects, he saved each alpha channel inside a separate PICT file. Then, he imported the PICT blobs and layered text files into a new After Effects document.

ANIMATING THE TEXT

To create the bubbling type inside After Effects, Hyde employed a technique called *track matting*, which involves the use of moving masks. He placed copies of his blob masks over the top of each of his text layers. Then, he assigned motion to the blobs by setting key frames.

"In After Effects, I can move elements by creating points in a motion path. In the first frame, I click on the little Position clock in the Time Layout window and drag the blob to the location where I want it to start in the preview. Then, I move the timeline marker to a key frame in the animation, and drag the blob to a different location. After Effects automatically connects the two locations with a motion path and gives me handles so I can change the way the path curves. The blob automatically moves along this path (18.18).

"At this point, it looks as if there's just a big blob moving around the screen, which isn't what I want. So, I go to the transfer control pop-menu and tell After Effects to take the alpha channel from the blob file and apply it to the text layer directly beneath it. This automatically hides the blob and applies it as a mask so the text is visible only when the blob passes over it." Because each layer has its own moving blob, the different text treatments appear to throb on and off when the movie is rendered (18.19).

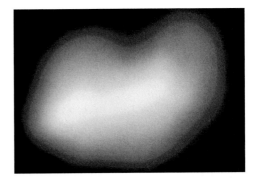

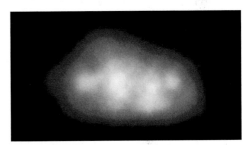

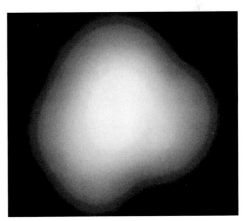

18.17

Obviously this technique requires a fair understanding of After Effects. "It's a weird program to get started with. But there isn't much you have to know to pull off this effect, and after you do it once or twice, it becomes pretty easy. I'm just applying one alpha blob after another to a dozen or so text layers. The point is, the text never moves. The alpha channels are the only items in motion, and they're invisible. It's sort of like moving a bunch of lenses over the image, focusing and warping your view of the text." To see a fragment from the finished commercial in motion, check out the QuickTime movie included on the CD.

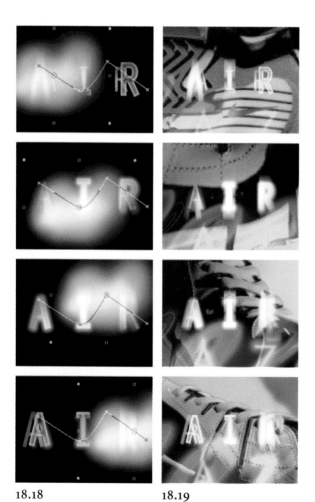

18.18   18.19

ROTOSCOPING WITH MASKS

"These days, most of what I do with Photoshop involves text. I'm basically using Photoshop as a source tool. My trade is typography — most of our work is distinguished by funky type treatments — so I'm preparing my type in Photoshop. But occasionally, I find other uses for the program. Like when I want to rotoscope something."

In the traditional world, rotoscoping is an animation technique that involves hand-tracing individual frames from a movie. A cel animator projects the frame onto a page or other surface, traces it, and shoots the traced images to create a contrived sequence with authentic form and motion.

Hyde is likewise tracing frames, but he's tracing with masks in order to isolate moving elements and superimpose them against a different background.

"In this one commercial, we had to assemble some soccer players and send them running around the Adidas logo. It wasn't feasible to shoot the players against a green screen. These are professional athletes, not tennis shoes. We only needed a few seconds of activity, so it was way easier to lift them out of an actual game.

"I opened a digitized version of a soccer game in After Effects and exported a few seconds worth of frames as individual images. Every frame became a numbered PICT file. Then, I opened the images one at a time in Photoshop (18.20) and traced around the player I wanted to mask inside the quick mask mode (18.21). When I finished, I copied the quick mask to a fourth channel and saved the PICT file."

Masking a hundred or so frames of soccer footage sounds like the sort of tedious activity that might put you off image editing for good. But Hyde claims he didn't waste much time on the project. "Video is extremely forgiving. When you look at a still frame (18.22), you can see the rough edges and maybe even pick out a few mistakes. But with 30 frames whipping by every second, you can't focus on the edges. It's not like someone's going to say, 'Hey, is that a little bit of green next to that guy's foot?' No player is onscreen for more than a couple of seconds.

"When I finished the masks, I imported the images back into After Effects as a PICT sequence, which is just like a QuickTime movie. PICT sequences are really cool because you can trade them back and forth between different programs." Why use a PICT sequence instead of, say, a Filmstrip file? "I don't think any professional uses Filmstrip. What's the point? You have to open up this enormous vertical file in Photoshop just so you can keep all the frames in one file. It's a dumb format.

"The funny thing about this ad is that this guy's kicking in the middle of a field of his teammates, but you'd never know it because I've destroyed them all with a few rotoscoped masks. Through the miracle of digital technology, I can lift a single player and send him moving through a totally different world. Even against an empty black background with some letters flowing through it, the player defines his space by running around it in a natural fashion (18.23). A person watching the ad never thinks for a second that it's real. But it looks cool. And that's pretty much what my job is about."

18.20(TOP), **18.21**(MIDDLE), **18.22**(BOTTOM)   **18.23**

CHAPTER 19
INVENTING PHOTO-REALISTIC WORLDS

E ric Chauvin has a dream job. From his home on the coast of northern Washington, about 45 minutes south of the Canadian border, he creates digital matte paintings for major studio movies and television shows. "I've created the mattes for every episode of *Babylon 5* that has a matte shot in it, with the exception of the original pilot." How did Chauvin land such a cushy client? "While I was working at Industrial Light & Magic (ILM), I was hired to do a single painting for the first regular episode of the show. I created this little 1MB painting entirely in Photoshop on my home computer and then e-mailed it down to the production in Los Angeles. Two weeks later a check arrived in the mail. It couldn't have gone any easier."

While at ILM, Chauvin worked on several feature film projects including *The Mask*, *Forrest Gump*, *Jumangi*, and *The American President*. After three years at ILM, he left to pursue his burgeoning freelance career. "By the end of the first season, I was averaging one painting for every episode. By the end of the second season, I was up to three or four shots per episode. It exponentially increased as the seasons progressed. They've also given me a great deal of creative latitude; very rarely will I turn something in and have them send it back and ask me to make some changes. As far as clients go, they're wonderful people to work with."

For the studio, hiring a talented artist with low overhead has its rewards as well. "Warner Brothers owns and distributes *Babylon 5*, but a team of independent producers really runs the show. They took over a warehouse in Sun Valley, retrofitted it to shoot sound, and built their own sets. Because of that, they can do

I use Photoshop to paint in elements, add shadows and haze, adjust the lighting, and fill in textures. I can take an entirely fabricated 3-D rendering and turn it into something that looks like a real set.

ERIC CHAUVIN

an episode — including all these effects shots — for under a million bucks. For an hour-long sci-fi show, that's a bargain."

From his house, Chauvin has also worked on all three recent *Star Trek* television series, as well as such films as *Sleepers* and the 20th anniversary *Star Wars: Special Edition* trilogy. When we first spoke with Chauvin he was working on the Robert Zemeckis film *Contact*, less than a month away from its scheduled debut. Having already seen three or four previews ourselves, we figured *Contact* would already be in the can. "Oh no, they'll be working on it until the absolute last minute. The shot that's going to kill me is due in seven days.

"I'm really fortunate. I knew at some point I'd be able to break away and work freelance. But I had no idea I'd be able to do it this soon. Almost all my peers have been doing matte painting longer than I have, and they're all very talented. My advantage is really

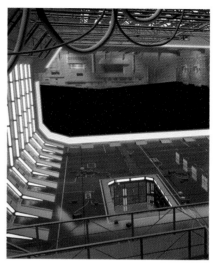

19.1   19.2

                                                                    19.3

THE EMPIRE STRIKES BACK™ *& © Lucasfilm Ltd. (LFL) 1980. All Rights Reserved.*

the computer. Programs like Photoshop have permitted me to be competitively priced, turn out a good product, and do it much quicker than I could if I were using older techniques and materials."

THE BASIC MATTE PROCESS

Up until five years ago, a matte painting was a still background image painted onto glass. But with the help of digital technology, modern mattes are actually short animated sequences that feature tiny people milling about, birds flying through the air, and water cascading over falls. Chauvin creates his digital scenes by constructing a three-dimensional wireframe model in Form•Z (19.1), rendering and sometimes animating elements from ElectricImage (19.2), editing and compositing the still portion of the backdrop in Photoshop (19.3), and putting the whole thing together in After Effects.

"I spend most of my time in Form•Z simply because the modeling is such an intricate process. The rest of my time is pretty evenly split between ElectricImage,

ARTIST:
Eric Chauvin

ORGANIZATION:
BlackPool Studios
P O Box 175
Bow, Washington 98232
360/766-6140
http://www.blackpoolstudios.com
echauvin@sos.net

SYSTEM:
PowerTower Pro 225 (Power Computing)
15GB storage

RAM:
500MB total
125MB assigned to Photoshop

MONITOR:
ViewSonic Pro Series 21-inch PT810 and
15-inch 15ES

EXTRAS:
Radius VideoVision, Exabyte 8mm tape
drive, Polaroid SprintScan, Wacom 9 × 12
inch ArtZ

Photoshop, and After Effects. The Photoshop work is probably the most subtle, but it's also some of the most important. Without Photoshop, the 3-D images would have a synthetic appearance that would immediately brand them as fake. I use Photoshop to paint in elements, add shadows and haze, adjust the lighting, and fill in textures. I can take an entirely fabricated 3-D rendering and turn it into something that looks like a real set."

CAN'T AFFORD THE HIGH-END?

Together, the full versions of Form•Z and ElectricImage cost somewhere in the neighborhood of $6,500, as much as a highly sophisticated computer system. Chauvin saved a little money by splitting the cost of ElectricImage with the producers of *Babylon 5*, but what's a mere mortal with limited means to do?

You could do the same thing Chauvin did when he was first starting out. Not so long ago, Chauvin did all his 3-D work in Specular International's Infini-D, an all-in-one 3-D program for the Mac that runs about $450. "A lot of the early episodes of *Babylon 5* feature mattes that I created in Infini-D. I haven't used Infini-D in about three years now, but I still look back on it fondly. It served my needs at the time, and it gave me the rudimentary knowledge I needed to create images using 3-D tools."

LITTLE IMAGES FOR BIG MOVIES

When you see a spectacular other-worldly landscape projected onto a massive two-story screen, you naturally assume that the resolution of the image must be fantastic. If a magazine cover equates to a 20MB file, a film image must be 10 or 20 times that large. But in fact, Chauvin's images are relatively modest in size. "Different studios have different pixel dimensions that they want you to work in, and they're all very secretive about it. But in general, we're talking in the neighborhood of 2,000 pixels wide × 1,000 pixels or less tall, depending on the aspect ratio of the movie." And because it's film, Chauvin spends all his time in RGB. This means the largest digital frame for a major film such as *Star Wars* weighs in at less than 10MB.

"That doesn't sound like many pixels when you think how big the image appears on screen. But the best you can do is to resolve at the resolution of the film. Even 70mm film stock is relatively small — each frame is less than three inches wide. The resolution we use makes the digital images look every bit as smooth as the live-action stuff." Sometimes too smooth. Occasionally, Chauvin has to add a little bit of noise so that his matte painting matches the graininess of the film.

VERSION USED:
Photoshop 5.0

OTHER APPLICATIONS:
Adobe After Effects, ElectricImage Animation System, Autodessys Form•Z

WORK HISTORY:
1987 — Hired at mortgage company — got so bored he spent most time writing golf statistic program in Lotus 1-2-3.
1989 — Entered graduate school, introduced to ILM matte painter who critiqued his paintings.

1991 — Got job as "glorified brush cleaner" for Steven Spielberg movie *Hook*; painted mattes for *Star Trek 5* and *Memoirs of an Invisible Man*.
1993 — Landed full-time job at ILM; used Photoshop for the first time to paint digital mattes for *Young Indiana Jones*; won Emmy for visual effects.
1995 — After moonlighting as matte artist for *Babylon 5*, eventually left ILM to freelance full time.

FAVORITE RIDING MOWER:
Craftsman 19.5HP ("With 2.5 acres of lawn, I really need it.")

19.4

THE EMPIRE STRIKES BACK™ & © *Lucasfilm Ltd. (LFL) 1980. All Rights Reserved.*

THE EMPIRE SHUTTLE BAY

A good example of the very least that Chauvin does in Photoshop is the shuttle bay matte he created for the rerelease of *The Empire Strikes Back* (19.4). "This shot is supposed to take place inside one of the big star destroyers. In the original movie, there was no shuttle bay shot of any kind, but George Lucas decided it was necessary to show Darth Vader moving from one scene to another. So they lifted a sequence of Vader walking down a gangplank that was originally shot for *Return of the Jedi*. They had me create this establishing scene to edit in front of it."

If the scene is new, why does it look so familiar? "The art director reasoned that the Empire liked to use a generic docking bay plan, so I modeled this scene after the old Death Star bays in *Star Wars* and *Return of the Jedi*. But they gave me total freedom to enhance the design and set the camera angle. I created the ceiling and gantry from scratch. I also added some cables and other elements to give the painting some depth. But the walls and floors are almost identical to the sets they built back in the '70s and '80s."

Although Chauvin modeled every cable, box, and crevice in Form•Z and rendered the surface textures from ElectricImage, he assembled the bits and pieces into a complex layered file in Photoshop (19.5). Why render groups of elements in a 3-D program and composite them in Photoshop when you can simply render the whole scene out of ElectricImage in one fell swoop? "It takes a little effort to break up the scene into pieces, but it doesn't take any more time for ElectricImage to do the rendering. Another plus is that Photoshop gives me a lot more flexibility by allowing me to isolate elements and apply different lighting effects. For example, in the case of the shuttle bay, I was able to quickly use the Levels command to make the walls a little lighter than the floor. I can also filter individual elements and make other minor tweaks that would involve a lot of work in ElectricImage."

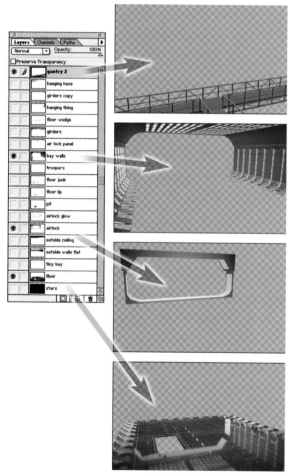

19.5

PAINTING THE VOID OF SPACE

One of the few elements that Chauvin created entirely in Photoshop was the layer of stars at the bottom of the stack. While his basic approach is similar to the one used by Greg Vander Houwen (Chapter 10), Chauvin's medium compels him to employ more subtlety. Chauvin's stars are projected onto huge movie screens, where a single pixel may grow to a half inch tall. If the stars are too numerous or too bright, the effect looks garish and fake. By contrast, Vander Houwen has to exaggerate his stars slightly so they survive dot gain and other darkening factors unique to the printing process.

That said, here's how Chauvin made his stars: He started by filling his background layer with black. Then he duplicated that layer and applied the Add Noise filter with a value of 68 set to Uniform. After pressing ⌘/Ctrl+F to reapply the filter and disperse the noise more evenly, he applied Image ➤ Adjust ➤ Threshold set to about 100 (19.6). He applied the Screen blend mode to the layer and set the Opacity to 50 percent to complete the dim background stars.

Next, he returned to the background layer and applied the Add Noise filter twice more with two whacks at ⌘/Ctrl+F. He again chose the Threshold command, but this time he set the value to 115 to create the effect of fewer bright stars. With Screen applied to the layer above, the work of combining bright and dim stars was already done (19.7), so he merged the two layers into one.

"If I were to send this directly to TV or film, these white and gray pixels would pop out like pinholes in the film. To fix this, I applied a little Gaussian Blur." Chauvin used a Radius value of 0.5. Then he chose the Levels command (⌘/Ctrl-L) and lowered the third Input Levels value to 70. This restored the brightness of the blurred stars (19.8).

Chauvin cautions that not all the starfields in *Star Wars* were created in this way. But in every star scene created by Chauvin, these are the stars you see. Who would have guessed that Luke Skywalker battles the Dark Force in a tumult of Add Noise?

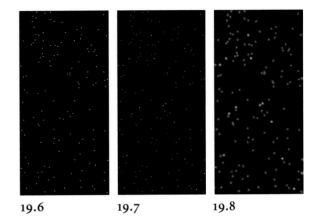

19.6   19.7   19.8

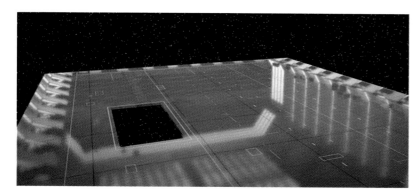

19.9

19.10

PLAYING WITH THE LIGHT

Chauvin spends a good half of his time in Photoshop adjusting lights and shadows. "It's very rare that I can set up my lights in ElectricImage exactly the way I want them. Also, ElectricImage doesn't do ray tracing, so it can't accurately match the way reflections look in real life. Sometimes I'll render an image with several different lighting variations and combine them inside Photoshop. I'll put the two renderings on different layers and just erase through one to reveal the other. I also spend a lot of time with the dodge and burn tools, which are great for creating highlights and shadows based on the original colors in the image. There's just no sense knocking yourself out over lighting in ElectricImage when you can create more realistic effects inside Photoshop."

The floor of the bay is an example of an area that required lots of image-editing attention (19.9). "First, I rendered the reflected light and floor onto separate layers. Then I created a separate file with noise in it. I used Layer ➢ Transform ➢ Perspective to splay the noise so it was larger at the bottom and smaller at the top. Then I applied it to the light layer as a displacement map (using Filter ➢ Distort ➢ Displace) to give the light a modeled look (19.10). I also created a gradient mask that went from white at the bottom to black at the top and then blurred the light within that mask. This way, the light grows less focused, and it moves farther away from the floor's surface."

Chauvin tells ElectricImage to automatically generate an alpha channel along with each rendered image. These alpha channels prove useful not only for compositing the rendered elements in Photoshop, but

also for adding lighting effects. "The lights around the air lock and bay walls looked a little flat right after I rendered them (19.11). So I generated alpha channels for the lights from ElectricImage.

"In Photoshop, I blurred the alpha channels to soften them a little (19.12). Then I loaded the side lights from the alpha channel as a selection and lightened these areas with the Levels command. This created the reflections along the wall (19.13). To get that blue glow around the air lock, I created a new layer and loaded the middle lights as a new selection. Then I filled the selection with light blue and applied the Screen mode."

THE TINY BAY ACROSS THE WAY

If you look closely at the final painting (19.14), you may spy a tiny bay on the far side of the shuttle entrance (highlighted orange in 19.14). "That's really just a distant shot of this same bay. In ElectricImage, I moved my camera so it was really far away from the model and looking in the opposite direction. Then I rendered it independently and added it to the Photoshop composition."

THE ARCHITECTURE OF CLOUD CITY

Chauvin also provided a couple of new matte paintings for the Cloud City sequence, home of Lando Calrissian and demise of Han Solo. "The Cloud City sequence features these humongous cylindrical buildings set against an orange sunset sky. Rather than trying to render the sky, I just went out and shot a few rolls of film with a 35mm camera (19.15)."

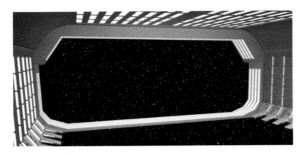

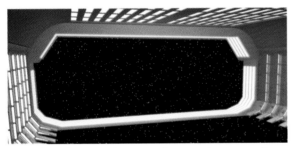

19.11 (top), 19.12 (middle), 19.13 (bottom)

19.14

19.15

ELIMINATING FILM GRAIN

Film grain on a still image is death at the box office. Normally, film grain is in constant motion because it changes from one frame to the next. But grain on a matte image just sits there. Even a hint of grain can make a still painting look like a cheesy backdrop. To kill the grain in his Cloud City sky, Chauvin took several pictures in a row and averaged them. He mounted a 35mm camera on a tripod and shot a dozen or more pictures to standard print film. Then he scanned them and layered the 10 best copies inside a single Photoshop document.

After aligning the images as best he could — "the registration wasn't exact, I just eyeballed them" — he adjusted the Opacity of each layer according to a secret formula hitherto known only at ILM. "The background layer is always opaque. You set the Opacity of the next layer up to 50 percent, then the layer above that to 33 percent, then 25, 20, 17, 14, 12, 11, and finally 10. In each case, you're taking the layer's number and dividing it into 100. So Layer 2 into 100 is 50 percent; Layer 3 into 100 is 33. You keep going until you get to Layer 10, which goes into 100 10 times."

Are 35mm pictures common elements in big-budget Hollywood movies? "Normally, I like to work from better source material than a handful of marginally registered snapshots. But clouds are pretty amorphous objects so a little softness didn't hurt them."

19.16

19.17

19.18

19.19

THE EMPIRE STRIKES BACK™ & © Lucasfilm Ltd. (LFL) 1980. All Rights Reserved.

ADDING BUILDINGS IN THE SKY

Chauvin designed the models for his Cloud City (19.16) from concept art provided by Lucasfilms. As with the shuttle bay art, Chauvin rendered his buildings in groups and assembled the pieces in Photoshop, starting with the background buildings (19.17) and working forward (19.18). "This gave me the freedom to change the relative locations of the foreground and background buildings. In the final version of the painting (19.19), you'll notice that I've moved the background buildings around and I have a lot more of them. In some cases, I copied and pasted parts of buildings to make the town look more crowded. I worked very carefully, of course; I don't think there are any two buildings that are absolutely identical. I may have spent close to an hour cloning elements in Photoshop, but it was a heck of a lot easier than rerendering the scene in ElectricImage."

TURNING DOWN THE LIGHTS

The issue of light raises its head in this painting just as it did in the shuttle bay scene. Most of the buildings had rings of office lights ringing their perimeters. Chauvin rendered the lights out of ElectricImage, but later decided he had gone a little overboard. "The original windows were too bright (19.20). It was like every office was filled to capacity with fluorescent bulbs. In print, the effect probably looks kind of cool. But you have to remember, the scale of these buildings on screen was gigantic. Sizzling windows would have really distracted from the foreground activity."

Naturally, Chauvin turned down the lights in Photoshop. "In ElectricImage, I turned off all my light sources and made the windows totally luminous. This made the windows white and everything else black. Then I rendered that view (19.21), brought it into Photoshop as an alpha channel, and loaded it as a selection."

The next step was to stroke black around the outline of the selection. Chauvin could have used Edit ≻ Stroke or he could have gone with Select ≻ Modify ≻ Border. But he had something slightly more elaborate in mind. "In my experience, Border does a terrible job of making an even antialiased edge. I used Select ➢ Modify ➢ Contract to make the selection slightly smaller, I think I feathered it to soften the edges, then I saved it to a separate channel." In the Channels palette, Chauvin ⌘/Ctrl-clicked the first channel to load it and ⌘/Ctrl+Option/Alt-clicked the second channel to subtract it from the first. Then he made a new layer and filled the selection with black (19.22). When composited at full opacity against the buildings, these window outlines had the magical effect of dimming the lights (19.23).

THE TEAMING MASSES

Every thriving metropolis swarms with activity, and Cloud City is no exception. "If you look closely at the finished painting, you'll notice that the floor of the balcony (lower right corner, 19.19) isn't very polished. That's because in the movie, this area is totally filled with people. This particular iteration of the scene appeared at the end of *Return of the Jedi,* where people across the galaxy are celebrating the Empire's defeat. You can't even see the railing through the crowds."

A hundred or so extras on the balcony wasn't deemed sufficient, so Chauvin was instructed to paint tiny crowds into the background. "Originally, I had painted a handful of tiny people in the lower courtyard off in the distance (19.24). But someone decided it didn't make sense for the background to be so sparse, so I added a ton of little specks to indicate the cheering crowds (19.25). I just scaled some noise and then painted on top of it."

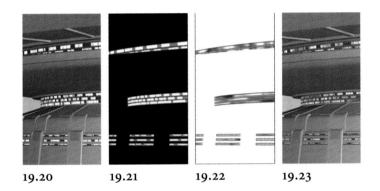

19.20   **19.21**   **19.22**   **19.23**

19.24 (TOP), 19.25 (BOTTOM)

19.26

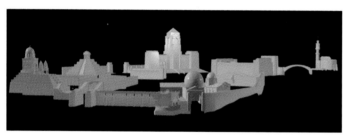

19.27

If you compare Chauvin's early rendered models (19.18) to the finished city (19.19), you'll see that he's also added tiny spotlights, shadows, rust drools, spindly roof paraphernalia, and literally hundreds of other subtle elements, all inside Photoshop. "I keep massaging the image until it looks real. Most of the time, *real* means uneven and scuffed up. I guess I could return to ElectricImage and render this kind of stuff, but it's almost always easier to add the finishing touches in Photoshop."

THE DINOSAUR MOVIE THAT NEVER GOT MADE

Not being acquainted with every one of Chauvin's matte paintings, it's terribly presumptuous of us to say this. But from what we've seen, Chauvin's masterpiece never made it to the big screen. "I created this painting (19.26) a couple of years ago for a movie version of *Dinotopia*, based on the children's book series by Jim Gurney. He's a very talented artist, so the illustrations in his book worked great as concept art. Unfortunately, the studio abandoned the project pretty early on so it was never finished. This is the first time I've ever displayed these images outside my demo tapes."

MODELING DINOTOPIA

"When I model something in Form•Z, I almost always work in the wireframe mode. After using the program more or less every day of my life, I'm pretty familiar with what I'm doing, so the pieces usually come out the way I expect them to. But this model was an exception. The Dinotopia city had become sufficiently complex that I found it helpful to take the model into ElectricImage and do a quick render while I was modeling. I even assigned a few parts different colors — like green and blue — so I could discern them from the purple walls and buildings around them (19.27).

"After importing the model into ElectricImage, I applied the basic texture maps (19.28). The nice thing about having assigned garish colors up front is that I can see right off the bat where I've applied textures and where I haven't. After adding 20 or so textures, it's very easy to get mixed up and accidentally leave something unmapped. This way, if I see something that's electric purple, I can say, 'Oh, there's something I forgot to map.' It makes for fewer surprises when I start playing with the image in Photoshop."

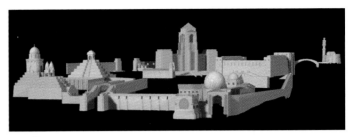

19.28

INTEGRATING THE NATURAL WORLD

"That's about as far as I took this in Form•Z and ElectricImage. I generally make my textures fairly generic, just enough to approximate the effect that I want. Then I go into Photoshop and age the walls, add the stains, paint the little statues, and generally add the realism. In this case, I also surrounded the city with a bunch of photographic elements like buildings, mountains, rocks, trees, and lots and lots of water. I suppose I could have tried to model this stuff, but it takes less time and ends up looking better if I do it in Photoshop.

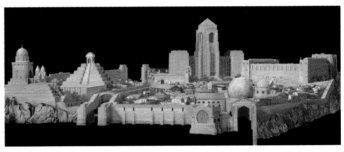

19.29

"The first thing I did in Photoshop was fill in the central area of the city (19.29). I actually lifted these little buildings out of a book, which raises an interesting point. I prefer to use my own photo reference or work from royalty free CDs. But it's sometimes necessary to reference copyrighted material.

"When I was at ILM, the company attorney spoke with us on the topic of sampling photographs. He explained that it was a gray area, but that it was kind of like sampling music, which he said is legal as long as the sample isn't too long and the song isn't dependent on the sample for its success. So on the rare occasions that I scan copyrighted material, I make sure I work the images until you can't find any specific similarities between the original photo and my edited version. In this case, I've cloned the buildings into different locations, scaled the buildings independently, combined two half buildings from different photos, painted in extra details, changed the lighting, and made absolutely every other modification I could think of." In effect, the original photograph serves as a template; Chauvin's finished piece is something altogether different.

19.30

19.31

"If the foothills in back of the city (19.30) look suspiciously like the Headlands in Marin County, California, it's because that's exactly what they are. This was back in the ILM days, so I just went out with my camera and took pictures of nearby hills that looked like they might go with the *Dinotopia* illustrations. The distant mountains are stock photos of the Swiss Alps."

THE CASCADING FALLS

"I spent a lot of time looking at the waterfalls in Gurney's paintings to try and determine which falls I needed to shoot and from which angles. I finally came to the conclusion that if I was going to get the right kind of water, I would have to go to Niagara Falls. So I called a cameraman friend of mine, and we were on a plane for Buffalo, New York, three days later. We scouted the whole thing out that afternoon, spent the night at the Holiday Inn near the Falls, shot the water elements I needed the next day, and were back on a plane that night. I had the film transferred to videotape so I could see which sections I wanted to digitize. Then I had to go back and scale them, paint on them, and make the masks so they all fit into place (19.31). The payoff is that it's all real water so it moves exactly like you'd expect it to."

Naturally, Chauvin can't add full-motion video inside Photoshop. "The water you see here is just for reference. I replaced it with the moving footage inside After Effects. Since After Effects retains Photoshop's layering scheme, I can just sandwich the various falls in between the layers of building and rock." To see the completed scene in motion, play the QuickTime movie included on the CD at the back of this book.

ERIC'S INTERMITTENT FLASHES OF FAME

You might envy Chauvin for the visibility of his work. After all, how many of us can name a piece we've done and hold out even a remote hope that someone has actually seen it? Yet here's a guy who can site a few examples and be relatively sure that no one in earshot has missed his paintings.

But Chauvin's work doesn't necessarily have the bang for the buck you might think. "If I had to create a complex matte painting from beginning to end without doing anything else, it would probably take me three weeks. Full time." And what are we talking about? Maybe a minute of film time? "No way. My work is usually measured in under 10 seconds. I've worked on shots that have been on screen for 2 seconds."

So just because we've all seen Chauvin's paintings doesn't mean we saw them for long. Good thing Mother Technology in Her infinite wisdom has equipped us with the Pause button.

melrose place

Today on E!

E! Program Guide

Original Shows

Old Faves

Personalities

Intl. Programs

couples & couplings

Amanda Woodward

Michael Mancini

Sydney Andrews

Kimberly Shaw

Billy Campbell

Jake Hansen

Jo Reynolds

Jane Mancini

Matt Fielding

Alison Parker

Navigator · Info

Color · Swatches

Who's slept with whom on *Melrose Place*: a brief history

by Alan Carter

Heather Locklear was at a loss. "There's no one else for Amanda to sleep with!" she told *Entertainment Weekly* last year. "They're going to have to bring in new people. I think she has slept with half of Los Angeles."

That, of course, is an exaggeration. *Melrose Place* fans know that Amanda has only been with around 49 percent of Los Angeles. And as long as we're keeping score, she hasn't even been as busy as Jake, the blue-collar stud who has trouble keeping his blue jeans on.

Just how do you keep all of this bed-hopping straight? (Speaking of straight--resident *Melrose* homosexual Matt is sorely in need of a relationship that lasts more than four episodes!) Well, it's not easy. So, as a service to fans old and new, we offer this handy, at-a-*glands* guide to who's done whom. (We avoided listing one-night stands. We don't have *that* much space.)

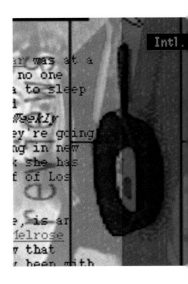

CHAPTER 20
CREATING IMAGES FOR THE WORLD WIDE WEB

T he World Wide Web is a truly wonder-ful, truly horrible medium. Its primary wonder is its ceaseless bounty. The Web is already so vast as to defy comprehen-sion, and yet it continues to grow at an incomprehensible rate. The Web also rates high marks for anarchy. Just plain folks can post sites for little money, and there are none of the space limita-tions inherent in, say, print media.

The horror is the speed. It doesn't matter what kind of modem or direct wiring you use, this is one ago-nizingly slow delivery vehicle. Consider this compari-son: When you pick up a traditional magazine, you can take in the entire full-color, high-resolution, uncompressed cover in the time it takes your brain to interpret reflected light. We're not physicists, but we're guessing that we're talking about a few nanoseconds, max. Now, imagine viewing that same full-color, high-resolution, uncompressed image posted on someone's Web site. We're not telecommu-nications experts, but if there was a race between that image and a snail crawling from Bangor to Tijuana, we'd put our money on the snail.

BEN WOULD KILL FOR A KILOBYTE

Having served on the launch teams for such promi-nent online magazines as *CNET* (20.1) and *E! Online* (20.2), full-time Web artist Ben Benjamin is all too familiar with the benefits and handicaps of packaging content for the Internet. On one hand, you can post pages until you're blue in the face and make them as long as you like. On the other hand, Benjamin wages a perpetual battle to make his images small.

Compress till it hurts.

BEN BENJAMIN

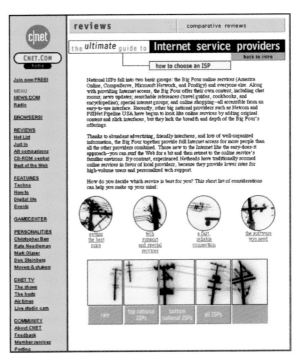

20.1

Reprinted with permission from CNET, Inc., ©1995–97

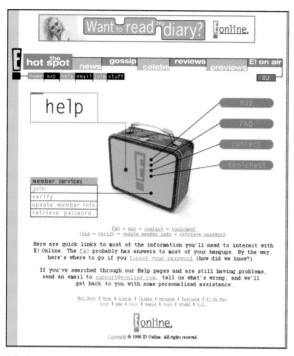

20.2

©1996 E! Online

"File size is absolutely the biggest constraint that I work under," Benjamin says. "I use Photoshop and Equilibrium's DeBabelizer to automate some of the chores — like deciding the optimal bit depth of a GIF palette or the amount of compression to apply to a JPEG file. But I often revisit the image inside Photoshop and do some tedious cleanup work. With GIF files in particular, I might zoom in to the image and examine which colors I can eliminate on a pixel-by-pixel basis. Like, say a block of pixels is mostly one shade of green with a red pixel in the middle. I'll probably use the pencil tool to change the red pixel to green, as well. That not only gets rid of a color, but it makes GIF's run-length-encoding compression more efficient."

Pixel-level editing is a pretty extreme measure. Why go to that effort to shave a few bytes off the file size? "Commercial sites enforce per-page maximums — file sizes that you can't go over. It varies from site to site, usually between 20K and 50K." When you consider that each character of text and HTML code takes up a byte, and a single icon-sized button weighs in at 1K, these maximums are rather prohibitive. In print, four 50K images could fit inside one square inch.

So, how do you make the cut? "Small size is generally considered more important than appearance. So you keep the pixel dimensions of the graphics as small as possible. And you compress till it hurts. You

ARTIST:
Ben Benjamin

ORGANIZATION:
Mr. Pants — A Design Firm
60 Thirteenth Street
San Francisco, CA 94107
415/863-9666
ben@superbad.com

SYSTEM:
PowerTower Pro 225 (Power Computing)
2GB storage

RAM:
128MB total
60MB assigned to Photoshop

MONITOR:
Apple 21-inch

EXTRAS:
Global Village 28K modem

VERSION USED:
Photoshop 4.0

keep nudging the bit depth or compression until the image looks awful. Then, you nudge it back one and leave it there." Good enough and speedy is better than beautiful and slow.

THE MELROSE MYSTERY

Not only has Deke never seen *Melrose Place*, he doesn't even know what channel it's on. Katrin, however, is a faithful viewer, as she makes clear in Chapter 17. Is it possible that we've uncovered a secret link between Photoshop users and Heather Locklear?

Benjamin couldn't say. "I know everybody says this, but I've really never watched the show either." We're certain the same goes for you, O chaste reader, but we'll all have to do our best to feign interest.

A TAWDRY LITTLE CYBERPLACE

"The *Melrose Place* story went up when we launched *E! Online* (20.3). Basically, it chronicles who slept with whom (20.4). It's a few years old now, so they've had to update the story to include new characters." We imagine the list of extramarital encounters has expanded as well.

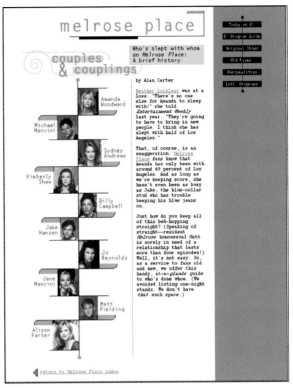

20.3

©*1996 E! Online*

OTHER APPLICATIONS:
Adobe Illustrator, Equilibrium DeBabelizer, Netscape Navigator, Bare Bones Software BBEdit, GifBuilder (shareware)

WORK HISTORY:
1990 — Hand-painted T-shirts and sold them to students at Indiana University.
1992 — Accepted one-day temp job shoveling dog food; created comic strip "Clod" for student newspaper.
1994 — Landed a job at Yo! Design; worked on Peachpit Press Web site back in the days of Netscape 1.0.

1995 — Joined CNET: The Computer Network as part of original launch team.
1996 — Hired as art director for *E! Online*, the Internet Entertainment magazine.

FAVORITE AMERICAN FOLKLORE HERO:
John Henry ("You have to admire the man's hatred of machines.")

20.4

©1996 E! Online

20.5

"This page went up before we had a photo editor or anything like that. So, all I had to work with was a badly digitized cast photo (20.5). It's pretty high-res, but it's a blurry, grainy, messed-up scan. But because we were posting the images online, it didn't really matter. I made it work by downsampling the heck out of it. Then, I indexed the image to the 216-color Web palette, without dithering (20.6)."

DESIGNING PAGES IN ILLUSTRATOR

Benjamin composed his basic page design in Illustrator (20.7). "I selected each of the faces in Photoshop and then dragged and dropped them over into the Illustrator document. Then, I added the body copy and designed the headlines and other text treatments."

Why use Illustrator for this purpose? Why not use PageMill or one of the other HTML editors? "I'm not in charge of generating the HTML files. I'm just making a design that the coders will work from. I export the design as a big GIF file and post it for the editorial folks to look at in L.A. After it's approved, I save all the graphics and send them down the assembly line."

In that case, why not use a page layout program such as QuarkXPress? "Illustrator handles single-

20.6

page designs really well, but it also permits me to add graphic elements and create special headline treatments. When I get the effect I want, I can export the graphics as GIF files, or drag and drop elements over to Photoshop. It's way more flexible than using a page layout program."

EXPORTING THE GIF IMAGE MAP

Benjamin exported a modified version of the "cast toolbar" — the column of characters' faces and names — as a GIF89a file (20.8). This toolbar was then tagged as an image map by the coding department. Each face became a button which would take you to a listing of the character's sexual exploits. (For the record, Illustrator 7 and 8 let you assign URLs to objects and save client-side image maps, but Benjamin was using Version 6 at the time.)

After exporting a GIF file from Illustrator, it's always a good idea to open it in Photoshop and make sure you like the results. "I usually export a few different versions of the graphic from Illustrator — one with antialiasing turned on, another with it turned off, one with dithering on, et cetera. Then, I combine the pieces I like into the final image inside Photoshop."

20.8

20.7

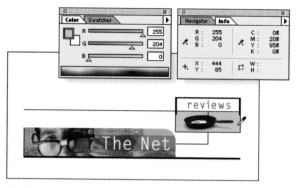

20.9

ANTICIPATING 256-COLOR MONITORS

As a Photoshop artist, you probably own a 16-bit or 24-bit monitor. But about half the people who visit your site will be looking at 8-bit monitors. When your image is viewed on an 8-bit screen, the browser redraws the image using the Mac or Windows system palette. The two palettes share 216 common colors, which make up the so-called Web palette.

"Any color in the graphic that falls inside the Web palette looks fine; any color that isn't in the palette appears dithered. Sometimes dithering is okay. With soft edges and continuous-tone photographs, dithering doesn't usually matter. But dithering looks crummy inside flat-colored areas, like the green shapes and the text in the cast toolbar."

The solution is to fill the flat areas with a Web-safe color. Illustrator 8 offers a built-in Web palette. And Photoshop lets you downsample to the Web palette using Image ➢ Mode ➢ Indexed Color. But the best trick is to memorize the RGB recipe for Web-safe colors, as explained in the sidebar "How Ben Anticipates 256-Color Monitors."

HOW BEN ANTICIPATES 256-COLOR MONITORS

Benjamin explains, "If each of the RGB values for a color is divisible by 51, then it's safe." That's a total of 6 permutations — 0, 51, 102, 153, 204, and 255 — in each of three channels. As it just so happens, $6 \times 6 \times 6 = 216$.

"When I reduce the bit depth of the image using Photoshop's Indexed Color command, I usually apply the Adaptive palette. Then, I go back and check the flat areas with the eyedropper to make sure they haven't changed (20.9). If a flat color has changed, I return to the RGB mode and use the paint bucket set to a Tolerance of 0 to make it Web-safe again."

EXPLOITING BROWSER CACHING

As we've said, Deke's experience with *Melrose Place* is nil, but it seems quite clear that the ambition of the show's cast is to put every known form of contraception through the most grueling test possible. To wit, each of the 10 characters had his or her own scorecard. We've grouped the headers for these pages into one big figure (20.10). As you can see, each header features a row of the characters' faces, along with elements highlighting the face and name of the character at hand.

If Benjamin had created each header as a separate graphic, the browser would have had to load a new image for each page, thereby slowing the user's enjoyment of the site. Luckily, Benjamin would have none of that. "The one common element in each header is the row of heads inside the little washing machine windows. So, I made that element a separate GIF graphic. That way, the browser downloads the image once, caches it, and doesn't have to load it again until the next session.

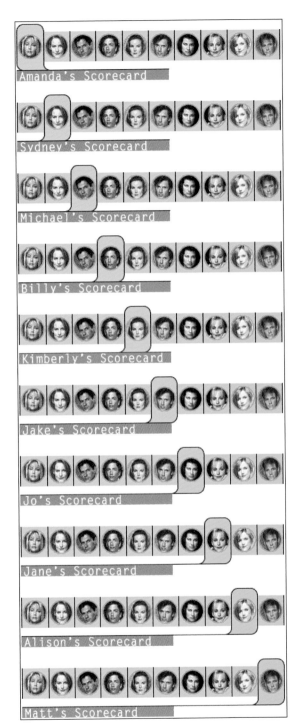

20.10

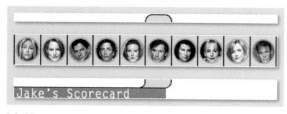

20.11

"The parts that change are the yellow cap above the washing machine heads and the yellow bit with the text below the heads (20.11). The cap is incredibly tiny. It's just three colors — yellow, black, and white — so that's a 2-bit GIF file with lots of flat areas for compression. Naturally, that's a Web-safe yellow. The bottom part is a little bigger, but I managed to get it down to a 4-bit palette.

"These elements have to line up perfectly, so I put together a layered file in Photoshop with the washing machine heads, all the caps, and all the bottoms. Then, I exported each layer to a separate GIF file. Because I cropped each element tight vertically, with no extra pixels hanging off above or below, they appear to merge into a single graphic inside the browser."

ANIMATED BANNER ADS

Banner ads are the current craze for advertising on the Web. They burst and sizzle at the top of your screen in an attempt to entice you to click on them. Some folks hate banner ads because they're intrusive, they prolong the overall download time, and they generally make a mockery of the original, civic-minded intentions of the Web. But we don't have any problem with them. Advertising is the fuel for just about every prevailing medium that's come down the pike. Without advertising, some excellent professional sites would have to fold up their tents. Even with advertising, some of these outfits are running on shoestring, loss-leader budgets. What we need is *more* advertising, not less!

HYPING TALK SOUP

Whatever your feelings are on this fascinating topic, you have Benjamin to thank for some of the banner ads you've seen. Included on the CD at the back of this book is an ad Benjamin created for the television show *Talk Soup*. In case you're not familiar with it, the show compiles sensational highlights from the current glut of fatuous daytime talk shows. It's like a *Reader's Digest* condensed guide to the daily sleaze. (Though Deke's never watched *Melrose Place*, he is guilty of having sat through entire episodes of *Talk Soup* with mouth agape like a motorist passing a train wreck.)

"E! wanted a simple animated banner for a contest they were running. It had to feature a little person rising from the *Talk Soup* bowl. That little person was you, if you won the contest.

"Like usual, I made a comp for the animation inside Illustrator (20.12)." To prepare the illustration, Benjamin set up the individual frames for the face, the soup bowl, and the shaking E! logo inside Photoshop. To keep things tidy, he painted each frame on a separate layer. Then, he dragged and dropped the layers into Illustrator. "I created this particular comp for myself so I could remember the order for the animation. I sent a more simplified version to E! for approval."

COMPILING THE FRAMES IN GIFBUILDER

After getting the idea accepted — "no one seemed to like how I made John Henson's eyes wiggle, but everything else was okay" — Benjamin set about compiling the frames in Yves Piguet's popular shareware utility, GifBuilder. "GifBuilder does a pretty good job of dithering and reducing file sizes. And in GifBuilder 0.5, you can drag and drop whole layers directly from Photoshop. That way, I don't have to worry about adjusting the Indexed Color settings or saving GIF files out of Photoshop."

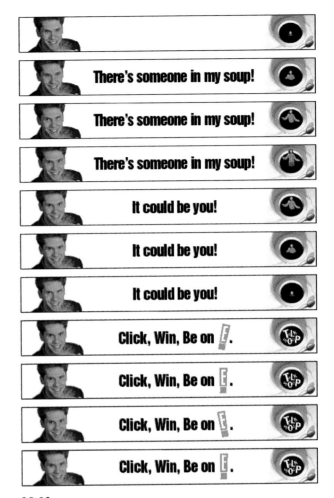

20.12

©1996 E! ONLINE

20.13

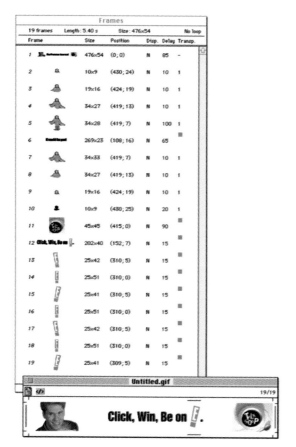

20.14

Benjamin started by dropping in the first frame of the animation, which included host John Henson's face on the far left side of the banner and the soup bowl on the far right (20.13). This frame served as a background for the remaining frames. Rather than drop in completed frames that measured the whole width of the banner, Benjamin dragged over different elements as separate pieces. One set of frames included different views of the bowl, another included alternate text, and the last was a thin set of frames that featured the red E! exclamation point.

GifBuilder's basic organization is a lot like Photoshop's Layers palette. The individual frames appear in a list with or without thumbnails (20.14). You can change the order of frames by dragging them up or down in the list. The program lets you specify the duration and coordinate positions of frames. You can even toggle the animation to loop repeatedly after it finishes playing the first time.

FILE SIZE, DIMENSIONS, AND DURATION

Of course, file size is as much of a concern when working with animated GIF files as it is when creating still images. "GifBuilder provides a command called *frame optimization* that dumps any pixel that's repeated from one frame to the next. If the file is still too big after that, I look at which frames I might be able to delete. The goal is to get the entire animation under 12K or so, which is sometimes a challenge."

File size isn't the only size limitation for banner ads. There's also the issue of pixel dimensions. "Up until very recently, banner ads were a total nightmare. Every single advertising venue had different banner specifications. This ad ran on *E! Online* and *CNET* at 476 × 54 pixels. Yahoo! needed 468 × 60. So, I'd have to do four or five different versions of the same ad. Nowadays, most sites have standardized at 468 × 60 pixels.

"But there are still weird parameters that you have to watch out for. At Yahoo!, a banner ad can't be more than 8K, and the animation can't last for more than four seconds." While that makes life difficult for the ad creators, it's wonderful news for Web content consumers. The ad loads in four seconds, plays for four seconds, and the pain is over. Personally, we're happy to give eight seconds of our time if it means keeping a site free.

LOOPING WITH A LOW SOURCE

If you write your own HTML code, you're probably aware of the `<LOWSRC>` tag, which instructs the browser to download a preliminary version of an image. For example, the TomGirl figure (20.15) illustrates the tag `<IMG SRC="zellweg.jpg" LOWSRC="zellmono.gif">`. This tag tells the browser to load the smaller monotone image first and then gradually display the larger JPEG file in its place. The mono file serves as a proxy until the real image loads.

Benjamin suggests that you can also use this tag with animated GIF files. "I saw this used really well with an animated bee. The `<LOWSRC>` tag loaded a file that showed the bee flying toward you. Then, the GIF switched out and it became looping animation with the bee flying in space. There's really no other way to pull that off without resorting to javascript or some sort of plug-in."

20.15

CHAPTER 21
BUTTONS, BUTTONS, BUTTONS

Computers have a way of completely transforming how we work in a small amount of time. Just as an example, perhaps you've seen the made-for-TV version of *The Shining* — you know, the Stephen King novel about the folks who spend the winter in a really scary hotel. The movie was inspired by and filmed at a hotel called the Stanley in Estes Park, Colorado. The story's theme is a bit gruesome — what with all the bleeding walls and killer topiary animals — but it's worth a few chuckles. It was especially comical when the mom and dad start freaking out about the snowmobile being wrecked and their being helplessly trapped, because in real life the Stanley is about a block away from a supermarket that's open all year. And supposedly, the hotel is poised at the edge of a blizzardy mountain pass that's closed over a span of about 200 miles, when clearly there isn't such a place even in Saskatchewan, much less Colorado.

But the least believable part comes right at the beginning. The lead character, Dad, is writing a play using a typewriter. King wrote the story in the 1970s, when typewriters were still common. But here it is 20 years later, and we're supposed to believe that an ex-

The best buttons are little pieces of art, as elegant and informative as characters in a typeface.

MICHAEL NINNESS

college professor in his mid-thirties hasn't managed to pick up a laptop somewhere along the way? How did he ever manage to wean himself off slide rules, rotary-dial phones, and 8-track tapes?

This is all a roundabout way of leading up to the topic of buttons. The point is, if we had shown you a collection of brightly colored buttons (21.1) three or four years ago, we would have fully expected you to utter a "Hm" or other bored commentary. Buttons are about as applicable to print-media designers as pressure-sensitive styluses are to stenographers. But

Study Agriculture **Learn a New Language** **You Can Be Mechanical** **Learn to Love Symbols**

21.1

nowadays, we'd be surprised if you didn't examine these buttons with at least a glimmer of curiosity. The latest computing rage — the World Wide Web — has turned armies of us into interface designers. Like it or not, buttons and onscreen iconography are fast becoming a part of our everyday lives.

In celebration of this phenomenon, we contacted a fellow whose only experience with typewriters was a tenth grade typing class. Young enough to have taken up desktop publishing in high school, Myke Ninness sees buttons as miniature artwork with a purpose. "Their real function is to guide visitors through your site, multimedia presentation, or whatever. The best you can hope is that the buttons are so intuitive that no one pays much attention to them. Or maybe someone thinks, 'Wow, this is a great site,' but they don't spend a lot of time pondering over each and every button. They just click and go.

"But if you take the time to look closely, the best buttons are little pieces of art, as elegant and informative as characters in a typeface. In fact, in many ways, electronic buttons are to the '90's what PostScript fonts were to the '80s — except you have a lot more options when creating them and they're a heck of a lot easier to make."

THE BASIC BEVELED SQUARE

"I'd like to stress up front that none of the button effects I use rely on third-party filters. You don't need Kai's Power Tools or any of those. All the 3-D stuff is done with two filters that are built into Photoshop — Emboss and Lighting Effects. And otherwise, it's all layers and channels."

Probably the easiest kind of button to create is a beveled rectangle or square. Ninness starts off by opening a texture file and sizing it to the desired shape. When creating a square button, he usually crops the texture to about 400 × 400 pixels. For best results, the image should have a low degree of contrast. "Because Lighting Effects exaggerates the amount of contrast in an image, you may want to mute the colors a few notches using Image ➤ Adjust ➤ Levels."

To define the beveled edge of the button, Ninness selects the entire image (⌘/Ctrl+A) and chooses Select ➤ Modify ➤ Border. "Enter a Width value of 40 pixels, or about one-tenth the width of the file. This expands the selection around the edges of the window. Then switch to the channels palette and click on the save selection icon (21.2) to convert the selection to a mask." Ninness names his channel Edge Mask.

ARTIST:
Michael Ninness

ORGANIZATION:
Extensis Corporation
1800 SW First Avenue, Suite 500
Portland, OR 97201
503/274-2020
mninness@extensis.com

SYSTEM:
Power Mac 7250/120
2GB storage

RAM:
32MB total (with RAM Doubler)
24MB assigned to Photoshop

MONITOR:
Sony 15-inch multisync

VERSION USED:
Photoshop 5.0

OTHER APPLICATIONS:
Macromedia FreeHand, Adobe Page-Maker, NetObjects Fusion, Bare Bones BBEdit

"At this point, you can deselect the image (⌘/Ctrl+D) or not. If you leave the selection intact, you'll get a flat button face. If you deselect the image, you get more depth, but it can be a little more difficult to control."

For purposes of this example, Ninness deselects the image and chooses Filter ➤ Render ➤ Lighting Effects. "Keep in mind, Lighting Effects is notorious for generating out-of-memory errors. To work on a 500K button, you'll need about 20MB of RAM assigned to Photoshop." He selects the Edge Mask channel from the Texture Channel pop-up menu at the bottom of the dialog box. Then, he turns off the White is High check box. "From there, it's just a matter of tweaking the spotlight and slider bars until you get the effect you want (21.3). When you press Return, Photoshop generates your beveled button automatically (21.4)."

MYKE SAYS, "WORK BIG"

Screen buttons are typically low-resolution images, rarely more than 60 pixels wide. But Ninness likes to start out with about ten times as many pixels as he ultimately needs. "It's always a good idea to work on a high-res file and then sample it down. Some filters are very difficult to control at low resolutions, and gradients can band. If you work big, you have a lot more wiggle room."

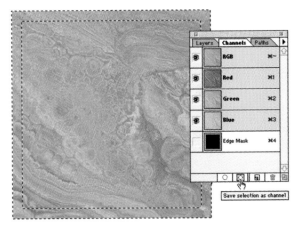

21.2

WORK HISTORY:
<u>1986</u> — Designed high school yearbook using Mac 512Ke and PageMaker 1.0.
<u>1990</u> — Paid way through design school training professionals to use Macs.
<u>1994</u> — Graduated from University of Washington with BFA in Graphic Design.
<u>1996</u> — Director of Computer Graphics Training Division at professional photo lab Ivey Seright.

FAVORITE FISH:
Clown fish ("They freakin' rock!")

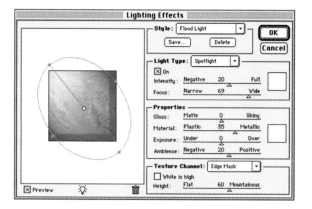

21.3 (TOP), 21.4 (BOTTOM)

MAKING BUTTONS WITH CLIPPING GROUPS

"Photoshop's clipping group function is a big help when creating buttons. You can place texture inside buttons and apply highlights and shadows, all with a simple Option-click." To demonstrate, Ninness starts with a simple collection of characters on a transparent layer (21.5). "If you're working with text, be sure to turn the Preserve Transparency check box off." He then creates a vibrant texture on a separate layer in front of the characters (21.6).

"The texture is a stock Noise and Motion Blur technique that's been around for ages. Just take a layer and fill it with whatever color you want — in this case, a reddish orange. Choose the Add Noise filter. Crank the noise as high as you want — higher values result in more streaks. Then, apply the Motion Blur filter at 45 degrees with a distance of 45 pixels. If you want, reapply the filter with the same angle but change the distance two or three times. This brings out the pattern a little bit more. Then, if you don't like the color, you can go into Hue/Saturation and modify the overall Hue. You have endless opportunities to change the overall look of this."

When you get the texture you want (and keep in mind, it doesn't have to be streaks — any texture will do), Option/Alt-click on the horizontal line between the two layers in the Layers palette to combine them

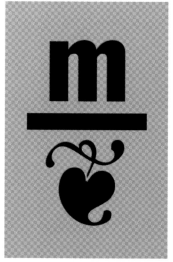

21.5

21.6

into a clipping group (21.7). Alternatively, you can press ⌘/Ctrl+G in Photoshop 4. Then, Ninness recommends that you merge the two layers together (⌘/Ctrl+E).

Next, Ninness duplicates the layer and fills the opaque portions with black (Shift+Option/Alt+Delete). This layer will serve as the highlights and shadows for the button. The Emboss filter will give the button depth, while Gaussian Blur will lend some softness to the effect. "By blurring the layer, you give the Emboss filter some soft edges to work with. Trust me, Emboss can do some ugly things to hard edges." Ninness applies a Radius value of about 6.0 for a 400 × 600 pixel image.

Next, Ninness chooses Filter ➤ Stylize ➤ Emboss. He sets the Angle value to 135 degrees. "I don't know why, but I like my light to come in from the upper left corner. Then, you match the Height value to the Radius you assigned for Gaussian Blur — in this case, 6. And the Amount is 300 percent (21.8).

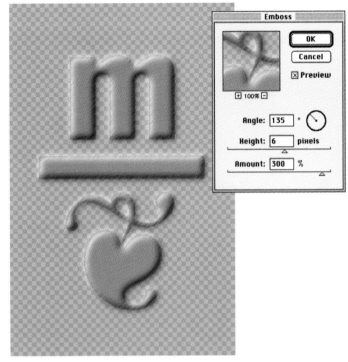

21.8

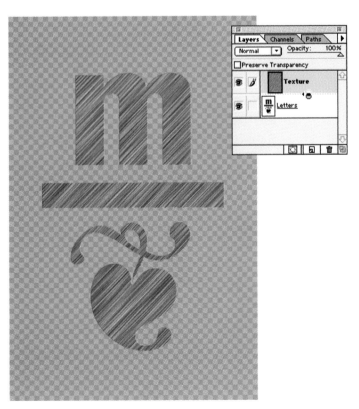

21.7

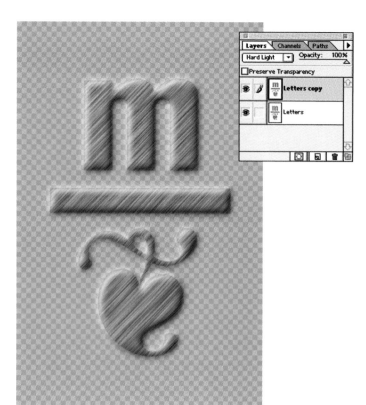

21.9

"After you apply the Emboss filter, you end up with this crappy gray effect. But we don't care about the gray; all we want are the highlights and shadows. So change the blend mode in the Layers palette to Hard Light. That nukes all the gray stuff and leaves the highlights and shadows intact (21.9)."

There's one final step. "Because you applied Gaussian Blur, you end up with this residue that drifts outside the original letters. If you don't like the shadow effect — sometimes it can be effective, other times not — then group the shadow with the layer below it, again by Option/Alt-clicking on the horizontal line or pressing ⌘/Ctrl+G." This will clean up the edge of the button. Then, add a drop shadow to taste.

"And here's a tip: If the highlights and shadows are too washed out, just duplicate the top layer and adjust the Opacity (21.10). Each copy of the layer remains inside the clipping group. With very little effort, you can have that button popping off the page."

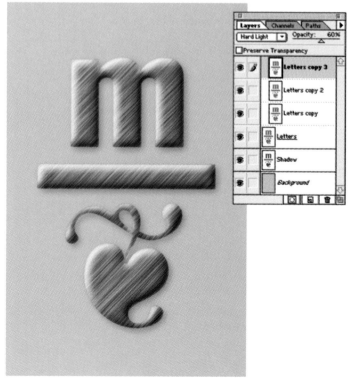

21.10

ETCHING TYPE INTO THE BEVELED SQUARE

"This clipping group technique is also a snazzy way to etch text into a button. For example, take the beveled square. A square by itself — that's not a button. But add some text and you've really got something."

Ninness sets the foreground color to 50 percent gray. Then, he uses Photoshop's type tool to add the words "Click Me" to a new layer. After he centers the text on the button, he turns off the Preserve Transparency check box (which permits blurring later). He also sets the blend mode in the Layers palette to Hard Light to make the gray text invisible.

Next, he duplicates the Click Me layer and fills it with black (by setting the foreground color to black and pressing Shift+Option/Alt+Delete). Ninness then applies the Gaussian Blur filter with a Radius value of 3.0. "The higher the radius, the deeper the etching."

After blurring, he chooses Emboss and sets the Height to 3 (matching the blur radius) and the Amount to 300 percent. "Unlike before, I'm digging the text into the button, so I rotate the Angle value to -45 degrees." The result is a soft-edged effect that looks like the type has melted into the button (21.11). To make the text nice and crisp, group the emboss layer with the text below it by pressing ⌘/Ctrl+G (21.12).

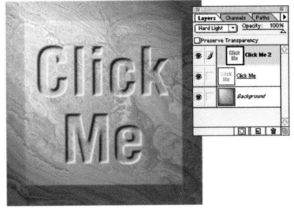

21.11 (TOP), **21.12** (BOTTOM)

MASS BUTTON PRODUCTION

"From a production standpoint, this technique can be a huge time saver. If you have a series of buttons on your Web site, and they're all going to be the same except for what they say, then you have one source file to go back and edit. Here, I just have to change the two text layers — which takes maybe five minutes — and export the modified button in the GIF89a format. That's because the GIF89a Export module saves just the visible layers.

"It also works in the other direction. If you change your mind about the color of the button, and you still have the original Photoshop file with the various text layers intact, you only have one layer to go back and edit — the Background layer. The text etches into the new background automatically."

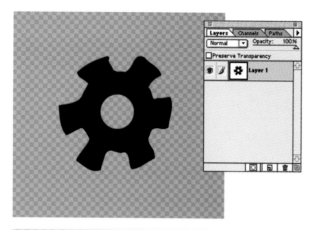

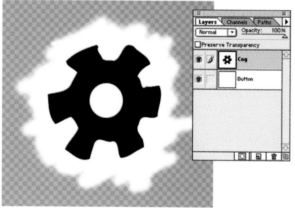

21.13 (TOP), 21.14 (BOTTOM)

CREATING A STAMPED BUTTON

"Clipping groups are a great way to add depth to complex shapes. But they aren't the only way to go. In fact, my favorite button technique doesn't involve clipping groups at all. Using layers and channels, you can stamp an icon so it looks like someone has branded it into a button shape." The buttons at the beginning of the chapter (21.1) are cases in point.

Ninness suggests two techniques for creating stamped buttons: one that involves the Emboss filter, and a more complicated but equally more realistic method that involves Lighting Effects.

THE SIMPLE EMBOSS APPROACH

Whether he decides to enhance his button with Emboss or Lighting Effects, Ninness starts off the same way. First, he creates a new image with the Contents set to Transparent. Then, he creates an icon for the button — shown here as a black cog (21.13) — on the default layer provided with the document. It's very important that the icon be black; even if you want to make it a different color later, use black for now.

Next, Ninness creates a new layer below the first and blocks out the shape of the button in white (21.14). "I just painted a few random strokes using the paintbrush tool with a soft brush. I figure, if the technique works with fuzzy brushstrokes, it'll work with anything." Again, it's very important that you use white for the button. You can always modify the color later.

If you're following along and creating your own button, this is a good point to save your work. In the next section, you'll start from this point when using the Lighting Effects filter. You may even want to duplicate the image so you don't harm the original.

Just so we're all on the same page, Ninness has two layers — one called Cog (black) in front of another called Button (white). With the Button layer active, he presses Option/Alt while choosing Layer ➢ Merge Visible. (On the Mac, you can alternatively press ⌘+Shift+Option+E.) This merges the contents of both layers onto the Button layer.

At this point, you could launch right into the Emboss filter. But again, Ninness suggests you start off with a little Gaussian Blur. "In this case, I'd go with something subtle, like a Radius of about 2.0."

Then, he chooses the Emboss filter. Because he's working with a layer of white pixels, Ninness sets the Angle value to -45 degrees to create the effect of light coming in from the upper left. "Then, I just experiment with the other settings. A Height of 3 and an Amount of 300 looks pretty good (21.15).

"That's it, really. From here, it's just a matter of assigning your button the proper colors." If you want to color the icon separately of the button, you can fill the icon with color by pressing Shift+Option/ Alt+Delete. Try setting the blend mode in the Layers palette to Hard Light. Then, adjust the Opacity setting as desired. As a general rule of thumb, cool colors tend to require higher Opacity settings than warm ones (21.16).

If you prefer to color the icon and button together, Ninness recommends that you leave the icon black and reduce the Opacity to about 50 percent. You can add an adjustment layer (by ⌘/Ctrl-clicking on the new layer icon along the bottom of the Layers palette) and set the layer to Hue/Saturation. Then, inside the Hue/Saturation dialog box, select the Colorize check box and adjust the Hue and Saturation values as desired.

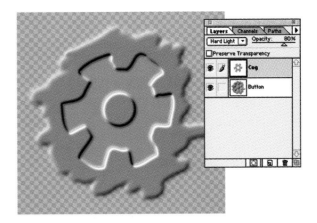

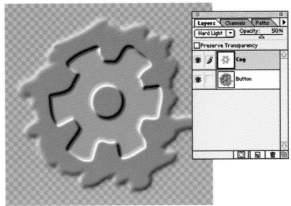

21.16

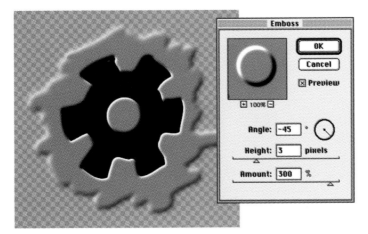

21.15

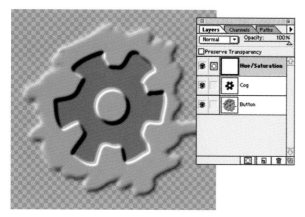

21.17

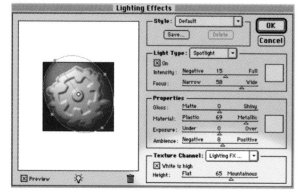

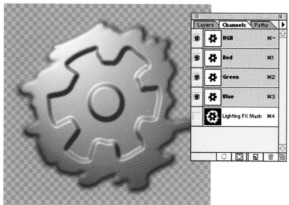

21.18 (TOP), **21.19** (BOTTOM)

"This is a great way to colorize the button (21.17) because you can always go back and modify your colors later. With your button layers set to neutral grays, your coloring options are virtually unlimited."

THE SLIGHTLY MORE ELABORATE LIGHTING EFFECTS METHOD

To light your button with the Lighting Effects filter, you start with the same two-layer file — black icon in the foreground and white button in the background. You'll apply Lighting Effects to the white button layer, but first, you need to create a mask to give the button some depth. "Lighting Effects creates the best results when you have a texture channel to work with. That's where the mask comes in."

In Photoshop, Ninness ⌘/Ctrl-clicks on the Button layer in the Layers palette to select the button outline. Then, he presses both ⌘ and Option, or Ctrl and Alt under Windows, and clicks on the Cog layer. This subtracts the cog outline from the selection. Finally, Ninness switches to the Channels palette and clicks the save selection icon to convert the selection to a channel.

To keep things tidy, Ninness names his mask "Lighting FX Mask." Then, he switches to the mask channel (⌘/Ctrl+4), deselects everything (⌘/Ctrl+D), and applies the Gaussian Blur filter, again with a Radius of 2.0.

Ninness switches back to the RGB composite view (⌘/Ctrl+tilde). With the Button layer active, he chooses Filter ➤ Render ➤ Lighting Effects. Then, he selects his Lighting FX Mask channel from the Texture Channel pop-up menu (21.18), and he leaves the White is High check box turned on. "Switch the angle of the light to wherever you want it. Again, I like it coming from the upper left, but it's up to you.

"If you plan on making a series of buttons using the same basic lighting and texture settings, you might want to take a moment and save your settings. Then, once you get an effect you like, go ahead and apply the filter by pressing Return or Enter." Although Lighting Effects is a more challenging filter to use than Emboss, it also delivers a more credible rendition of depth (21.19). The figure shows the Button layer on its own, with Cog temporarily hidden.

"To color the button, do the same thing you did with the Emboss effect. Set the Opacity of the icon layer to 50 percent and apply Hue/Saturation on an adjustment layer (21.20).

"You can use the buttons as is, against a white HTML page. Or use the mask channel to clean up the edges of your buttons and then add drop shadows (21.21). This effect takes some effort the first few times you run through it. But with a little practice, you'll be cranking out buttons in no time."

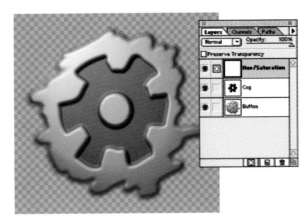

21.20

 <u>**When Good Steer Go Bad**</u>

 <u>**Cowhands of the Orient**</u>

 <u>**I Was a Gear-Head Cowpoke**</u>

 <u>**@Home.OnThe/Range.html**</u>

21.21

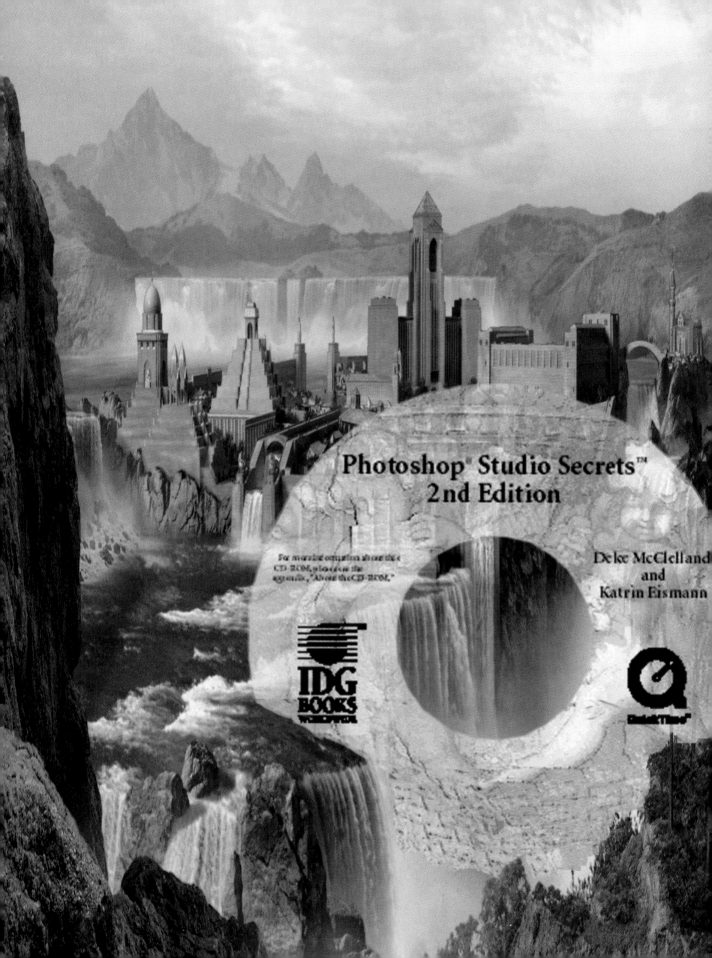

Photoshop® Studio Secrets™
2nd Edition

For more information about this
CD-ROM, please see the
appendix, "About the CD-ROM."

Deke McClelland
and
Katrin Eismann

IDG
BOOKS
WORLDWIDE

ABOUT THE CD-ROM

By your genial CD curator, Deke McClelland

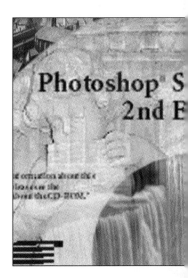

The CD at the back of this book contains just 60 files, approximately 0.000000143 percent as many as you'll find on most CDs at the back of most computer books. However, although they're few in number, they're mighty powerful. These 60 files still manage to consume more than 300MB of disk space. It's sort of the Alamo of CD content.

All 60 files fall under the heading of "custom content." In stark contrast to the oft reproduced plug-ins and demo utilities that serve as the backbone for a proud industry of CDs at the back of Photoshop titles, all 60 files on this CD are unique to this book.

These 60 files are shockingly relevant to the information conveyed in the text. Strange as this may sound, the content on the CD actually has a bearing on the topics covered in the book.

To highlight the noble purpose of this CD, I've chosen as its icon the eye of an owl (A.1). Famous as the symbol for Great Intellectual Prowess — as popularized in Winnie the Pooh books and other dramatic folklore — the owl's eye serves as a signpost for high-minded artistry. It is sheer coincidence that I was in a hurry and I came across an owl in the first stock photo collection I looked at.

The 60 files of which I speak so highly are for the most part self-evident. Just double-click a file and watch it go. The following sections quickly walk you through the lot.

THE CONTENTS

Stick the CD in your computer. Double-click the owl-eye icon to display the contents of the CD. Depending

A.1

on your platform, you will see one of two independent partitions, one for the Mac (A.2) and the other for the PC (A.3). Now you'll discover the multimedia side of *Photoshop Studio Secrets, 2nd Edition*.

The CD content is divided into seven folders and three loose QuickTime files. The QuickTime files are big — 320 by 240 pixels at 15 frames per second — so they work best on Power Mac and Pentium computers. They'll still play on 040 and 486 models, but occasional frames may hang and the sound may not sync properly with the video.

Here's a complete rundown on the files:

- **DigGuru.mov:** As many of you know, I occasionally host a cable television show called "Digital Gurus" (A.4). It appears sporadically in 30 or so million households, but that still leaves a few billion without. Luckily, Jones Entertainment Company has generously donated this 15-minute segment, minus

TIP

If a video plays slowly or unevenly, you can speed up performance by copying the Quick-Time movies to your hard drive. You'll need QuickTime 3 to see all the movies; if you don't have it, run the installer program inside the QuickTime VR folder.

commercials. Open the DigGuru.mov file and click the Play button to see Adobe's Russell Brown demonstrate Photoshop 4's adjustment layers. Okay, so Photoshop 5 is out now, but Russell is forever entertaining and even moderately educational, thanks to my eagle-eyed supervision. Think of it as a 22nd chapter — one you don't have to read.

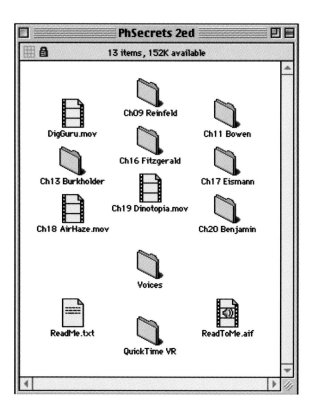

A.2

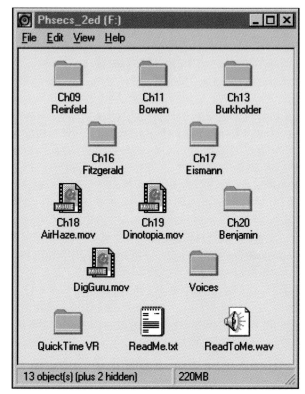

A.3

■ **Reinfeld:** This folder contains four silent QuickTime movies, all of which show moving type effects created by Eric Reinfeld (Chapter 9). These are the only files you can find elsewhere, specifically on the CD included with Reinfeld's own book, *Real World After Effects* (Peachpit Press). If nothing else, check out Trippy.mov. No mind-altering chemicals needed.

■ **Bowen:** Double-click this folder to access two versions of Robert Bowen's stereoscopic view of New York City (Chapter 11). If you have a monster system with scads of RAM, open the Huge3-D.psd file. Otherwise, open Med3-D.psd instead. Then get yourself a pair of 3-D glasses and put them on with the red lens over your left eye and the blue over your right. (You can hear Bowen personally explain the file by running his movie in the Voices folder.)

■ **Burkholder:** If you want to follow along with Dan Burkholder's imagesetting techniques (Chapter 13), check out this folder. Instead of glitzy images, you'll find two Curves dialog box settings and three graduated step wedges.

■ **Fitzgerald:** Inside this folder, you'll find 15 QuickTime VR movies created by Janie Fitzgerald (Chapter 16). Drag inside the movies and watch the world spin around. Press Shift to zoom in, press Ctrl to zoom out. Don't expect to see the stereotypical photographic panoramic views; Fitzgerald proves that art has a place in the virtual world.

■ **Eismann:** Coauthor and artist, Katrin decided to grace this CD with some content from her chapter on digital photography (Chapter 17). All four of these QuickTime VR movies were created by stitching together pictures from digital cameras.

■ **AirHaze.mov:** Here is the finished spinning shoe sequence from Will Hyde's Air Haze commercial for Nike (Chapter 18).

■ **Dinotopia.mov:** Run this movie to see Eric Chauvin's vision of Dinotopia live and breathe (Chapter 19). The water comes from Niagara Falls; music and sound effects come from Denver-based musician David Schmal.

A.4

■ **Benjamin:** Because Ben Benjamin (Chapter 20) creates his images to be viewed on screen, I figure you should see them on screen. Nine of the files are screen shots of his finished Web pages from CNET and E! Online. The tenth file, TalkSoup.gif, is an animated banner ad. You can open it up inside a Web browser such as Netscape Navigator or a GIF animation utility such as GifBuilder. (Neither of these programs is included with the *Photoshop Studio Secrets, 2nd Edition* CD.)

■ **Voices:** This folder includes snippets from my phone interviews with the 16 original *Photoshop Studio Secrets* artists (A.5). Lasting one to two minutes apiece, these QuickTime conversations explore technical topics, personal background, and just plain goofiness. Hear a bit of calming digital camera advice from Katrin Eismann. Find out why Michael Ninness is known to his friends as "Myke with a Y."

Keep in mind, all the conversations in the Voices folder were pieced together from telephone recordings, so the quality is a little choppy. If you have speakers attached to your computer, crank the volume. If you don't, go out and buy some. They're cheap and they make computing much more enjoyable.

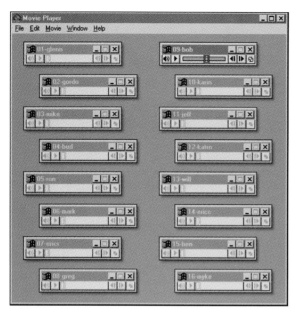

A.5

CD TECHNICAL SUPPORT

If you have any problems getting the CD to work with your computer, it's very likely that some of your settings files or drivers are not working properly. For assistance, call IDG's technical support hotline at 1-800-762-2974. This is also the number to call if your CD is damaged.

INDEX

A

abstract expressionism, 95–109
  channel experimentation for, 98–102, 103
  color use for, 102–103
  magic wand for, 106, 109
  with scanned-in Pres Type, 96, 98
acetate for fine-art printing, 166
Add Noise filter, 138, 153
Adobe Gamma monitor calibration utility, 179
advertising (with high-resolution imaging), 145–159
  "cartoon physics" for, 156–157
  CMYK files and RGB transparencies for, 150
  examples by Robert Bowen, 150–157
  file size and poster art, 149–150
  role of illusion in, 145
  spontaneous snapshot looks, 154–156
  texturing gradient skies in ads, 153
  trompe l'oeil images, 145, 150
  unreal and outrageous images, 145–147
advertising on the Web, 306–309
After Effects program for video art, 30, 31, 273, 275, 277–283
airbrushing
  for budget 3-D characters, 35, 38
  Dissolve mode for, 75, 77
alien creatures, facial distortions for. See distortions, face
Alien Skin Software
  Eye Candy plug-in collection, 12
  Motion Trail filter, 219–220
aligning vector art with imagery, 24
alpha channels used to create abstract art, 103
alterations and "base camps," 129–130
anaglyphs, 158
animal photography, 199–205
animated banner ads for the Web, 306–309
Apple QuickTime Virtual Reality, 235–257
  commercial work done with, 236–239
  defined, 235, 243–244
  experimentation with, 254–255
  personal work done with, 240–241
  as photographer's tool, 235–236
  Photoshop production for, 245–247
  proportion and color with, 248–251
  shooting photographs for, 244–245
  unreal images with, 252–253
  viewing high- or low-resolution QTVR files, 238
  virtual galleries, 256–257

Web site, 241–242
Apply Image command, 120, 122–123, 124
archiving issues, 74, 130, 271
arrow keys, 141
artist profiles
  Benjamin, Ben, 300–301
  Bowen, Robert, 146–147
  Burkholder, Dan, 176–177
  Chan, Ron, 72–73
  Chauvin, Eric, 286–287
  Claesson, Ulrik, 96–97
  Eismann, Katrin, 262–263
  Fitzgerald, Janie, 236–237
  Goto, Hiroshi, 54–55
  Hyde, Will, 276–277
  Mitsui, Glenn, 4–5
  Moore, Mark, 86–87
  Ninness, Michael, 312–313
  Pawlok, Werner, 214–215
  Peen, Bud, 42–43
  Reinfeld, Eric, 116–117
  Schewe, Jeff, 200–201
  Schminke, Karin, 162–163
  Strassburger, Mike, 34–35
  Studer, Gordon, 20–21
  Vander Houwen, Greg, 130–131

B

backgrounds
  creating unique, 61–62
  mixing static, 24
  shadows in, 12–13
  sky images, 138–140, 153
banner ads on the Web, 306–309
"base camps" and alterations, 129–130, 141, 142
Benjamin, Ben
  artist profile, 300–301
  on Web images, 299–309
Berman, Howard, 151, 157
beveled electronic buttons, 312–313
beveled outlines, 12
bitmaps, 191–192
black paper, fine art printing on, 168
blend modes
  Difference blend mode, 121, 228
  Hard Light blend mode, 123, 124, 125
  Multiply blend mode, 38, 64, 133
  Normal blend mode, 38, 64
  Overlay mode, 124
  painting shadows and, 38
  Screen blend mode, 38, 133, 134
  Soft light blend mode, 189

blends in Illustrator, 74
block eraser, 56, 58
blurring and dodging type, 119
Bowen, Robert
  artist profile, 146–147
  on high-resolution imaging, 145–159
bristol board, 43
broadcast design, 273–283
  fundamentals, 274–277
  Photoshop as a tool for, 273
  real-time editing, 277
  rotoscoping with masks, 282–283
  setting up text effects in Photoshop, 277–282
Burkholder, Dan
  artist profile, 176–177
  on fine-art digital photography, 175–197
burn tool, 38
buttons, electronic, 311–321
  basic beveled square, 312–313
  clipping group function for, 314–317
  as elegant and informative art, 312
  Emboss filter for creating, 318–320
  faces as, 303
  high-res files for, 313
  Lighting Effects filter for creating, 320–321
  stamped, 318–321

C

CalComp printer
  for fine art printing, 163
  price of, 171
Calculations command, 120
calibration, 179
cameras, digital, 259–271
  archiving photos shot with, 271
  catalogs produced with, 263
  cost of, 260
  Dicomed BigShot, 262
  evaluating, 266–267
  film cameras versus, 259, 262, 265
  Fisher-Price Fun Photo Maker, 183
  Kodak DCS420, 259
  Leaf Digital Camera Back II, 260
  long-term forecast for, 259
  low-end, 268
  Polaroid PDC-2000, 267
  quality issues, 259, 262, 264
  savings with, 265
  shooting and editing photos, 267–270
  time-saving advantages of, 262
cameras as notebooks, 181
Canvas Size command, 44, 166

cartoon characters in budget 3-D, 33–39
  airbrush tool for, 34, 35, 38
  creating layers for, 36
  drawing paths for, 36
  Glass Lens filter from Kai's Power Tools for, 39
  painting highlights and shadows for, 38
  pen tool for, 35
  rasterizing artwork inside Photoshop, 35
  sketching trial versions in Illustrator, 34
cast shadows, 38
Chan, Ron
  artist profile, 72–73
  on Illustrator versus Photoshop, 71, 74, 82–83
channel experimentation for abstract art, 98–102, 103
Channel Mixer feature, 182
Channels palette, 79
Chauvin, Eric,
  artist profile, 286–287
  on digital matte paintings, 285–297
Claesson, Ulrik
  on abstract expressionism, 95–109
  artist profile, 96–97
  on commercial design, 110–112
  on scanning in Pres Type, 96, 98
  simulated moonscape by, 99–100
client-artist relationship
  advice on taking risks, 155
  communication in, 7
  concept development and, 7
  initial contact with client, 6–7
  scanned sketch as visual contract, 142
  submitting sketches and final work, 11, 68
Clipboard
  copying files to, 218
  memory, 138
clipping group function
  for electronic button design, 314–317
  for type treatments, 118
Clockwork Web design company, 95, 97
clone tool, 185
CMYK conversions, 50, 59, 150
CMYK preview mode, 59, 150
color
  in abstract art example, 102–103
  CMYK files and RGB transparencies, 150
  fashion photography and, 218–220
  matching, 50, 68, 150
  for paintings merged with Photoshop, 59–60
  for type effects, 127
Color Balance and Hue/Saturation technique, 59–60, 66
Color Range command, 210
Color Table command, 14, 16
colorizing
  with different hues, 14
  photographs, 25

commercial art process, 3–17
  communicating with client, 7
  concept development, 7, 9–10
  initial contact with client, 6–7, 11
  for medical conference brochure cover, 7–17
  rasterizing and tracing in Photoshop, 11–12
  scanned sketch as visual contract, 142
  submitting one sketch for approval, 11
  tracing sketches in FreeHand, 11
commercials, television, 273–283
  broadcast design fundamentals, 274–277
  Photoshop as a tool for, 273
  real-time editing, 277
  rotoscoping with masks, 282–283
  setting up text effects in Photoshop for, 277–282
communicating with clients, 7
compositing
  fashion photography images, 226–227
  Hiroshi Goto's artwork, 63–64
  roughing out compositions by, 130, 132–133
  scanned logos against backgrounds, 134
computers
  freedom to experiment and, 50
  limitations of, 41, 43
  Power Macs, 30, 150
concept development
  for fashion ad campaigns, 215–216
  sketching for, 9–10
converting to CMYK, 50, 59, 150
corporate identity, designing a, 110–112
cost of digital cameras, 260
cost of Photoshop, 3
curved type, 13–14
Curves feature
  for fine-art photography, 186, 188, 189, 191
  for manipulating mask transitions, 135, 137

D

DeBabelizer program, 300
Difference blend mode, 121, 228
Difference Clouds filter, 102
digital cameras, 259–271
  archiving photos shot with, 271
  catalogs produced with, 263
  cost of, 260
  Dicomed BigShot, 262
  evaluating, 266–267
  film cameras versus, 259, 262, 265
  Fisher-Price Fun Photo Maker, 183
  Kodak DCS420, 259
  Leaf Digital Camera Back II, 260
  long-term forecast for, 259
  low-end, 268
  Polaroid PDC-2000, 267
  quality issues, 259, 262, 264
  savings with, 265
  shooting and editing photos, 267–270

  time-saving advantages of, 262
digital matte paintings. *See* paintings, digital matte
digital photography, 267–270
  adjusting lighting irregularities, 268–269
  fixing as little as possible in Photoshop, 267
  fixing rainbows, 269
  with low-end cameras, 268
  using special effects, 270
digital photography, fine-art, 175–197
  calibrating monitor for, 179–180
  cameras as notebooks, 181
  Channel Mixer feature for, 182
  experimentation done by artist Burkholder, 178–179
  galleries that exhibit, 197
  Iris prints versus platinum prints, 197
  light and drop shadows for, 188–190
  matching film grain, 187–188
  Photoshop as darkroom for, 184–186
  preparing file for final output, 191–192
  platinum versus regular prints, 175, 177
  pricing of, 197
  scanning in film for, 182–183
  service bureaus and, 193
  step wedges for, 179–180, 193
  tweaking files for, 193–195
distortion blurs, cleaning up, 91
distortions, face, 85–93
  cranium, 90–91
  ears, 88
  eyes, 89–90
  masking features, 88–89
  mouth, 92
dithering in Web images, 304
dodge tool, 38
dragging and dropping, 138
dragging paths from Illustrator, 75–76
drop shadows, 26, 109
Duralene, translucent, 43
Dust & Scratches filter, 56

E

editing commercial photography, 199–211
  of animals, 199–201
  of glass and water, 208–210
  matching backgrounds, 201–203
  mixing multiple live elements, 203–205
  playing with scale, 205–206
  Spherize filter for, 201, 209
Eismann, Katrin
  artist profile, 262–263
  on digital cameras, 259–271
electronic buttons. *See* buttons, electronic
emboss effects for type, 121–126
Emboss filter
  for creating electronic buttons, 318–320
  for type treatments, 121, 122
End key, 223
enhancing vector artwork, 71–83

adding depth, 80–82
adding textures, 75–80
aligning vector art with imagery, 24
Epson StylusColor 3000 printer, 171
eraser, block, 56, 58
ethics of repurposing photos, 21
Extensis Mask Pro plug-in, 188, 189
Extensis PhotoTools plug-in, 115
Eye Candy (Alien Skin Software), 12
eye distortions, 89–90
eyedropper, 76

F
face distortions. *See* distortions, face
faces from "Retro" stock photography collection, 19–21
Fantastic Forest, National Geographic's, 51
fashion photography, 213–233
  adding color to black-and-white photos, 218–220
  compositing images for, 226–227
  concepts for ads, 215–216
  film choices for, 216
  hair mask technique for, 228–232
  layouts, 224–225
  retouching, 220–223
  scanning, 218
  shooting with digital process in mind, 216
fear of Photoshop, 74, 83
file size management
  Illustrator versus Photoshop and, 74, 83
  for large, high-resolution images, 149–150
  removing channels and flattening layers in abstract art, 103
film
  for fashion photography, 216
  for platinum prints, 182, 187
film grain
  digital fine-art photography and, 187–188
  on matte images, 291
filters
  Add Noise filter, 138, 153
  Dust & Scratches filter, 56
  Emboss filter, 121, 122, 318–320
  Find Edges filter, 121
  from Kai's Power Tools, 14, 39
  Lens Flare filter, 16
  Lighting Effects filter, 39, 320–321
  Maximum filter, 118
  Minimum filter, 118, 119
  Pinch filter, 85, 88, 209
  Shear filter, 14, 159
  Solarize filter, 59, 62
  Spatter filter, 126
  Spherize filter, 85, 91, 201, 209
  Find Edges filter, 121
fine-art photography, digital, 175–197
  calibrating monitor for, 179–180
  cameras as notebooks, 181

Channel Mixer feature for, 182
clone tool for, 185
Curves feature for, 186,188–189
experimentation done by artist Burkholder, 178–179
galleries that exhibit, 197
Iris prints versus platinum prints, 197
light and drop shadows for, 188–190
matching film grain, 187–188
Photoshop as darkroom for, 184–186
preparing file for final output, 191–192
platinum versus regular prints, 175, 177
pricing of, 197
scanning in film for, 182–183
service bureaus and, 193
step wedges for, 179–180, 193
tweaking files for, 193–195
fine-art printing, 161–173
  on black paper, 168
  creating background for inset image, 165
  creating inset superimage, 165
  creating the subimage, 164
  mixing digital and traditional media, 163, 173
  overprinting inset image, 166–168
  painting onto printed template, 169
  printing onto acrylic, 169
  printing onto liquid photo emulsion, 170–171
  printing the subimage, 164–165
  protecting ink-jet artwork, 171
  shopping for a fine-art printer, 171–173
  testing overprint with acetate, 166
Fisher-Price Fun Photo Maker digital camera, 183
Fitzgerald, Janie
  artist profile, 236–237
  on QuickTime Virtual Reality photography, 235–257
Fractal Design Painter
  creating watercolors in, 41
  natural media tools in, 78
  texturing capabilities in, 16
Free Transform command, 119, 141
FreeHand, 11, 110–111
friskets for Photoshop's airbrush, 35
furniture design, 50–51

G
Gallery Effects filters added to Photoshop 4, 126
gallery-photographer partnerships, 197
Gaussian Blur filter
  for ad with depth of field, 157
  for corporate identity design manipulation, 111
  for enhancing vector artwork, 74, 80, 81
  for glowing edges, 219
  for soft edges in photos, 204

for softening shadows in photos, 190
for texturing gradient skies, 153
for type treatments, 119, 121, 126
Gaussian Glow filter in Kai's Power Tools, 184
GifBuilder shareware utility, 307–309
glass and water, photographing, 208–210
Goto, Hiroshi
  artist profile, 54–55
  on submitting work to clients, 68
  on traditional technique combined with PhotoShop, 53–67
  on watercolor painting, 67–68
gradient layer masks, 135
gradient tool, 135, 137
graphic art combined with stock photography, 19–31
  aligning vector art with imagery, 24
  colorizing photos, 25
  ethics of repurposing photos, 21
  faces from "Retro" collection, 19–21
  free-form image chopping, 29–30
  geometric look for, 23–29
  hands, 28
  trend toward stock photos, 21, 23
  with Version 5 of Photoshop, 30–31

H
hands, stock photography of, 28
Hard Light blend mode, 123, 124, 125
Hewlett-Packard 560c printer, 173
HI! Seisaku-Shitsu design firm, 53, 54
highlights, painting, 38
high-resolution imaging for ads, 145–159
  "cartoon physics" and, 156–157
  CMYK files and RGB transparencies, 150
  examples by Robert Bowen, 150–157
  file size and poster art, 149–150
  spontaneous snapshots and, 154–156
  texturing gradient skies in ads, 153
  trompe l'oeil images, 145, 150
  unreal and outrageous images, 145–147
Home key, 223
Hue/Saturation command, 14, 59–60, 66
huge file sizes
  Illustrator versus Photoshop and, 74, 83
  for large, high-resolution images, 149–150
  removing channels and flattening layers in abstract art, 103
  World Wide Web images and, 300–301
Hyde, Will
  artist profile, 276–277
  on broadcast design, 273–283

I
iconography (electronic buttons), 311–321
Illustrator
  blends, 49, 74, 77

Continued

Illustrator *(continued)*
  brush tool, 47
  dragging paths from, 75–76
  versus Photoshop, 71, 74, 82–83
  Place Art command, 24
  Trim filter, 75
  for type creation, 115
  for Web pages, 302–303
image chopping, free-form, 29–30
Indexed Color command, 14
  for Web art, 304
Info Palette, 179
Inner Bevel filter, 12
Internet artwork, 299–309
  animated banner ads, 306–309
  anticipating 256-color monitors and, 304
  exploiting browser caching, 305–306
  exporting GIF files from Illustrator, 303
  file size, 300, 309
  Illustrator for, 302–303
  LOWSRC tag for, 309
  pixel-level editing of, 300
Iris prints versus platinum prints, 197

J

JPEG file format, 50, 74

K

Kai's Power Tools, filters from, 14, 39
keyboard shortcuts in Photoshop 5.0, 223

L

Lab Color mode, 269
lasso and layer masking, 137
layer masks, tonal adjustments in, 135–138
layer options, 133–135
layered type, 119
layering, 129–142
  adding depth to vector artwork by, 80–82
  "base camps" and alterations, 129–130, 141, 142
  for budget 3-D cartoon characters, 36
  example using Vander Houwen's techniques, 138–142
  roughing out a composition, 130–133
  tonal adjustments in layer masks, 135–138
  using layer options, 133–135
Lens Flare filter, 16
Letraset Pres Type, 96, 98
Levels command, 130, 138
Lighting Effects filter
  creating electronic buttons with, 320–321
  creating shadows inside a sphere with, 39
limitations of Photoshop, 41, 43, 83, 129

M

Macs, Power, 30, 150
magic wand
  for abstract expressionism, 106, 109
  fashion photos and, 228

layer masking and, 137
marquee tool, 36
masking facial features, 88–89
masking hair, 228–232
masks, from sketches to, 56–58
matte paintings, digital. *See* paintings, digital matte
Maximum filter for type treatments, 118, 120
Media Composer 1000, 277
medical conference brochure cover, 7–17
MetaCreations products, 184
Minimum filter for type treatments, 118, 120
Mitsui, Glenn
  artist profile, 4–5
  on client-artist relationship, 6–7, 11
  range of styles used by, 3–6
Modern Dog design firm, 33, 34
monitor calibration utility, 179
moonscape, simulated, 99–100
Moore, Mark
  artist profile, 86–87
  on distortions, 85–93
Motion Blur filter, 61, 119, 138
Motion Trail filter (Alien Skin software), 219–220
mouse-headed man ad, 145–146
mouths, distorting, 92
movies, matte paintings for. *See* paintings, digital matte
moving around images (keyboard shortcuts), 223
moving through layers, 121
Multiply blend mode, 133

N

natural media integration, 41–51. *See also* fine-art printing; paintings merged with Photoshop
  benefits of, 43
  coloring inside Photoshop, 45–46
  combining line art and watercolor in Photoshop, 44
  JPEG files for, 50
  preparing watercolors for scanning, 43–44
  quill-pen illustrations, 46–49
  stigma of working outside computers and, 41
  watercolors on National Geographic Web site, 51
navigation shortcuts in Photoshop 5.0, 223
Nihon-ga paintings, 67
Ninness, Michael
  artist profile, 312–313
  on buttons, 311–321
Normal blend mode, 38, 64

O

outlines of image elements, 12
outlining type, 121
Overlay mode, 124

P

Page Down key, 223
paintbrush tool, 132
Painter, Fractal Design
  creating watercolors in, 41
  natural media tools in, 78
  texturing capabilities in, 16
paintings, digital matte, 285–297
  for *Babylon 5,* 285
  basic matte process, 286–287
  Cloud City mattes for *Return of the Jedi,* 290–294
  Dinotopia city example, 294–296
  eliminating film grain from, 291
  shuttle bay matte for *The Empire Strikes Back,* 288–290
  visibility of, 297
paintings merged with Photoshop, 53–68
  adding color to image, 59–60
  compositing, 63
  creating backgrounds, 61–62
  Japanese culture as inspiration for, 54, 65–67
  masking out image elements, 56–58
  signing or sealing, 64
  sketches as templates for, 55
  watercolor painting without Photoshop, 67–68
paths
  for budget 3-D characters, 36
  for commercial photos, 204
  dragging paths from Illustrator, 75–76
  instead of watercolor, 47–49
Paths palette, 76
Pawlok, Werner
  artist profile, 214–215
  on fashion photography, 213–233
Peen, Bud
  artist profile, 42–43
  on natural media, 41–51
pen tool. *See also* paths
  as fashion photographer's favorite selection tool, 229
  shaving images into cartoon shapes with, 30
  tracing with, 12, 35
perspective, violating, 12–13
petroglyphs, 9, 10
PhotoDisc image library, 12, 19, 21
photography, digital fine-art, 175–197
  calibrating monitor for, 179–180
  cameras as notebooks, 181
  Channel Mixer feature for, 182
  experimentation done by artist Burkholder, 178–179
  galleries that exhibit, 197
  Iris prints versus platinum prints, 197
  light and drop shadows for, 188–190
  matching film grain, 187–188
  Photoshop as darkroom for, 184–186
  preparing file for final output, 191–192

platinum versus regular prints, 175, 177
pricing of, 197
scanning in film for, 182–183
service bureaus and, 193
step wedges for, 179–180, 193
tweaking files for, 193–195
photography, editing, 199–211
of animals, 199–201
of glass and water, 208–210
matching backgrounds, 201–203
mixing multiple live elements, 203–205
playing with scale, 205–206
Spherize filter for, 201, 209
photography, fashion, 213–233
adding color to black-and-white photos,
218–220
compositing images for, 226–227
concepts for ads, 215–216
film choices for, 216
hair mask technique for, 228–232
layouts, 224–225
retouching, 220–223
scanning, 218
shooting with digital process in mind, 216
photography, QuickTime Virtual Reality,
235–257
commercial work done with, 236–239
defined, 235, 243–244
experimentation with, 254–255
personal work done with, 240–241
as photographer's tool, 235–236
Photoshop production for, 245–247
proportion and color with, 248–251
shooting photographs for, 244–245
unreal images with, 252–253
viewing high- or low-resolution QTVR
files, 238
virtual galleries, 256–257
Web site, 241–242
photography, stock, 19–31
aligning vector art with imagery, 24
colorizing photos, 25
ethics of repurposing photos, 21
faces from "Retro" collection, 19–21
free-form image chopping, 29–30
geometric look for, 23–29
hands, 28
trend toward, 21, 23
with Version 5 of Photoshop, 30–31
Photoshop
cost of, 3
as darkroom, 184–186
digital matte paintings with, 285–297
as editing tool, 71, 83
fashion photography with, 213–233
fear of, 74, 83
fine-art printing with, 161–173
high-resolution imaging with, 145–159
versus Illustrator, 74, 82–83
as industry standard, 71
layering, 129–142

limitations of, 41, 43, 83, 129
as a moneymaker, 210, 286
photographing for, 199–211
platinum prints with, 175–197
on Power Macs, 150
from sketch to execution in, 3–17
for television commercials, 273–283
3-D characters with, 33–39
traditional media and, 41–51, 53–68
Web art with, 299–309
Photoshop 5
changes in artist's life with, 30–31
filling artwork with white in, 26
layer effects, 127
navigation shortcuts, 223
undos with, 31
PhotoTools, 115
platinum prints. *See* prints, platinum
plug-ins
Extensis Mask Pro, 188, 189
Extensis PhotoTools, 115
Eye Candy from Alien Skin software, 12
Kai's Power Tools filters, 14, 39
Motion Trail filter, 219–220
Polaroid SprintScan 35Plus, 182
polygon lasso tool, 132
Power Macs, 30, 150
Pres Type, 96, 98
Preserve Transparency check box, 38, 119
price of Photoshop, 3
price range for digital cameras, 260
printers, fine-art, 171–173
printing fine art, 161–173
creating background for inset image, 165
creating inset superimage, 165
creating the subimage, 164
mixing digital and traditional media, 163,
173
overprinting inset image, 166–168
printing onto acrylic, 169
painting onto a printed template, 169
printing onto liquid photo emulsion,
170–171
printing the subimage, 164–165
protecting ink-jet artwork, 171
shopping for a fine-art printer, 171–173
testing overprint with acetate, 166
prints, platinum, 175–197
calibrating monitor for, 179–180
cameras as notebooks, 181
Channel Mixer feature for, 182
experimentation done by artist Burkholder,
178–179
gallery-photographer relationship and, 197
Iris prints versus platinum prints, 197
light and drop shadows for, 188–190
matching film grain, 187–188
Photoshop as darkroom for, 184–186
preparing file for final output, 191–192
platinum versus regular prints, 175, 177
pricing of platinum prints, 197

scanning in film for, 182–183
service bureaus and, 193
step wedges for, 179–180, 193
tweaking files for, 193–195

Q

QuickTime Virtual Reality, 235–257
commercial work done with, 236–239
defined, 235, 243–244
experimentation with, 254–255
personal work done with, 240–241
as photographer's tool, 235–236
Photoshop production for, 245–247
proportion and color with, 248–251
shooting photographs for, 244–245
unreal images with, 252–253
viewing high- or low-resolution QTVR
files, 238
virtual galleries, 256–257
Web site, 241–242
quill-pen illustrations, 46–49

R

rainbows in digital photography, 269
rasterizing
adding depth to vector artwork, 80–82
adding textures to vector artwork, 75–80
budget 3-D cartoon characters, 35
after tracing sketch in FreeHand, 11–12
Ray Dream Designer program, 14
Reinfeld, Eric
artist profile, 116–117
on type stylizing, 115–127
retouching fashion photography, 220–223
RGB
transparencies for clients, 150
working in, 50, 127, 150
rotoscoping with masks, 282–283
roughing out a composition, 130–133
rubber stamp for retouching fashion photography, 220, 222

S

scanners
PaperPort scanner, 183
Polaroid SprintScan 35Plus film scanner,
182
scanning
fashion photos, 218
fine-art photography, 182
paintings, 56
Pres Type, 96, 98
watercolors, 44
Schewe, Jeff
artist profile, 200–201
on photographing for Photoshop, 199–211
Schminke, Karen
artist profile, 162–163
on fine art printing, 161–173
Screen blend mode, 133, 134

service bureaus, 193
shadows
    drop, 26, 109, 189–190
    for fine-art photography, 189–190
    painting, 38
    inside a sphere, 39
Shear filter
    for creating vertical waves, 159
    for faking 3-D effects, 14
Shift-arrow, 141
shooting commercial animal photography,
        199–205
    creating a centaur, 203–205
    dressing up a pig, 199–201
    finding a photogenic bull's head, 203
shooting digital camera photos, 267–270
    adjusting lighting irregularities, 268–269
    fixing as little as possible in Photoshop and,
        267
    fixing rainbows, 269
    with low-end cameras, 268
    using special effects after, 270
shooting fashion ads, 213–233
    adding color to black-and-white photos,
        218–220
    compositing images for, 226–227
    concept development and, 215–216
    film choices for, 216
    hair mask technique with Photoshop,
        228–232
    layouts, 224–225
    retouching, 220–223
    scanning of photos into Photoshop, 218
    shooting with digital process in mind, 216
shopping for a digital camera, 259–271
    Dicomed BigShot, 262
    film versus digital cameras, 259, 262, 265
    Fisher-Price Fun Photo Maker, 183
    guidelines for, 266–267
    Kodak DCS420, 259, 269
    Leaf Digital Camera Back II, 260
    long-term forecast for digital cameras, 259
    Polaroid PDC-2000, 267
    price range, 260
    quality issues, 259, 262, 264
    savings from use of digital cameras, 265
    time-saving advantages of digital cameras,
        262
    tips for working with low-end cameras, 268
shopping for a fine-art printer, 171–173
shortcuts in Photoshop 5.0 for navigating
        images, 223
sketches
    for concept development, 9–10
    submitting sketches for approval, 11
    as templates, 55
    as visual contracts with clients, 142
sky images
    Add Noise filter and Gaussian Blur for,
        138–140

layering lightning against clouds, 133–135
    texturing gradient skies in ads, 153
smudge tool, 138
snapshots, crafting spontaneous, 154–156
Soft light blend mode, 189
Solarize filter, 59, 62
Spatter filter, 126
special type effects, 115–127
Spherize filter, 85, 91, 201, 209
stamped electronic buttons, 318–321
static backdrops, mixing, 24
step wedges
    creating, 179–180
    defined, 179
stereo pictures, 159
stock photography combined with graphic
        art. *See* photography, stock
Stonehenge cotton rag paper, 163
Strassburger, Mike
    artist profile, 34–35
    on budget 3-D characters, 33–39
StrataStudio Pro, 34, 39
Streamline tracing program, 47, 49
Studer, Gordon
    artist profile, 20–21
    on stock photography with graphic art,
        19–31
stylizing type. *See* type
subimages in fine art compositions
    creating, 164
    printing, 164–165
submitting work to clients, 11, 68
    advice on doing modifications and, 155
    communication with client and, 7
    concept development and, 7
    scanned sketch as visual contract, 142

T

Tarashikomi painting method, 67–68
television and movies, matte paintings for.
        See paintings, digital matte
television commercials, 273–283
    broadcast design fundamentals, 274–277
    Photoshop as a tool for, 273
    real-time editing, 277
    rotoscoping with masks, 282–283
    setting up text effects in Photoshop,
        277–282
textures
    adding textures to vector artwork, 75–80
    for gradient skies in ads, 153
3-D characters, budget approach to, 33–39
    airbrush tool for, 34, 35, 38
    creating layers for, 36
    drawing paths for, 36
    Glass Lens filter from Kai's Power Tools for,
        39
    painting highlights and shadows for, 38
    pen tool for, 35
    rasterizing artwork inside Photoshop, 35

sketching trial versions in Illustrator, 34
3-D effects, Shear filter for, 14
3-D software programs
    ad for 3-D program by Glenn Mitsui, 5
    StrataStudio Pro, 34, 39
    using Photoshop instead of, 33
tonal adjustments in layer masks, 135–138
tracing programs
    Adobe Streamline, 47, 49
    FreeHand, 11
traditional media integration, 41–51. *See also*
        fine art printing; paintings merged with
        Photoshop
    benefits of, 43
    coloring inside Photoshop, 45–46
    combining line art and watercolor in
        Photoshop, 44
    JPEG files for, 50
    preparing watercolors for scanning, 43–44
    quill-pen illustrations, 46–49
    stigma of working outside computers and,
        41
    watercolors on National Geographic Web
        site, 51
Transform command, 190
Transform options, accessing, 190
trash icon, 118
trompe l' oeil images, 145, 150
type, 115–127
    colors for, 127
    creating, 115, 119
    distorting text with Shear filter, 13–14
    emboss effects, 121–126
    filling type with image surrounded by halo,
        117–119
    layered, 119
    outlines, 121
    Pres Type, 96, 98
    quill pen artwork as, 49
    with sharp edges, 127
    on TV Guide cover art, 71–73
    for video, 277–282
    weight variations, 120

U

undos, 31, 129
Unique Editions, 161
UV-protective glass for artwork, 166

V

Vander Houwen, Greg
    artist profile, 130–131
    on layering, 129–142
vanishing point, consistent, 157
Variations command, 25, 28
varnish for protecting artwork, 166
vector artwork, 71–83
    adding depth to, 80–82
    adding textures to, 74, 75–80
    aligning vector art with imagery, 24

video art, 273–283
    broadcast design fundamentals, 274–277
    Photoshop's role in, 273
    real-time editing, 277
    rotoscoping with masks, 282–283
    setting up text effects in Photoshop,
        277–282

W

watercolors, Hiroshi Goto's method of paint-
    ing, 67–68
watercolors, modifying, 41–51. *See also*
    paintings merged with Photoshop
    advantages of using Photoshop for, 41, 43
    coloring inside Photoshop, 45–46

    combining line art and watercolor in
        Photoshop, 44
    JPEG file format for, 50
    preparing and scanning watercolors, 43–44
watercolors on National Geographic Web
    site, 51
Web images, 299–309
    animated banner ads, 306–309
    anticipating 256-color monitors, 304
    designing pages in Illustrator, 302–303
    exploiting browser caching, 305–306
    exporting GIF files from Illustrator, 303
    file size, 300, 309
    <LOWSRC> tag for, 309
    Melrose Place pages on E! Online, 301–306

    pixel-level editing of, 300
Web palette, 304
Web site buttons, 311–321
    basic beveled square, 312–313
    clipping group function for, 314–317
    as elegant and informative art, 312
    Emboss filter for creating, 318–320
    faces as, 303
    high-res files for creating, 313
    Lighting Effects filter for creating, 320–321
    stamped, 318–321
weight variations, type, 120

Z

Zip files, 31, 74

ABOUT THE AUTHORS

Deke McClelland is a contributing editor for *Macworld* and *Publish* magazines. He has authored more than 50 books on electronic publishing and the Macintosh computer, and his work has been translated into more than 20 languages. Deke also hosts *Digital Gurus*, a syndicated TV show about personal computing, from his home base in Colorado. He started his career as artistic director at the first service bureau in the United States.

Deke won a Society of Technical Communication Award in 1994, an American Society for Business Press Editors Award in 1995, and the Ben Franklin Award for Best Computer Book in 1989. He is also a five-time recipient of the prestigious Computer Press Award.

Deke is the author of the following books published by IDG Books Worldwide, Inc.: *Macworld Photoshop 5 Bible*, *Photoshop 5 for Windows Bible*, and *Web Design Studio Secrets;* and *Real World Illustrator 8* (Peachpit Press). The previous edition of *Photoshop Studio Secrets* won the Computer Press Award for the best advanced how-to book of 1997.

Katrin Eismann is an internationally recognized educator and speaker on the subject of imaging and the impact of emerging technologies on the professional photographer. Katrin is coauthor of *Web Design Studio Secrets* (IDG Books Worldwide) and is the conference chairperson for the Thunder Lizard Productions Photoshop Conferences. Her company, PRAXIS Digital Solutions, teaches and lectures throughout Europe, North America, and the Asian-Pacific region.

Katrin's creative work is based on investigating concepts and working with the appropriate technologies to create intriguing images. Her images have appeared in the books *Photoshop WOW!, Photoshop 4 Studio Secrets, Essentials of Digital Photography, Make Your Scanner a Great Production Tool,* and *Essentials of Computing* and in the magazines *Macworld, PhotoDistrictNews, American Photo, Photonics, Computer Artist, Image World, International Photography, IdN,* and *Mac Art & Design.*

COLOPHON

This book was produced electronically in Foster City, California. Microsoft Word 97 was used for word processing; design and layout were produced using QuarkXPress 4.03 and Abobe Photoshop 5 on Power Macintosh computers. The typeface families used are Minion, Myriad Multiple Master, Prestige Elite, Symbol, Trajan, and Zapf Dingbats.

Acquisitions Editor: **Andy Cummings**
Development Editors: **Amy Thomas Buscaglia, Katharine Dvorak**
Technical Editor: **Marc Pawliger**
Copy Editor: **Ami Knox**
Project Coordinator: **Ritchie Durdin**
Book Designer: **Margery Cantor**
Cover Design: **Kate R. Shaw**
Cover Images: **D'pix © Amber Productions, Inc.**
Graphics and Production Specialists: **Jude Levinson, Linda Marousek, Hector Mendoza**
Quality Control Specialists: **Mick Arellano, Mark Schumann**
Illustrator: **Hector Mendoza, Mark Schumann**
Proofreader: **York Production Services**
Indexer: **York Production Services**

IDG BOOKS WORLDWIDE, INC.
END-USER LICENSE AGREEMENT

<u>Read This</u>. **You should carefully read these terms and conditions before opening the software packet(s) included with this book ("Book"). This is a license agreement ("Agreement") between you and IDG Books Worldwide, Inc. ("IDGB"). By opening the accompanying software packet(s), you acknowledge that you have read and accept the following terms and conditions. If you do not agree and do not want to be bound by such terms and conditions, promptly return the Book and the unopened software packet(s) to the place you obtained them for a full refund.**

1. <u>License Grant</u>. IDGB grants to you (either an individual or entity) a nonexclusive license to use one copy of the enclosed software program(s) (collectively, the "Software") solely for your own personal or business purposes on a single computer (whether a standard computer or a workstation component of a multiuser network). The Software is in use on a computer when it is loaded into temporary memory (RAM) or installed into permanent memory (hard disk, CD-ROM, or other storage device). IDGB reserves all rights not expressly granted herein.

2. <u>Ownership</u>. IDGB is the owner of all right, title, and interest, including copyright, in and to the compilation of the Software recorded on the disk(s) or CD-ROM ("Software Media"). Copyright to the individual programs recorded on the Software Media is owned by the author or other authorized copyright owner of each program. Ownership of the Software and all proprietary rights relating thereto remain with IDGB and its licensers.

3. <u>Restrictions On Use and Transfer</u>.

(a) You may only (i) make one copy of the Software for backup or archival purposes, or (ii) transfer the Software to a single hard disk, provided that you keep the original for backup or archival purposes. You may not (i) rent or lease the Software, (ii) copy or reproduce the Software through a LAN or other network system or through any computer subscriber system or bulletin-board system, or (iii) modify, adapt, or create derivative works based on the Software.

(b) You may not reverse engineer, decompile, or disassemble the Software. You may transfer the Software and user documentation on a permanent basis, provided that the transferee agrees to accept the terms and conditions of this Agreement and you retain no copies. If the Software is an update or has been updated, any transfer must include the most recent update and all prior versions.

4. <u>Restrictions On Use of Individual Programs</u>. You must follow the individual requirements and restrictions detailed for each individual program in the appendix, "About the CD-ROM," of this Book. These limitations are also contained in the individual license agreements recorded on the Software Media. These limitations may include a requirement that after using the program for a specified period of time, the user must pay a registration fee or discontinue use. By opening the Software packet(s), you will be agreeing to abide by the licenses and restrictions for these individual programs that are detailed in the appendix, "About the CD-ROM," and on the Software Media. None of the material on this Software Media or listed in this Book may ever be redistributed, in original or modified form, for commercial purposes.

5. Limited Warranty.

(a) IDGB warrants that the Software and Software Media are free from defects in materials and workmanship under normal use for a period of sixty (60) days from the date of purchase of this Book. If IDGB receives notification within the warranty period of defects in materials or workmanship, IDGB will replace the defective Software Media.

(b) IDGB AND THE AUTHORS OF THE BOOK DISCLAIM ALL OTHER WARRANTIES, EXPRESS OR IMPLIED, INCLUDING WITHOUT LIMITATION IMPLIED WARRANTIES OF MERCHANTABILITY AND FITNESS FOR A PARTICULAR PURPOSE, WITH RESPECT TO THE SOFTWARE, THE PROGRAMS, THE SOURCE CODE CONTAINED THEREIN, AND/OR THE TECHNIQUES DESCRIBED IN THIS BOOK. IDGB DOES NOT WARRANT THAT THE FUNCTIONS CONTAINED IN THE SOFTWARE WILL MEET YOUR REQUIREMENTS OR THAT THE OPERATION OF THE SOFTWARE WILL BE ERROR FREE.

(c) This limited warranty gives you specific legal rights, and you may have other rights that vary from jurisdiction to jurisdiction.

6. Remedies.

(a) IDGB's entire liability and your exclusive remedy for defects in materials and workmanship shall be limited to replacement of the Software Media, which may be returned to IDGB with a copy of your receipt at the following address: Software Media Fulfillment Department, Attn.: *Photoshop Studio Secrets, 2nd Edition*, IDG Books Worldwide, Inc., 7260 Shadeland Station, Ste. 100, Indianapolis, IN 46256, or call 1-800-762-2974. Please allow three to four weeks for delivery. This Limited Warranty is void if failure of the Software Media has resulted from accident, abuse, or misapplication. Any replacement Software Media will be warranted for the remainder of the original warranty period or thirty (30) days, whichever is longer.

(b) In no event shall IDGB or the authors be liable for any damages whatsoever (including without limitation damages for loss of business profits, business interruption, loss of business information, or any other pecuniary loss) arising from the use of or inability to use the Book or the Software, even if IDGB has been advised of the possibility of such damages.

(c) Because some jurisdictions do not allow the exclusion or limitation of liability for consequential or incidental damages, the above limitation or exclusion may not apply to you.

7. U.S. Government Restricted Rights. Use, duplication, or disclosure of the Software by the U.S. Government is subject to restrictions stated in paragraph (c)(1)(ii) of the Rights in Technical Data and Computer Software clause of DFARS 252.227-7013, and in subparagraphs (a) through (d) of the Commercial Computer — Restricted Rights clause at FAR 52.227-19, and in similar clauses in the NASA FAR supplement, when applicable.

8. General. This Agreement constitutes the entire understanding of the parties and revokes and supersedes all prior agreements, oral or written, between them and may not be modified or amended except in a writing signed by both parties hereto that specifically refers to this Agreement. This Agreement shall take precedence over any other documents that may be in conflict herewith. If any one or more provisions contained in this Agreement are held by any court or tribunal to be invalid, illegal, or otherwise unenforceable, each and every other provision shall remain in full force and effect.

Learn the Secrets of the Photoshop Masters

These conferences will make you

to Photoshop what Godzilla was

to Tokyo—a raging, inexorable

thunder lizard of an image maker,

letting nothing stand in your way.

Photoshop Conference 1999

GET THE DETAILS:

www.thunderlizard.com

Fax: **206/285-0308**

Web: **www.thunderlizard.com**

Email: **tlp@thunderlizard.com**

Voice: **800/221-3806**

1619 Eighth Ave. North
Seattle, WA 98109
206/285-0305

Thunder
Lizard
Productions

Publish

THE MAGAZINE FOR ELECTRONIC PUBLISHING PROFESSIONALS

FREE 101 Tips Book!

Pixel-Perfect Scans

Managing Color: Get Consistent Results From Start To Finish

The Next Generation of Publishing Software

Affordable Big-Screen Monitors

Top Products of the Year

Choose The Right Paper For Dramatic Effect

Can You Trust Onscreen Proofing?

Acquisition & Imaging — Design & Illustration
Online & Onscreen — Layout & Type

101 BEST electronic publishing TIPS

To receive your FREE ISSUE and FREE *101 TIPS* book, simply detach this postcard return it today. No purchase required.

CUT HERE – MAIL NOW – NO POSTAGE NECESSARY

1 FREE ISSUE AND A FREE BOOK
absolutely free

Yes, I'd like to sample 1 issue of *Publish*. I understand that I'll also receive 101 Best Electronic Publishing Tips FREE just for trying Publish. If I like my sample issue, I'll pay just $29.95 for 11 more issues (for a total of 12 issues). I'll save $29. That's 50%!– off the annual cover price.

If I don't choose to subscribe, I'll return your subscription bill marked "cancel" and owe nothing.

The FREE issue and 101 TIPS book will be mine to keep – free.

**Trial only.
Don't send money.
Just mail this card!**

Name

Title

Company

Address

City   State   Zip

E-mail

H80111

Just an hour a month with *Publish*

gives you the edge in mastering your electronic publishing tools– from design to → print → web screen → or CD-ROM!

With today's explosion of new electronic publishing technologies, you have more options than ever before. To keep up, you need the magazine that pioneered the digital publishing revolution... and still sets the pace for graphics professionals.

It's *PUBLISH*. Month after month, *PUBLISH* improves your skills at every step in the electronic publishing process.

PUBLISH provides the ongoing education you need to save time and money in today's competitive world of electronic publishing. Our experts not only discuss new digital technologies, they show you how to use design and imaging tools to achieve spectacular results.

Yours FREE fo **trying** *Publish*

We're giving this free gift to catch your eye and call your attention to our no-risk, no-commitment offer of 1 FRE ISSUE.

The electronic publishing secrets in 101 Best Electronic Publishing Tips guarantee you'll ignite your creativity and shorten the learning curve for your favorite programs. They're FREE just for mailing the reply card. Do it today. Don't wait

- Acquisition & Imaging Tips
- Design & Illustration Tips
- Layout & Type Tips
- Online & Onscreen Tips

Tips apply to the current versions of programs on both Macintosh and Windows platforms of -

- Fractal Design Painte
- Adobe Photoshop
- Adobe PageMaker
- QuarkXPress
- Macromedia FreeHand
- Adobe Illustrator
- Corel Draw
- And more!

NO POSTAGE NECESSARY IF MAILED IN THE UNITED STATES

BUSINESS REPLY MAIL
FIRST CLASS MAIL PERMIT NO. 237 BRENTWOOD, TENNESSEE

POSTAGE WILL BE PAID BY ADDRESSEE

SUBSCRIPTION DEPARTMENT
P.O. BOX 5039
BRENTWOOD, TN 37024-9815

my2cents.idgbooks.com

Register This Book — And Win!

Visit http://my2cents.idgbooks.com to register this book and we'll automatically enter you in our fantastic monthly prize giveaway. It's also your opportunity to give us feedback: let us know what you thought of this book and how you would like to see other topics covered.

Discover IDG Books Online!

The IDG Books Online Web site is your online resource for tackling technology — at home and at the office. Frequently updated, the IDG Books Online Web site features exclusive software, insider information, online books, and live events!

10 Productive & Career-Enhancing Things You Can Do at www.idgbooks.com

- Nab source code for your own programming projects.

- Download software.

- Read Web exclusives: special articles and book excerpts by IDG Books Worldwide authors.

- Take advantage of resources to help you advance your career as a Novell or Microsoft professional.

- Buy IDG Books Worldwide titles or find a convenient bookstore that carries them.

- Register your book and win a prize.

- Chat live online with authors.

- Sign up for regular e-mail updates about our latest books.

- Suggest a book you'd like to read or write.

- Give us your 2¢ about our books and about our Web site.

You say you're not on the Web yet? It's easy to get started with IDG Books' *Discover the Internet*, available at local retailers everywhere.

CD-ROM INSTALLATION INSTRUCTIONS

Stick the accompanying CD in your CD-ROM drive. Double-click the owl-eye icon to display the contents of the CD. Depending on your platform, you will see one of two independent partitions, one for the Mac and the other for the PC.

The CD content is divided into seven folders and three loose QuickTime files. You need QuickTime 3 to see all the movies; if you don't have it, run the installer program inside the QuickTime VR folder.

Here's a complete rundown on the files:

- **DigGuru.mov:** Double-click the file to open it and then click the play button.
- **Reinfeld:** This folder contains four silent QuickTime movies. Double-click each file to play each movie.
- **Bowen:** This folder contains two versions of Robert Bowen's stereoscopic view of New York City (Chapter 11). If you have a monster system with scads of RAM, open the Huge3-D.psd file. Otherwise, open Med3-D.psd. Then get yourself a pair of 3-D glasses and put them on with the red lens over your left eye and the blue over your right. (You can hear Bowen personally explain the file by running his movie in the Voices folder.)
- **Burkholder:** This folder contains two Curves dialog box settings and three graduated step wedges. Double-click the files to open them.
- **Fitzgerald:** This folder contains 15 QuickTime VR movies. Double-click the files to open them. Drag inside the movies and watch the world spin around. Press Shift to zoom in, press Ctrl to zoom out.
- **Eismann:** This folder contains four QuickTime VR movies. Double-click the files to open them.
- **AirHaze.mov:** Double-click this QuickTime movie to play it.
- **Dinotopia.mov:** Double-click this QuickTime movie to play it.
- **Benjamin:** This folder contains ten files. Nine of the files are screen shots of Ben Benjamin's finished Web pages from CNET and E! Online; simply double-click to view each file. The tenth file, TalkSoup.gif, is an animated banner ad. You can open it up inside a Web browser such as Netscape Navigator or a GIF animation utility such as GifBuilder. (Neither of these programs is included with the *Photoshop Studio Secrets, 2nd Edition* CD.)
- **Voices:** This folder contains 16 QuickTime conversations with the original *Photoshop Studio Secrets* artists. Double-click to play each QuickTime movie.